THE
GREAT
CANADIAN
BOOK
OF
LISTS

T0119138

THE
GREAT
CANADIAN
BOOK
OF
LISTS

GREATESTSEXIEST**STRANGEST**BEST**WORST**HIGHEST**LOWEST**LARGEST

MARK KEARNEY
& RANDY RAY

THE DUNDURN GROUP
A HOUNSLOW BOOK
TORONTO · OXFORD

Publisher: Anthony Hawke
Design: Scott Reid
Printer: Webcom Ltd.
Cover photos: Paul Gross photographed by Jeffrey Newbury
The Butchart Gardens photo courtesy of The Butchart Gardens

Canadian Cataloguing in Publication Data

Kearney, Mark, 1955–
The great Canadian book of lists

ISBN 0-88882-213-8
1. Canada — Miscellanea. I. Ray, Randy, 1952– . II. Title.
FC51.K42 1999   971'.002   C99-932145-5   F1008.K42 1999

1   2   3   4   5   03   02   01   00   99

We acknowledge the support of the **Canada Council for the Arts** for our publishing program. We acknowledge the support of the **Ontario Arts Council.** We acknowledge the financial support of the Government of Canada through the Book Publishing Industry Development Program (BPIDP) for our publishing activities.

Printed and bound in Canada .Printed on recycled paper.

www.dundurn.com

Dundurn Press
8 Market Street
Suite 200
Toronto, Ontario, Canada
M5E 1M6

Dundurn Press
73 Lime Walk
Headington, Oxford,
England
OX3 7AD

Dundurn Press
2250 Military Road
Tonawanda NY
U.S.A. 14150

Contents

BUSINESS   57

ENVIRONMENT AND NATURE   75

MUSIC   185

SCIENCE 253

SPORTS 265

TRAVEL AND LEISURE 301

When it comes to dedicating this book, we have our own list:

Janis.
Catherine.
All the Rays.
All the Kearneys.
The late Carol Ray who taught her sons the meaning of determination.
The late Kevin Stevenson (1952–1991), who would have enjoyed this book.
The Dock at Ray's Rock, where many an idea has been spawned, and Watson the dog whose desire for long walks led to moments of inspiration.

Preface

One of Prime Minister Wilfrid Laurier's most quotable quotations in the early 1900s was about the twentieth century belonging to Canada. His optimistic statement has reverberated across the country during the past one hundred years, and while it may be argued that if the century "belonged" to anyone it was probably to our good neighbours to the south, there is no doubt that the twentieth century saw Canada come into its own as a prosperous nation that has played an increasingly significant role in the world.

As we looked back at the twentieth century while putting together *The Great Canadian Book of Lists*, we wanted to do more than just create a shopping list of key achievements and events from the past one hundred years. We wanted to chronicle the century in a way that would give readers plenty of details and a clear sense of why each and every item in this book is important to what we've become as a people and how the country has been shaped as Canada heads into the new millennium. You'll also find several statistical snapshots throughout the book: these are designed to provide a better understanding of the various trends over different years and show how much the face of Canada has changed since Laurier's time. You'll notice that in comparing some statistics over the years the headings often differ. While it may seem like apples and oranges, we've kept it that way to give a better idea of how the gathering of information has changed over time, too. We've also selected different years for certain lists to give you a flavour of what Canada was like at specific times. And look for this camera logo and the word "Snapshot" sprinkled randomly throughout the book for some quick, interesting information.

We don't pretend to be experts on every aspect of Canada in the twentieth century, so that is why we decided to draw on others' knowledge to prepare many of the lists you'll find in these pages. We also know that list books are supposed to be fun and entertaining, too; that's why we asked a handful of celebrities to provide their favourites from the past one hundred years and why we went off the beaten path somewhat to draw up lists you might not expect to find in a book such as this. For example, we have lists that look at various aspects of Canada that we take for granted — from the point of view of two contributors who were born and raised in the United States but spent part of their lives here.

We've done our best to provide a generous mix of the serious and the silly, the tragic and the heroic, and the entertaining and the enlightening. So you'll find Canada's ten most romantic couples alongside the country's worst disasters, our best beers, the worst television shows, biggest news events, and the country's most accomplished athletes. In some cases the same people and events appear on different lists; that's an inevitable part of any list book that covers such a wide range of topics and strives to serve up a complete picture of an entire century. We've numbered the items in each list, but that doesn't always indicate a specific order. When it does, we indicate it.

Perhaps most importantly we hope *The Great Canadian Book of Lists* will delight, surprise, educate, and intrigue you. We also expect that it will start more arguments than it settles. Even though our lists are the result of many months of research and interviews, coupled with input from hundreds of Canadians, young and old, from all corners of the country, there's bound to be disagreement. We know some of you will wonder what we or those who helped us prepare some of the lists were thinking when choosing one person over another, mentioning one event and not something else, or picking some accomplishment you might think is minor instead of one you believe is crucial. Such is the nature of list books — that's what makes them fun and, dare we say, provocative.

Innovations and flops, successes and failures, comebacks and breakthroughs, record setters and trend setters: you'll find them all in *The Great Canadian Book of Lists*. So turn the page and let the debate begin.

Arts & Entertainment

GREAT READING ...
TEN BEST CANADIAN NOVELS
(in alphabetical order)

1. *As For Me and My House* by Sinclair Ross.
2. *Cat's Eye* by Margaret Atwood.
3. *The English Patient* by Michael Ondaatje.
4. *Famous Last Words* by Timothy Findley.
5. *Fifth Business* by Robertson Davies.
6. *Joshua Then and Now* by Mordecai Richler.
7. *More Joy in Heaven* by Morley Callaghan.
8. *The Stone Angel* by Margaret Laurence.
9. *The Tin Flute* by Gabrielle Roy.
10. *Who Has Seen the Wind* by W.O. Mitchell.

List prepared by Holly McNally, co-owner of McNally-Robinson Books Ltd.

TOP FIVE CANADIAN FICTION BOOKS

1. *Stone Angel* by Margaret Laurence.
2. *Diviners* by Margaret Laurence.
3. *Fifth Business* by Robertson Davies.
4. *The Edible Woman* by Margaret Atwood.
5. *Who Has Seen the Wind* by W.O. Mitchell.

Based on a poll of the delegates at the 1999 Canadian Booksellers Association convention.

Robertson Davies wrote many wonderful novels, including *Fifth Business*.
Photo by Pete Paterson

TEN BEST CANADIAN NON-FICTION BOOKS
(in chronological order)

1. *The Gutenberg Galaxy: The Making of Typographic Man* by Marshall McLuhan, 1962.

2. *Lament for a Nation: The Defeat of Canadian Nationalism* by George Grant, 1965.

3. *Canada: Year of the Land.* Edited by Lorraine Monk, 1967.

4. *The Republic of Childhood: A Critical Guide to Canadian Children's Literature in English* by Sheila Egoff, 1967.

5. *The Selected Journals of Lucy Maud Montgomery, Volumes 1 to 4.* Edited by Mary Rubio and Elizabeth Waterston, 1985 to 1998.

6. *Historical Atlas of Canada* by Geoffrey Matthews, R. Cole Harris, Deryck Holdsworth, and Donald Kerr, 1987.

7. *The Canadian Encyclopedia.* Edited by James Harley Marsh, 1988.

8. *Dictionary of Newfoundland English.* Edited by G.M. Story, W.J. Kirwin, and J.D.A. Widdowson, 1990.

9. *Voltaire's Bastards: The Dictatorship of Reason in the West* by John Ralston Saul, 1992.

10. *A Story Sharp as a Knife: An Introduction to Classical Haida Literature* by Robert Bringhurst, 1999.

List prepared by Celia Duthie, president of Duthie Books in Vancouver, British Columbia.

HAVE YOUR READ THESE?
THE FIRST TEN WINNERS OF THE GOVERNOR GENERAL'S LITERARY AWARD FOR FICTION

1. 1936: *Think of the Earth* by Bertram Brooker.

2. 1937: *The Dark Weaver* by Laura G. Salverson.

3. 1938: *Swiss Sonata* by Gwethalyn Graham.

4. 1939: *The Champlain Road* by Franklin Davey McDowell.

5. 1940: *Thirty Acres* by Ringuet (Philippe Panneton).

6. 1941: *Three Came to Ville Marie* by Alan Sullivan.

7. 1942: *Little Man* by G. Herbert Sallans.

8. 1943: *The Pied Piper of Dipper* by Thomas Raddall.

9. 1944: *Earth and High Heaven* by Gwethalyn Graham.

10. 1945: *Two Solitudes* by Hugh McLennan.

TEN GREAT CANADIAN MAGAZINES NO LONGER PUBLISHING

1. *The Atlantic Advocate*
2. *The Canadian Magazine*
3. *The City* magazine (*Toronto Sunday Star*)
4. *The Globe* magazine
5. *The Idler*
6. *The Last Post*
7. *Liberty*
8. *Quest*
9. *Star Weekly*
10. *Weekend* magazine

THE FIFTEEN GREATEST CANADIAN MAGAZINES OF THE CENTURY
(in alphabetical order)

1. *l'Actualité:* Like its counterpart *Maclean's* is in English, *l'Actualité* is ubiquitous and relied upon among Francophones. When waves are to be made in Quebec, it makes them.

2. *The Canadian Forum:* The granddaddy of left-liberal magazines, still in there punching.

3. *Canadian Living:* The queen of the meatloaf zeitgeist. Its homespun charm connected with its audience in ways that most magazines dream of.

4. *Chatelaine:* Recently they've put 10,000 volts through it, before which it had mostly rested on its laurels. But what laurels! Particularly under Doris Anderson's editorship in the sixties, it helped to stoke the feminist revolution.

5. *The Globe* magazine: A tabloid with an often weird look, but it did some excellent journalism. Never seemed to catch on as a commercial proposition, but respected and remembered fondly by readers and writers.

6. *Harrowsmith:* Started on a kitchen table, never made a dime, discovered and defined an audience nobody else knew existed — urban wannabe back-to-the-landers. Now a shadow of its former self, but remembered fondly.

7. *The Idler:* Even if you didn't like its arch right-wingedness, or the fact that it lasted only a few years, you had to admire its retro charm, style, and audacity.

8. *The Last Post:* On the left, nobody did it better; a short-lived combination of muckraking style and substance. It should be on this list for its coverage of Quebec and the October crisis, if nothing else.

9. *Liberty:* In its day, the most popular magazine in the country, driven by the megalomania and showmanship of Jack Kent Cooke.

10. *Maclean's:* It is almost as old as the century and managed to reinvent itself successfully. In earlier days, *Maclean's* was a large-format general feature magazine. In later days, a news weekly. No Canadians remember when it wasn't there and outside of Toronto's chattering classes, it is like a household utility.

11. *Saturday Night:* Award winner, with reason. In the list for brinksmanship, but also for continuing to do the kind of general interest journalism that has all but died out elsewhere. Lately, it has oozed attitude, and has always taken itself seriously.

12. *Star Weekly:* Set a high standard for journalism and magazine fiction. Killed by television.

13. *Toronto Life:* A survivor. More lives than a cat. Now a bit smug and self-satisfied, but thereby accurately reflecting its intended audience.

14. *Vancouver:* A controlled circulation magazine that never acted like it. If an eye needs a finger put in it, *Vancouver* still does so.

15. *Weekend* magazine: The last of the great rotogravures. Like a candle that burns brightest as it is about to go out, it made huge waves towards the end and was known for its ground-breaking journalism and design.

Lists prepared by D.B. Scott, president of Impresa Communications Limited and longtime editor and magazine publishing consultant. Scott has been a frequent judge in the National Magazine Awards.

KIDS' STUFF ... TWELVE GREAT CANADIAN FICTION BOOKS FOR YOUNG CANADIANS

(Stories that should be on the bookshelf of every Canadian youngster.)

1. *Anne of Green Gables* by L. M. Montgomery: This classic tale, published in 1908, about an orphaned girl in PEI is beloved throughout the world and is arguably the most famous book ever written by a Canadian.

2. *The Incredible Journey* by Sheila Burnford: Who could forget the homecoming scene in this pet tale of love and loyalty featuring two dogs and a cat. This popular book from 1961 became a family-favourite movie.

3. *A Prairie Boy's Winter* by William Kurelek: The author's memories of a Ukrainian-Canadian childhood in the 1930s combined with marvellous illustrations made this one of Canada's most successful books when it was published in 1973. It was the first Canadian book to be chosen as the illustrated book of the year (1973) by *The New York Times*.

4. *Alligator Pie* by Dennis Lee: This best-selling collection of nonsense rhymes ("Alligator pie, Alligator pie, If I don't get some I think I'm gonna die") was created partly because Lee didn't like what was currently available to read to his own children. His book boosted Canadian children's writing when it was published in 1974, and it's lots of fun.

5. *The Olden Days Coat* by Margaret Laurence: Like the character Sal, who travels back in time by trying on an old coat, this holiday classic from 1979 takes young readers to a Christmas long ago. It was reissued in 1999 with new art by the original illustrator.

6. *Up to Low* by Brian Doyle: In this 1983 Canadian Library Association Book of the Year award winner, Doyle writes with great confidence about the kid in himself. His honest and often humorous voice makes him a great success with young readers.

7. *The Hockey Sweater* by Roch Carrier: This book (1984 edition) scores high with hockey fans young and old. *The Toronto Star* described it as "not only sweet and funny, but a wise parable about Quebec and English Canada."

8. *Mama's Going to Buy You a Mockingbird* by Jean Little: This inspiring author had already received the 1974 Vicky Metcalf Award for a Body of Work when this book about a young boy coping with death won her the 1985 Canadian Library Association Book of the Year Award and the Ruth Schwartz Children's Book Award.

9. *The Cremation of Sam McGee* by Robert Service: Pierre Berton introduced the 1986 version by writing "This book represents a happy marriage between the most eloquent of the Yukon poets and the most brilliant of the Yukon artists" (Robert Service and Ted Harrison). Generations have thrilled to the chill of this tale.

10. *Love You Forever* by Robert Munsch: This heart-warming 1986 tale of love between a mother and son is Canada's best-selling picture book and treasured by many.

11. *Home Child* by Barbara Haworth-Attard: This critically acclaimed historical piece of fiction from 1996 led to many elderly home children (a "home child" was a child exported by Britain to Canada as cheap farm labour before the Great Depression) contacting the author because the novel opened a door and allowed them to tell their families of their own experiences.

12. *One is Canada* by Maxine Trottier: The most important number in this lyrical counting book from 1999 is "one" for unity. The author had to keep her hopes high when writing it because the 1995 referendum was taking place.

List prepared with the assistance of "The Book Lady" Margot Griffin, author and syndicated columnist who specializes in writing about children's books.

SIX GREAT CANADIAN NON-FICTION BOOKS FOR YOUNG CANADIANS

(The Canadian children's publishing industry, especially in recent years, has excelled at factual books. These are among the best.)

1. *Never Cry Wolf* by Farley Mowat: This 1963 tale of life among Canada's wolves changed the way people of all ages regarded these marvellous creatures. The book later became a popular movie.

2. *The Story of Canada* by Janet Lunn: Novelist Lunn knew how to find and tell the stories in Canadian history. This outstanding book won her the 1992 IODE Book Award, the 1993 Information Book Award, and the 1993 Mr. Christie's Book Award.

3. *North Star to Freedom* by Gena K. Gorrell: This book from 1996 details the extraordinary spirit of the many escaped slaves who followed the Underground Railroad to freedom and the brave men and women who helped them.

4. *The Kids Book of Canada* by Barbara Greenwood: The author met her vision to create "an at-a-glance pictorial first-look at Canada organized by province and territory for quick reference." It quickly became a Canadian bestseller in 1997.

5. *The Kids Book of Canadian Prime Ministers* by Pat Hancock: Full length, full-colour portraits, intriguing anecdotes, and handy information boxes in this 1998 book introduce young Canadians to our twenty prime ministers in a lively and interesting way.

6. *Boldly Canadian, The Story of the RCMP* by Joann Hamilton-Barry: The author had to battle the Disney corporation (which holds the rights to the Mountie image) before this 1999 tribute to the Mounties and her father could be published.

List prepared with the assistance of "The Book Lady" Margot Griffin, author and syndicated columnist who specializes in writing about children's books.

ON THE TUBE ...
TEN BEST CANADIAN TV SERIES

1. "This Hour Has Seven Days" (CBC)
2. "Road to Avonlea" (CBC)
3. "Due South" (CTV)
4. "SCTV" (CBC-Global)
5. "Wojeck" (CBC)
6. "The Newsroom" (CBC)
7. "The Nature of Things" (CBC)
8. "Traders" (Global)
9. "The National Dream" (CBC)
10. "Don Messer's Jubilee" (CBC)

THE TEN WORST CANADIAN TV SERIES

1. "Jalna" (CBC)
2. "Party Game" (CHCH-TV)
3. "Half the George Kirby Comedy Hour" (CTV)
4. "Not My Department" (CBC)
5. "Side Effects" (CBC)
6. "Police Surgeon" (CTV)
7. "Ein Prosit" (CHCH-TV)
8. "Delilah" (CBC)
9. "Stars on Ice" (CTV)
10. "The Trouble with Tracey" (CTV)

Lists prepared by Jim Bawden, television columnist for Starweek *magazine.*

TALKING HEADS ... TOP TEN CANADIAN BROADCASTERS

1. **Lorne Greene**: The "Voice of Doom," as he was known, had a distinctive, mellifluous voice familiar to Canadians during World War II, not long after the CBC had been established in 1936. Greene later became an international celebrity as the leading figure on the TV series "Bonanza."

2. **Larry Henderson**: Henderson was CBC television's first network newscaster. His personality became familiar to Canadians after he entered their homes daily through the electronic medium. He had a special talent for memorizing the news script and because of his travels as a correspondent brought an international perspective to early TV news in Canada.

3. **Harvey Kirck**: The CTV newscaster deserves credit for his longevity. He read the news over a twenty-year period. As he noted in his memoirs with Wade Rowland, *Nobody Calls Me Mr. Kirck*, his first newscast was delivered from Ottawa on December 3, 1963, and his last in Toronto on April 27, 1984.

4. **Lloyd Robertson**: Robertson has consistently read a network newscast in a most effective manner. His early CBC training as an announcer has been shown in his capacity to communicate the stories informatively and with variation.

5. **Peter Kent**: Kent's considerable talents in the field as a journalist paid off in the credibility he has brought to newscasts as a mature news anchor. His breadth of experience in Canadian private and public television, and in the United States, has provided him with a credible background for his role as a newscaster.

Lorne Greene broadcasting over the CBC in 1942. *Photo courtesy of National Archives of Canada: PA116178.*

6. **Barbara Frum**: Some of the most effective journalism performed by the late Frum was on radio as the early host of the CBC program "As It Happens" in the early 1970s. Frum was in the vanguard of a movement that saw the ascendance of female announcers. Her talent for interviewing seemed to be at one with the new style of talk radio that "As It Happens" introduced to Canadian listeners.

7. **Pamela Wallin**: Undoubtedly one of the best interviewers in broadcasting that Canada has seen. Wallin has informed and entertained Canadians on both the privately owned CTV network and the CBC, the public broadcaster. Perhaps her greatest strength is the considerable research she brings to a range of interviews.

8. **Foster Hewitt**: When it came to hockey on radio and television, the name of the late Foster Hewitt could hardly be overlooked. His signature, "He shoots, he scores," had a simplicity and economy of language that was unbeatable, especially on radio.

9. **Danny Gallivan**: The former broadcaster for the Montreal Canadiens had a remarkable command of the English language when he described the play-by-play of a game. His even manner on air and his background commentary, beyond the actual description of the action, often seemed as stylish as the play of the Canadiens.

10. **Johnny Esaw**: As sports director of CFTO-TV, Toronto, the flagship station of the CTV network, Esaw had a profound influence on the coverage of sports on Canadian television. Through his initiative, the sport of figure skating received a great deal of prominence on Canadian television, and the exposure it received was to have a lasting impact on Canadians.

List prepared by Michael Nolan, who teaches in the Journalism Program at the University of Western Ontario and in the Political Science department at King's College, an affiliate of Western.

ARTHUR BLACK'S TEN WEIRDEST INTERVIEWS

1. Skunk Control Officer, Gimli, Manitoba.

2. Linda Montano, performance artist. (Tied herself to a man with a six-foot rope for one year.)

3. Judy Williams, spokeswoman for the Wreck Beach Nudist Society. (Interview performed on the beach. In the nude.)

4. Imre Somogyi, psychic toe reader.

5. Jeannie "M," who makes stuffed rats to hang from Christmas trees.

6. Paulu Rainbowsong. This guy makes didgeridoos (Australian Aborigine wind instruments) out of PVC plumbing pipe.

7. Lydia Hibby, pet psychic. Treats dogs, cats, horses, iguanas, etc., telepathically.

8. Marge's Muffs, product of "Marge the Rancher" of Redvers, Saskatchewan. The muffs are err, ballmuffs — cold weather protection for bulls' scrotums.

9. Trevor Weekes, editor: *Teaching Chickens to Fly: The Manual.*

10. Harold Fiske. Don't ask — listen to the show.

Arthur Black is the longtime host of CBC Radio's "Basic Black" program.

TOP TEN RADIO/TELEVISION COMMERCIALS

1. A Household Finance Corporation radio commercial in the 1930s declared, "Never borrow money needlessly, just when you must; borrow then where loans are a specialty from folks you trust. Borrow confidently from HFC!" Advertising a loan company in a way that encouraged trust in times of hardship was a good way to make people feel more comfortable about having to borrow money.

2. Lux soap's radio sponsorship of Roy Ward Dickson's radio programs which originated in Toronto in the 1940s and 1950s. The tie-in of the product with the celebrity was a harbinger of things to come.

3. In the late 1970s and early 1980s, a series of TV commercials for Labatt's Blue beer highlighted activities many viewers had never dreamed of, such as walking in a huge clear balloon over the surface of a lake. These commercials emphasized good health, fresh air, and fun, and encouraged the viewer to join the party.

4. A Chesebrough Pond's Canada TV commercial in 1984 showed a Q-tip cotton swab being used to make a sooty rose beautiful and fresh-looking. This was a fine example of Canadian understatement.

5. Canadian dairy industry TV commercials in the 1980s featured butter dancing with various partners such as vegetables or bread. Simple animation and music encouraged the viewer to see butter as a sensual product.

6. Two Canadian Tire commercials featuring young lads. The first, produced in the 1980s, featured a young hockey player named Albert who was shown being picked last for a game of pick-up hockey. The camera flashed forward a few years later, and Albert was a hockey star, his name chanted by fans. The second, produced in the 1990s, featured soft colours, and showed a little boy and his anticipation of receiving a new bike from his father. All of these elements contributed to a deeply felt nostalgia for the "good old days."

7. A Business Depot back-to-school TV commercial in the late 1990s portrayed a father who was happy that the kids were returning to school after the summer holidays. His joy, and the contrasting faces and feelings of the kids, hit a familiar note with most parents and kids.

8. Heritage Minutes, which began airing on TV in 1998, and were very successful. They are a great way to bring Canadian history alive to Canadians,

in small, gentle doses — which is the way we do things in Canada. We never want to boast about our heritage or our history.

9. In the 1998 Majesta bathroom tissue TV commercial, a little boy used a pile of rolls of tissue to protect his puppy, who was eagerly running on the polished floor and, we assume, smashing into the wall, every time he heard the can opener. The sweetness and acting ability of the boy, and the cuteness of his pet, tied in with the injuries we thought the poor puppy was suffering, made this a memorable commercial.

10. A Purina MAXX cat litter TV commercial in 1998 featured a cat holding its breath while using the litter box — computer animation or real? The cat was so lifelike that it was difficult to tell what was real and what wasn't — which is the way it is with so many things today!

List prepared by Claudine Goller, a Toronto consultant in media literacy.

EIGHTEEN CATCHY ADVERTISING SLOGANS (AND THEIR PRODUCTS)

1. "Always got time for Tim Hortons." (donuts)

2. "At Speedy you're a somebody." (mufflers)

3. "Canada, the world next door." (Tourism Canada)

4. "Ever been to sea, Billy?" (Cap'n Highliner foods)

5. "Ex says it all." (Beer)

6. "Harvey's makes a hamburger a beautiful thing." (fast food)

7. "Hey Mabel, Black Label." (beer)

8. "Home of the handyman." (Home Hardware)

9. "It's mainly because of the meat." (Dominion grocers)

10. "It's the next best thing to being there." (long distance telephone)

11. "Me 'n the boys and our 50." (beer)

12. "Only in Canada? Pity." (Red Rose Tea)

13. "Pep 'er up with Primrose." (gasoline)

14. "The Champagne of Ginger Ales." (Canada Dry)

15. "We've licked them at the front, you lick them at the back." (World War I slogan for Thrifty Stamps).

16. "We who make whisky say: 'Drink moderately.'" (Seagrams' campaign in 1934).

17. "Where you give like Santa and save like Scrooge." (Canadian Tire)

18. "Wouldn't a Dow go good now?" (beer)

THE ENVELOPE PLEASE ...
CANADIAN ACTRESSES NOMINATED FOR OR WINNERS OF OSCARS
(in chronological order)

1. **Mary Pickford**: Winner in 1929 for Best Actress in *Coquette*. The Toronto-born actress also received an honorary award in 1975.

2. **Norma Shearer**: Won in 1930 for Best Actress in *The Divorcée*. The Montreal native was also nominated in the same category that same year for *Their Own Desire*, in 1931 for *A Free Soul*, in 1934 for *The Barretts of Wimpole Street*, in 1936 for *Romeo and Juliet*, and in 1938 for *Marie Antoinette*.

3. **Marie Dressler**: The Cobourg, Ontario, star won in 1931 for Best Actress in *Min and Bill*. She was nominated in the same category the following year for *Emma*.

4. **Deanna Durbin**: The Winnipeg-born actress was one of the best-known young stars in the thirties and forties, and was awarded a miniature Oscar in 1938 for "bringing to the screen the spirit and personification of youth." Her films included *Three Smart Girls* and *One Hundred Men and a Girl*.

5. **Genevieve Bujold**: The Montreal performer was nominated in 1969 for Best Actress in *Anne of the Thousand Days*.

6. **Meg Tilly**: Raised in Victoria, she was nominated for Best Supporting Actress in 1985 for *Agnes of God*.

7. **Kate Nelligan**: The London, Ontario, native was nominated in 1991 for Best Supporting Actress in *The Prince of Tides*.

8. **Jennifer Tilly**: The Vancouver actress matched her sister Meg with a nomination for Best Supporting Actress for her role in *Bullets Over Broadway*.

CANADIAN ACTORS NOMINATED FOR OR WINNERS OF OSCARS

(in chronological order)

1. **Walter Huston:** The Toronto-born actor was first nominated in 1936 for Best Actor for *Dodsworth*. He was nominated in the same category in 1941 for *All That Money Can Buy*. He got the nomination for Best Supporting Actor in 1942 in *Yankee Doodle Dandy*, and won in that category in 1948 for *Treasure of Sierra Madre*.

2. **Gene Lockhart:** The London, Ontario, native was nominated for Best Supporting Actor in 1938 for *Algiers*.

3. **Raymond Massey:** The Toronto actor received a Best Actor nomination in 1940 for *Abe Lincoln in Illinois*.

4. **Walter Pidgeon:** From Saint John, New Brunswick, Pidgeon was nominated for Best Actor in 1942 for *Mrs. Miniver* and in the same category the following year for *Madame Curie*.

5. **Alexander Knox:** The Strathroy, Ontario, native was nominated in 1944 for Best Actor in *Wilson*.

6. **Hume Cronyn:** From London, Ontario, Cronyn was nominated in 1944 as Best Supporting Actor in *The Seventh Cross*.

7. **Harold Russell:** The Sydney, Nova Scotia, native was nominated and won in 1946 for Best Supporting Actor in *The Best Years of Our Lives*. A war amputee (Russell was missing both arms), he also received a special Oscar that year for "bringing hope and courage to his fellow veterans" with his appearance in the film.

8. **John Ireland:** The actor from Vernon, British Columbia, was nominated for Best Supporting Actor in 1949 for *All the King's Men*.

9. **Chief Dan George:** Hailing from the Burrard Indian Reserve in North Vancouver, George was nominated in 1970 for Best Supporting Actor in *Little Big Man*.

10. **Dan Aykroyd:** The Ottawa-born comedian was nominated in 1989 for Best Supporting Actor in *Driving Miss Daisy*.

11. **Graham Greene:** Born at the Six Nations Reserve near Brampton, Ontario, Greene received a Best Supporting Actor nomination in 1990 for *Dances With Wolves*.

TOP TEN CANADIAN FILMS OF ALL TIME

(Listed alphabetically with director and year of release.)

1. *The Apprenticeship of Duddy Kravitz*, Ted Kotcheff, 1974.
2. *Les Bons Débarras,* Francis Mankiewicz, 1980.
3. *Crash*, David Cronenberg, 1996.
4. *Dead Ringers*, David Cronenberg, 1988.
5. *Le Déclin de l'Empire Américain (The Decline of the American Empire)*, Denys Arcand, 1986.
6. *Goin' Down the Road*, Don Shebib, 1970.
7. *The Grey Fox*, Phillip Borsos, 1983.
8. *Jesus de Montréal (Jesus of Montreal)*, Denys Arcand, 1989.
9. *Mon Oncle Antoine*, Claude Jutra, 1971.
10. *The Sweet Hereafter*, Atom Egoyan, 1997.

List prepared by Wyndham Wise, publisher and editor-in-chief of Take One, *Canada's finest film magazine.*

FILMS WITH THE MOST GENIE AWARDS*

1. *Un Zoo la Nuit* won thirteen in 1988.
2. *Jésus de Montréal (Jesus of Montreal)* won twelve in 1990.
3. *Dead Ringers* won ten in 1989.
4. (tie) *The Changeling* won eight in 1980.
   Les Bons Débarras won eight in 1981.
   Le Déclin de l'Empire Américain (The Decline of the American Empire) won eight in 1987.
   Naked Lunch won eight in 1992.
   Exotica won eight in 1994.
   The Sweet Hereafter won eight in 1997
10. (tie) *Les Plouffe* won seven in 1982.
   The Grey Fox won seven in 1983.

* Prior to the Genies being established in 1980, *Mon Oncle Antoine* won eight Canadian Film Awards in 1971, *J.A. Martin Photographe* and *The Best Damn Fiddler from Calabogie to Kaladar* each won seven in 1977 and 1969 respectively.

Fabulous Fact

The only film to capture Best Actor, Best Actress, Best Supporting Actor, and Best Supporting Actress Genies was 1996's *Long Day's Journey into Night*.

TWELVE SIGNIFICANT CANADIANS IN THE SILENT FILM ERA

1. **Mary Pickford**: Born in Toronto, but known as "America's Sweetheart," she co-founded United Artists and was arguably the most important actress of the silent film era. Among her supporting actors in her first silents was Dell Henderson, a Canadian who later became a director.

2. **Florence Lawrence**: In the early days of movies, the powers that be were reluctant to give actors on-screen credit for their work. Although Lawrence's film career was not as distinguished as others, the Hamilton, Ontario-born actress bucked the trend of anonymous actors, and became known in 1910 as the "Biograph Girl." Thanks to a publicity stunt, she was pivotal in introducing the star system in the business.

3. **Mack Sennett**: The king of early film comedy, Sennett, from Danville, Quebec, produced hundreds of movies, and his Keystone Kops are still a symbol of and an influence on the slapstick humour prevalent then and still around today. Sennett was the first to hire Charlie Chaplin as well as other stars such as Fatty Arbuckle, Mabel Normand, and Gloria Swanson. Fellow Canadian Harry Edwards also directed for Sennett in the 1920s.

4. **Allan Dwan**: One of the top directors of the silent era, Dwan worked with every major star of the day, including Douglas Fairbanks, whose screen personality he helped develop. Dwan, who was born in Toronto, also made a successful transition to sound film, making movies up until the mid-1960s.

Mary Pickford: America's Sweetheart but still a Canadian. *Photo courtesy of National Archives of Canada: C16958.*

5. **John S. Robertson**: Known as the best-liked director in Hollywood during the 1920s, the London, Ontario, native got his start as an actor but made a successful transition behind the camera. He worked with such top performers as John Barrymore, Mary Pickford, and Greta Garbo and turned out such silent classics as *Dr. Jekyll and Mr. Hyde*, *The Enchanted Cottage*, and *Tess of the Storm Country*, which starred Pickford.

6. **Norma Shearer**: Before she won her Academy Award as Best Actress in 1930, Shearer, from Montreal, appeared in dozens of silent films. Perhaps best known as the wife of MGM mogul Irving Thalberg, she had a distinguished film career from the 1920s to the 1940s.

7. **Fay Wray**: Though most famous for her work in the talkie *King Kong*, the Cardston, Alberta-born actress made her first impact as a silent movie star in such films as *Wedding March* and *Street of Sin*.

8. **Al Christie**: A London, Ontario-born comedy director and producer who rivalled Sennett, Christie acquired the first studio in Hollywood, Nestor Company. Among his notable films were *So Long Letty* and *Charley's Aunt*.

9. **Sidney Olcott**: A pioneering film director from Toronto who directed many silent films around the world and in Hollywood from its earliest days. He was the chief director of the Kalem Company, known for its willingness to travel abroad to shoot movies on location. His first film was *Ben-Hur* in 1907, which was later re-made by other directors.

10. **The Holland Brothers**: Andrew and George Holland were entrepreneurs from Ottawa who opened the world's first Kinetoscope parlour in New York in 1894. (A Kinetoscope was a device that was a key forerunner to the development of motion pictures.) Two years later in their hometown, they promoted what is believed to be the first public showing of a movie in Canada.

11. **Marie Dressler**: The Cobourg, Ontario, native was a well-respected and loved comic actress. *Tillie's Punctured Romance* was one of her best silent films, and she acted in many others before successfully making the transition to talkies.

12. **Louis B. Mayer**: Though not Canadian-born, he grew up in New Brunswick and was a key force in the movies for more than thirty years. He built his first studio in 1917 and then formed Metro-Goldwyn-Mayer in 1924. He remained vice-president in charge of production until 1951.

LIGHTS, CAMERA, ACTION ... TOP TEN HOLLYWOOD FILM DIRECTORS FROM CANADA (SOUND ERA)

1. **Norman Jewison**: Arguably the best director Canada has produced, Jewison has been behind the camera for such films as *The Cincinnati Kid; The Thomas Crown Affair; The Russians are Coming, The Russians are Coming; In the Heat of the Night; Fiddler on the Roof; Rollerball; And Justice for All; A Soldier's Story; Moonstruck;* and *In Country*. He received the Irving G. Thalberg Award from the Academy of Motion Picture Arts and Sciences in 1999.

2. **Sidney Furie**: The Toronto-born director enjoyed success in Britain and Canada as well as Hollywood. Among his films are *The Ipcress File, The Naked Runner, Lady Sings the Blues, Little Fauss and Big Halsy, Gable and Lombard, The Boys in Company C*, and *The Entity*.

3. **Ted Kotcheff**: Born in Toronto, he worked in Britain making such films as *Life at the Top*, and in Australia where he made *Outback*. Kotcheff returned to North America, where he made, among other films, *The Apprenticeship of Duddy Kravitz, Who Has Been Killing the Great Chefs of Europe, Fun With Dick and Jane, First Blood*, and *Uncommon Valor*.

4. **Arthur Hiller**: Hailing from Edmonton, Hiller, who has served as the president of the Academy of Motion Picture Arts and Sciences for several years, has directed such notable films as *The Americanization of Emily, Plaza Suite, The Hospital, Love Story, Silver Streak*, and *Outrageous Fortune*.

5. **Daniel Petrie**: The Glace Bay, Nova Scotia, native got his start in television before going on to direct such films as *A Raisin in the Sun, The Bramble Bush, Fort Apache the Bronx, The Besty, The Bay Boy*, and *Rocket Gibraltar*.

6. **James Cameron**: Best known for directing the highest-grossing film of all time (as of mid-1999), *Titanic*, Cameron's other films include *The Terminator, The Abyss*, and *True Lies*.

7. **Ivan Reitman**: A successful director of comedies that include *Ghostbusters, Meatballs, Stripes, Junior, Kindergarten Cop*, and *Dave*.

8. **Mark Robson**: The versatile Montreal-born director made such films as *Champion, Home of the Brave, The Bridges of Toko-Ri, Peyton Place, The Inn of Sixth Happiness, Valley of the Dolls, Von Ryan's Express*, and *Earthquake*.

9. **David Cronenberg**: The master of horror and off-beat films, his most notable works are *Scanners*, *The Dead Zone*, *The Fly*, *Dead Ringers*, *Naked Lunch*, and *Crash*.

10. **Edward Dymtryk**: The Grand Forks, B.C. native made several movies before becoming a victim of the McCarthy era and leaving for Britain. He eventually returned to Hollywood. Among his films were *Murder My Sweet*, *Crossfire*, *The Caine Mutiny*, *Raintree County*, *The Carpetbaggers*, *Anzio*, and *Bluebeard*.

ELWY YOST'S FIFTEEN FAVOURITE CANADIAN ACTORS AND ACTRESSES IN HOLLYWOOD

(*including favourite performances*)

1. Hume Cronyn: *Shadow of a Doubt* (1943) and *People Will Talk* (195l).

2. Kate Reid: *Atlantic City* (1980) and *The Andromeda Strain* (1971).

3. Dan Aykroyd: *Trading Places* (1983) and *Driving Miss Daisy* (1989).

4. Deanna Durbin: *Three Smart Girls* (1936).

5. Raymond Massey: *The Scarlet Pimpernel* (1935) and *East of Eden* (1955).

6. Walter Huston: *The Treasure of the Sierra Madre* (1948).

7. Walter Pidgeon: *Mrs. Miniver* (1942) and Fritz Lang's *Man Hunt* (1941).

8. Donald Sutherland: *The Day of the Locust* (1975) and *Klute* (1971).

9. Fay Wray: *King Kong* (1933).

10. John Candy: *Splash* (1984) and *Only the Lonely* (1991).

11. Catherine O'Hara: *Beetlejuice* (1988) and *Home Alone* (1990).

12. Glen Ford: *The Big Heat* (1953).

13. Douglas Dumbrille: *The Lives of a Bengal Lancer* (1935).

14. Lois Maxwell: With Sean Connery in all those James Bond films.

15. Jack Carson: *Roughly Speaking* (1945).

List prepared by Elwy Yost, longtime host of TVOntario's "Saturday Night at the Movies." "I dedicate this list to the memory of Canadian actor Ned Sparks who I saw in 1933 in Lady for a Day, *a Frank Capra classic, when I was 8."*

THE PLAY'S THE THING ...
THE TEN MOST SIGNIFICANT PLAYS OF THE CONTEMPORARY
CANADIAN THEATRE
(in chronological order)

1. *Anne of Green Gables* (1965) by Don Harron, Norman Campbell, Mavor Moore, and Elaine Campbell: The most consistently popular show in Canadian theatre history, as successful today as it was thirty-five years ago. It showed that Canadians could write a hit musical. No other show has ever come along to rival it.

2. *The Ecstasy of Rita Joe* (1967) by George Ryga: Very much a work of its time, it captured perfectly the mood and feel of the Pacific Coast in the late sixties. It became the first Canadian play to form a powerful bond with its immediate constituency, and dared to address our society's unfair treatment of the Native community.

3. *Les Belles Soeurs* (1968) by Michel Tremblay: The play that told Quebec — and the rest of Canada — what Quebec was really thinking. It not only introduced us to Michel Tremblay, but it brought a whole new theatrical vocabulary onto the stage. Tremblay's later plays would say it better, but this one said it first.

4. *Leaving Home* (1972) by David French: This straightforward, naturalistic script took a form that the Americans and British had mastered decades ago, and used it to study the people and concerns of this country. Still a moving piece in its own right, it also made possible all the variations on this theme that continue to this day.

5. *Ten Lost Years* (1974), a collective creation based on the book by Barry Broadfoot: The "collective" was an important part of the Canadian theatre scene, and still is today to a lesser degree. It involved a company working on a theme or source material to yield a richly theatrical final result. None was better than this one, thanks to the strength of the original material, and the profound appeal of the story of people trying to survive against impossible odds: in this particular case, the Great Depression.

6. *Les Canadiens* (1977) by Rick Salutin ("with an assist from Ken Dryden"): This was an illustration of how good things can be when a talented author — Rick Salutin — found a perfect metaphor — hockey — to analyze a political issue of great concern — Quebec. Guy Sprung's inventive production took the best elements of collective theatre and set them at the service of a fine script.

7. *Billy Bishop Goes to War* (1978) by John Gray with Eric Peterson: Another popular form of the period was the "one-man show." Here, there were two men, with author-composer Gray at the piano, and the incredibly versatile Eric Peterson as World War I flying ace Billy Bishop and dozens of other characters. The play had wit, style, form, and something lasting to say about the nature of heroism. A successful revival twenty years later proved that this work would continue to endure.

8. *Automatic Pilot* (1980) by Erika Ritter: Another example of a play that perfectly encapsulates its time and place: in this case, Toronto at the start of the eighties. Ritter's play was deftly written in the hit-American-comedy mode, and its feminist slant and outspoken — for the time — sexual attitudes made it a hip commercial success. In the past two decades, unfortunately, no one else has mined this vein as successfully.

9. *Doc* (1984) by Sharon Pollock: For fifteen years, Sharon Pollock wrote an impressive assortment of plays that alternated between the political and the personal. The political plays seem to have had little impact after their initial productions, but her personal work - in particular, *Doc* — will endure. This is both a memory play and a family tragedy, two genres well-worn by time, but given lasting fire in the passion of Pollock's writing.

10. *Suburban Motel* (1998-9) by George F. Walker: George F. Walker has been the most-produced English language Canadian playwright in our times, but of all his many works, this collection of six one-act plays stands out. All are set in a seedy motel on the outskirts of a large North American city. The themes and characters vary, but as a portrait of this society at the end of the millennium, they are frighteningly accurate.

List prepared by Richard Ouzounian, writer, broadcaster, and critic, who has worked at most major Canadian theatres, the CBC, and TVOntario.

ACTORS/ACTRESSES WHO HAVE WON MORE THAN ONE DORA MAVOR MOORE AWARD

(The Doras have been given out each year since 1979–80 to recognize excellence in theatre in Toronto.)

1. Nancy Beatty: *Love and Anger* in 1990, *Stories* in 1991, *The Faraway Goodbye* in 1995, and *Risk Everything* in 1999.

2. Martha Burns: *Trafford Tanzi* in 1984 and *The Miracle Worker* in 1986.

3. Brent Carver: *Unidentified Human Remains* and *The True Nature of Love* in 1990, *Bent* in 1992, *Kiss of the Spiderwoman — The Musical* in 1993, and *High Life* in 1996.

4. Nicola Cavendish: *Shirley Valentine* in 1992 and *Later Life* in 1996.

5. Patricia Collins: *The Europeans* in 1990 and *White Biting Dog* in 1994.

6. Paulina Gillis: *Assassins* in 1995 and *The Barber of Seville* in 1996.

7. Robert Haley: *Singers* in 1992 and *Death and the Maiden* in 1994.

8. Stuart Hughes: *On the Verge* in 1989 and *The Collected Works of Billy the Kid* in 1990.

9. Frances Hyland: *The Heiress* in 1986 and *2000* in 1997.

10. Heath Lamberts: *A Funny Thing Happened on the Way to the Forum* in 1982, *Cyrano de Bergerac* in 1985, and *One for the Pot* in 1996.

11. Mary Ann MacDonald: *The Al Conell Story* in 1981 and *The Tyrant of Pontus* in 1992.

12. Sheila McCarthy: *Really Rosie* in 1983 and *Little Shop of Horrors* in 1985.

13. Seana McKenna: *Saint Joan* in 1991 and *Valley Song* in 1998.

14. Richard McMillan: *Prague* in 1985, *The Stone Angel* in 1993, and *Assassins* in 1995.

15. Stephen Ouimette: *Danny and the Deep Blue Sea* in 1986, *B-Movie: The Play* in 1987, and *7 Stories* in 1991.

16. Louise Pitre: *Blood Brothers* in 1989 and *Piaf* in 1994.

17. Fiona Reid: *Six Degrees of Separation* in 1995 and *Fallen Angels* in 1993.

18. Julian Richings: *The Man Himself* in 1987 and *Coming Through Slaughter* in 1990.

19. Martha Ross: As part of an ensemble for *Paranoia* in 1989 and *The Attic, the Pearls and 3 Fine Girls* in 1995.

20. Maria Vacratsis: *2nd Nature* in 1991 and as part of the company in *The Lorca Play* in 1993

21. Colm Wilkinson: *The Phantom of the Opera* in 1990 and *Les Misérables* in 1999.

22. Susan Wright: *New World* in 1985 and *A Lie of the Mind* in 1988.

Fabulous Fact

Several actors have also won awards for directing and writing including Ken McDougall, Linda Griffiths, and Richard Greenblatt.

Arts & Entertainment

CURTAIN CALL ...
BARRY MacGREGOR'S TEN BEST THEATRICAL STAGES IN CANADA

1. **The Stratford Shakespearean Festival Theatre**: This stage requires a truth from the actor in a way proscenium stages do not. That is, a deeper truth, because there is nowhere to hide.

2. **The Stratford Shakespearean Avon Theatre**: An excellent acoustic quality, especially for singing without electronic support.

3. **The Shaw Festival Theatre**: The auditorium demands an openness from the actor that automatically enhances the work. It has an acoustic quality that is a joy for both performer and audience member.

4. **The Grand Theatre, London**: This is the most exquisite theatre in the country, and a great theatre to perform in.

5. **Perspehone Theatre, Saskatoon**: Started by Susan Wright and friends, there is an amazing rapport between artist and audience, which, when you consider it was built as a place of worship, makes it a theatre that is a communicative joy to work in.

6. **The Citadel Theatre, Schoctor Stage, Edmonton**: There is not a bad seat in the house, and an openness on the stage that complements the work and the viewing. The architect did a superb job.

The beautiful arch over the stage at the Grand Theatre in London, Ontario — "the most exquisite theatre in the country." *Photo courtesy of the Grand Theatre.*

7. **The Elgin Theatre, Toronto**: A great auditorium served by an adequate stage. But the grandiose and elegant auditorium with boxes takes one back to the twenties and the feel of theatre as it once was.

8. **The Bluma Appel Theatre, Toronto**: There is a utilitarian look to the auditorium, but this fools you as it is a very intimate house.

9. **The Grand Theatre, Kingston**: The sister to the London Grand and not as well-maintained, but a good house to perform in.

10. **The Royal Alexandra Theatre, Toronto**: A majestic building of large proportions, but capable of housing large musicals and intimate theatre.

Barry MacGregor celebrated fifty years of acting on the stage in 1999.

FREEZE FRAME ... FIFTEEN OF CANADA'S MOST MEMORABLE PHOTOGRAPHS FROM THE TWENTIETH CENTURY

Frank Lennon's photograph of Paul Henderson's winning goal in the 1972 Canada-Russia hockey series is one of Canada's most memorable photographs.
Photo courtesy Frank Lennon
© "Goal of the Century"

1. Paul Henderson's winning goal in the 1972 Canada-Russia hockey series: Taken by Frank Lennon of *The Toronto Star*, this is arguably the most famous photograph in Canadian sports history. It captured Henderson and his teammates' elation in winning a series that was just the beginning of the fierce rivalry between teams from North America and Soviet Bloc countries.

2. Nose-to-nose confrontation between a Mohawk warrior and a soldier during a standoff at Oka, Quebec: The photo, taken in 1990 by Shaney Komulainen of the Canadian Press in Montreal, shows a young soldier standing his ground against an angry native while being verbally abused during a tense confrontation.

3. Conservative Leader Robert Stanfield fumbling a football during the 1974 federal election campaign: The photo received national play and is widely believed to have hurt Stanfield's image and contributed to his election loss. It was taken by Doug Ball, Canadian Press.

4. A backlit and silhouetted Terry Fox running just ahead of a police car on an early summer morning during his Marathon of Hope cross-Canada run in 1980: The photograph, by Peter Martin of United Press Canada, depicts the image of Fox that most Canadians still remember today.

5. A silhouette of former prime minister John Diefenbaker reclining on a beach in the Caribbean in the 1970s by *Toronto Star* photographer Boris Supremo: The photo shows Diefenbaker writing his memoirs as he heads into the sunset of his life.

6. The Dionne Quintuplets: This photograph, taken in 1938 at the quints' birthplace in Callandar, Ontario, shows Annette, Emilie, Cécile, and Marie sadly saluting a flag, which is being held by their sister Yvonne. The five youngsters, who were perhaps the most famous Canadians in the world at the time, are about four years old in the photo and are wearing matching uniforms. The photographer is unknown.

7. Marilyn Bell touches the seawall at Toronto after completing her 1954 swim across Lake Ontario, the first person ever to do so: The photographer was Ted Dinsmore of the *Toronto Telegram*, who had someone hold his legs while he leaned out over the water in the darkness waiting for Bell to come into view.

8. Off to World War II: A young boy in New Westminster, BC, reaches for his father as his dad marches off to war with The Duke of Connaught's Own Rifles Regiment. This shot captured the reality of young men leaving their families behind to serve Canada in the Second World War. The photo was taken in 1940 by Claude Dettloff and graces the cover of the book *Six War Years 1939–1945: Memories of Canadians at Home and Abroad* by Canadian writer Barry Broadfoot.

9. Yousef Karsh's Winston Churchill: This classic portrait of the British prime minister, minus his trademark cigar — which Karsh removed from Churchill's mouth prior to taking the photograph — was taken at Paliament Hill in 1941 while Churchill was visiting Canada. It ran on the cover of *Life* magazine and brought Karsh international fame.

10. The Stanley Cup riots, 1955: Roger St.-Jean of *La Presse* in Montreal captured National Hockey League president Clarence Campbell clutching his hat while Montreal Forum security staff restrained a protester who was incensed over Campbell's suspension of Montreal Canadiens' player Rocket Richard.

11. Massacre of fourteen women at École Polytechnique in Montreal: *Montreal Gazette* photographer Allan McInnis's photograph through a window shows a

dead student slumped in a chair in the cafeteria at the university engineering school in 1989.

12. The Halifax Explosion: This 1917 photograph shows the devastation caused in Halifax when the French munitions ship *Mont Blanc* collided with the Belgian relief ship *Imo* in Halifax Harbour causing an explosion which killed more than 1,600 people and left 6,000 people homeless. Photographer unknown.

13. Pierre Trudeau does a pirouette behind the Queen's back in 1977 as other world leaders stroll toward a dining room at Buckingham Palace: This photograph was taken by Doug Ball of Canadian Press.

14. The Springhill Mine Collapse: Amherst News photographer Ted Jolly's 1958 photograph shows draegermen being outfitted to go into the Springhill mine to aid in the rescue of one hundred men who survived the disaster. Seventy-four others died.

15. René Lévesque, accompanied by his wife Corinne, waves sadly to the crowd at the Paul Sauvé Arena in Montreal as he acknowledges defeat in the 1980 referendum: Many photographers captured this shot.

List prepared with the assistance of photographers Doug Ball, Rick Eglinton, Tim McKenna, Sam McLeod, Bill Ironside, and George Blumson, writer Pat Currie, and Brian Cantley of the Canadian Newspaper Association.

IT'S A BIRD, IT'S A PLANE ...
SEVEN CANADIAN SUPERHERO COMIC BOOK CHARACTERS

1. **Superman**: Co-created by Toronto-born Joe Shuster, with friend Jerry Siegal, the Man of Steel is one of the most famous cartoon characters in the world. Superman debuted in Action Comics #1, and more than sixty years later is the longest continuously running comic in the field.

2. **Freelance**: Created by Ed Furness in 1941, this superhero, who battled Nazis, was a popular comic among youngsters during World War II.

3. **Nelvana of the Northern Lights**: A comic book heroine created by Toronto artist Adrian Dingle in 1941, she was the beautiful protectress of the Eskimo people, fighting spies and villains. She was one of the earliest female superheroes.

4. **Johnny Canuck**: Created by Leo Bachle (now known as Les Barker) as a sixteen-year-old high school student during World War II. He had no superpowers, but battled secret agents and fought for democracy.

5. **Captain Canuck**: Created in 1975 by Richard Comely, later illustrated by the brilliant comic book artist George Freeman. This superhero worked for the Canadian International Security Organization defending Canada against evil. He was twice as strong and fast as normal humans. Captain Canuck was resurrected in the 1990s with a different storyline.

6. **Alpha Flight**: A Canadian team of superheroes, created by Canadian/American comic artist John Byrne, that defends Canada and the planet from wrongdoers. Alpha Flight first appeared in 1983 and is one of the most popular comics in North America.

7. **Fleurs de Lys**: This superhero was based in Montreal, protecting Canada from crime. Fleurs de Lys, created by Gabriel Morrissette and Mark Shainblum, debuted in 1984 and lasted until 1990.

TEN CANADIAN ANIMATED CHARACTERS

1. **Prince Valiant**: Created by Hal Foster of Halifax, Nova Scotia, this comic strip, which details the story of a fictional prince in the time of King Arthur, first appeared in 1937 in the United States. The strip provides a mix of artistic realism and fantasy, and is read by some 44 million people.

2. **Herbie**: This luckless, and chinless, Canadian cartoon soldier from World War II had a penchant for getting into scrapes and was a favourite with Canadian troops overseas. Created by Bing Coughlin, Herbie first appeared in 1944.

3. **Elmer the Safety Elephant**: A symbol of the national safety program for children, Elmer has been used as a mascot by the Canada Safety Council since 1949.

Elmer the Safety Elephant, symbol of Canada's national safety program for children since 1949. *Photo courtesy of Canada Safety Council.*

4. **Nipper**: The mischievous young boy was created by Doug Wright and appeared in *Weekend Magazine* in the 1950s and 60s. The comic strip, which didn't use dialogue, was later renamed Doug Wright's Family and appeared in the Canadian magazine.

5. **Jasper**: The friendly bear with the all-too-human characteristics, created by Jim Simpkins, was a regular feature of *Maclean's* magazine in the 1950s and 60s.

6. **Herman**: One of the most popular cartoon strips in North America, Herman was a character created by Jim Unger in 1974. Prior to that Unger had been doing editorial cartoons for the *Mississauga Times*.

7. **Peter Puck**: An impish character created by Toronto author/broadcaster Brian McFarlane in 1974 to teach hockey basics and safety tips to young hockey fans on "Hockey Night in Canada."

8. **Cerebus the Aardvark**: The satirical aardvark, who first appeared in late 1977 and was created by Dave Sim, is featured in the longest-running Canadian comic book. It's also the longest-running alternative comic book in the history of the medium.

9. **The Patterson family**: This family, featured in the popular and widely syndicated *For Better or For Worse* comic strip by Lynn Johnston, has been a familiar fixture on funny pages for many years.

10. **Mavis and Bill**: These two senior citizens are the work of Ben Wicks, who began featuring them in his comic strip *The Outcasts* around 1980. Mavis was a gentle liberal while Bill was a conservative curmudgeon.

TOP TEN CANADIAN WORKS OF ART BY VALUE SOLD AT AUCTION
(date of sale included)

1. *Untitled* (1955) by Jean-Paul Riopelle: $1.61 million, 1989.

2. *Lake Superior III* (1924) by Lawren Harris: $1.056 million, 1999.

3. *Untitled* (1950) by Jean-Paul Riopelle: $798,000, 1989.

4. *Untitled* by Jean-Paul Riopelle: $700,00, 1991.

5. *L'Autriche* (1954–55) by Jean-Paul Riopelle: $532,000, 1989.

6. *Bull Ring* by James Wilson Morrice: $520,000, 1995.

7. *Filets Frontiere* (1951) by Jean-Paul Riopelle: $462,000, 1988.

8. *...et plus...* (1959) by Jean-Paul Riopelle: $456,000, 1989.

9. *Mountains in Snow* by Lawren Harris: $450,000, 1986.

10. *The Ice Harvest* (1913) by Clarence Gagnon: $450,000, 1989.

List prepared by the Canadian Art Sales Index.

ART AND ACRIMONY — TEN CONTROVERSIAL MOMENTS IN CANADIAN ART

1. 1916, Toronto: J.E.H. MacDonald, *Tangled Garden*: Just three years after Montreal ridiculed John Lyman out of town for his "crude," unnaturalistic renderings of the human figure, Toronto hurled jibes at J.E.H. MacDonald's "crude" vision of a garden. Hector Charlesworth, most vociferous of the critics, accused the artist of having "thrown his paint pots in the face of the public."

2. 1931, Toronto: Bertram Brooker, *Nudes in a Landscape*: Accepted by the jury for the Ontario Society of Artists' exhibition of 1931, *Nudes in a Landscape* barely saw the wall before it was removed by officials concerned about the effect the content might have on young visitors. Brooker, disgusted, lashed out against such parochialism in "Nudes and Prudes," his written response to the incident. Thirty-five years later attitudes had progressed, but with dire consequences. Dorothy Cameron had no qualms about exhibiting in her gallery nudes by John Gould and Mark Prent in *Eros-65*, but the show garnered her a conviction on obscenity charges.

3. 1948, Montreal: Paul-Emile Borduas, *Refus global*: An aesthetic tract with political overtones, *Refus global*, produced by a group of francophone artists led by Borduas, was a scathing indictment of the society in French Quebec as dominated by the Roman Catholic Church. When the manifesto (all 400 copies of it) hit the stands, it exploded, effectively ending Borduas's official career in Quebec, but also rallying many to the defence of freedom of artistic expression.

4. 1968, Montreal: Greg Curnoe, *R-34*: Curnoe's mural dealing with the history of flight was being installed at Dorval Airport when U.S. Customs officials spied a likeness of President Johnson in the pilot figure dropping bombs. Unappreciative of such criticism of American imperialism, especially during the Vietnam War, they demanded the mural be removed *pronto*. The Canadian Department of Transport, which had commissioned Curnoe, complied.

5. 1982, Toronto: Michael Snow, *Flight Stop* (1979): The "ribbon caper" made it clear to corporate culture that one doesn't mess with artists. The Eaton Centre's decorating of Snow's sculpture of geese suspended from its ceiling provoked the ire and indignation of both artist and public alike. For the Centre, the red bows tied around the bird's necks created a festive atmosphere. Snow, who had not been consulted about the tampering, sued, claiming breach of copyright. The case, heard in the Ontario Supreme Court, was resolved in the artist's favour.

6. 1984, Toronto: Oscar Nemon, Canadian Airmen's Memorial (1978–1984): The fact that a private individual could commission a monument for city property, thus imposing his own interests and aesthetic tastes on the public, jolted many awake to the realities if not the shortcomings of civic process. The episode of "Gumby Goes to Heaven" (as the sculpture is still disparagingly called), prompted a host of inquiries into issues in public art.

The Canadian Airman's Memorial in Toronto, aka "Gumby Goes to Heaven," is one of the most controversial pieces of art this century.
Photo by Mark Kearney.

7. 1991, Regina: John Nugent, *Louis Riel* (1967): Nugent's bronze sculpture of the leader of the Northwest Rebellion — dressed in a simple cloak but with his genitals exposed — stood on the grounds of the Saskatchewan Legislature for a quarter of a century until it was removed in 1991 at the insistence of the Métis Society of Saskatchewan. One could hardly argue with the contention that a statue of Sir John A. Macdonald, similarly naked, would be similarly degrading. The offending statue of Riel has been relegated to the vaults of the Norman Mackenzie Art Gallery.

8. 1991, Ottawa: Barnett Newman, *Voice of Fire* (1967): The $1.8-million price tag for this painting — described as one that could have been painted by any child — outraged many. The painting is about eighteen feet high by eight feet wide, and was made up of three vertical stripes — a red one in the centre with blue ones on either side. The fact that the artist was an American didn't help the position of the National Gallery of Canada, which vigorously defended its acquisition in the press and in public roundtable discussions. Shades of 1966, when the $100,000 price tag on an abstract bronze sculpture (*The Archer*, by British artist Henry Moore) for Toronto's new City Hall caused an uproar.

9. 1991, Ottawa: Jana Sterbak, *Vanitas: Flesh Dress for an Albino Anorectic*: Versions of *Flesh Dress* had been publicly exhibited without controversy in Canadian and other cities since 1987, but the National Gallery of Canada's sponsorship of a dress made of 23 kilograms of raw meat at a cost of $300 — only to have it rot — hit a nerve. Citing rising hunger and poverty in Canada, as well as the nation's mounting deficit, critics (which included Opposition MPs and officials of the Ottawa Food Bank) grabbed the opportunity to score political points.

10. 1992, Toronto: Eli Langer, Solo Exhibition at Mercer Union Gallery: Langer's drawings and paintings of the sexual abuse of children precipitated the most heated debate to date in Canada about art censorship. Both Langer and Mercer Union Gallery's director were charged under Canada's recently implemented child-pornography law, and the works seized. Although the charges were later dropped, Langer's images became the subject of Canada's first forfeiture hearing under the new law. The Crown's application to have the artworks destroyed was unsuccessful.

List prepared by Canadian and Contemporary Art Departments, Art Gallery of Ontario.

CANADA'S TEN MOST NOTABLE TWENTIETH-CENTURY BUILDINGS
(for better or worse)

The CN Tower soars over Toronto as the world's tallest freestanding structure. *Photo by Mark Kearney.*

1. **CN Tower** (1975): The world's tallest free-standing phallic symbol got Toronto on the cover of *The Guinness Book of World Records*, but what it might really tell us is that T.O. suffers from a bad case of the edifice complex.

2. **Canadian Museum of Civilization** (1988): Douglas Cardinal's masterpiece, a sprawling complex of carved stone and curves in Hull, Quebec, can truly be called unique. It fits into its site like some giant rock outcropping, a landmark facing the Ottawa River. Too bad Hull is on the other side; no wonder Cardinal ignored it.

3. **National Gallery of Canada** (1988): Designed by Moshe Safdie, he of Expo 67 Habitat fame, this is the cultural institution reinvented as see-through cathedral. Despite its interior awkwardness, the building is one of Ottawa's architectural highlights. Safdie succeeded in paying homage to the capital's Gothic heritage while bringing it into the transparent present.

4. **SkyDome** (1989): A dinosaur from the moment it was completed, this bloated technological marvel in Toronto with the retractable roof never quite lived up to expectations. Bigger isn't always better, but the echo is terrific.

5. **Toronto City Hall** (1965): Designed by Finnish architect Viljo Revell after he won an international competition, this is the only building in Canada that deserves to be called an icon. Its appearance marked the end of Toronto's long provincial slumber. Not surprisingly, it has become the symbol of that city.

6. **West Edmonton Mall** (1981-86): Maybe it should have been called West Edmonton Sprawl; this is the architecture of consumerism writ large, very large. Future generations will look back on it as the Circus Maximus of shopping, the last gasp of a civilization that suffocated beneath the weight of its own acquisitiveness.

7. **The Eaton Centre** (1978): A little bit of suburbia transplanted into the heart of downtown Toronto. Maybe that's why it has become that city's most popular tourist destination, drawing 800,000 visitors weekly. Recently the mall underwent a major facelift that gives it a more urban appearance and a stronger sense of belonging. Architect Eberhard Zeidler did both the original and its make-over.

8. **Mississauga Civic Centre** (1987): One of the few totally convincing examples of post-modernist architecture to be built anywhere in the world, this is a masterpiece. The designers, Edward Jones and Michael Kirkland, gave civic architecture a contemporary language. Most Mississaugans hate it, of course, but that may be because it reveals the rest of their city for the mess it is.

9. **Olympic Stadium** (1973-87): Monumentalism gone monumentally wrong, this hubristic conceit, designed by French architect Roger Taillebert, is one of Montreal's biggest eyesores. Beauty may be only skin deep, but ugliness, at least in this case, goes from top to bottom.

10. **First Canadian Place** (1975): The seventy-two-storey bank tower in downtown Toronto has more Carrera marble — the translucent white stone preferred by Michelangelo — but still barely manages to rise above its own banality. If bigger is better, lighter must be brighter.

List prepared by Christopher Hume, the art and architecture critic of The Toronto Star.

Business

DOLLARS AND CENTS ...
TWELVE IMPORTANT BANKING AND FINANCE EVENTS

1. August 1914: Canada went off the gold standard, breaking forever the link between national gold reserves and the money supply.

2. August 1923: The Home Bank failed. This was a major event because there were losses to depositors as well as shareholders. The failure led to creation of the federal office of the Inspector General of Banks.

3. March 1935: Founding of the Bank of Canada as Canada's central bank.

The Bank of Canada in Ottawa.
Photo by Andrew Ray.

4. August 1935: William Aberhart was elected premier of Alberta on a Social Credit platform and began issuing his own money in the form of prosperity certificates which could be used as currency. However, the Supreme Court of Canada disallowed the practice, ruling that banking and money fell under the control of the federal government.

5. March 1954: Banks were authorized to make residential mortgage loans for the first time and also to take "chattel mortgages," which led banks to offer automobile financing.

6. June 1961: The "Coyne Affair." Prime Minister John Diefenbaker fired James Coyne as Governor of the Bank of Canada because the government felt his monetary policy was too tight.

7. September 1963: Citibank bought the Mercantile Bank. This takeover resulted in a confrontation with Finance Minister Walter Gordon because Citibank ignored Gordon's advice not to buy Mercantile, which was the only foreign bank with a charter.

8. September 1964: Canada imposed a 10 percent limit on foreign bank ownership.

9. June 1967: The federal government removed the 6 percent ceiling on interest rates charged by banks.

10. 1980: Federal legislation allowed 100 percent owned foreign banks to set up shop in Canada.

11. 1980: Creation of the Canadian Payments Association, which in addition to banks included trust companies, credit unions, and *caisses populaires* in the process of clearing and settling cheques, direct deposits, and other paper and electronic payments.

12. December 1998: The federal government rejected proposed bank mergers that would have united the Canadian Imperial Bank of Commerce with the Toronto-Dominion Bank and the Royal Bank with the Bank of Montreal.

CANADA'S TEN LEADING TRADE PARTNERS IN 1902
(in order)

1. United States	$ 192 million
2. Great Britain	$166.5 million
3. Germany	$ 13.5 million
4. France	$ 8 million
5. West Indies	$ 5.4 million
6. Belgium	$ 4.1 million
7. Newfoundland	$ 3.5 million
8. South America	$ 3.4 million
9. China/Japan	$ 2.5 million
10. Holland	$ 1.2 million

CANADA'S TEN LEADING TRADE PARTNERS IN 1997
(in order)

1. United States	$ 245 billion
2. Japan	$ 11 billion
3. United Kingdom	$ 3.8 billion
4. South Korea	$2.99 billion
5. Germany	$ 2.7 billion
6. People's Republic of China	$2.37 billion
7. Hong Kong	$ 1.7 billion
8. France	$1.67 billion
9. Netherlands	$1.67 billion
10. Brazil	$1.67 billion

Snapshot

Canadian Investment Abroad:

1925: $ 212 million
1946: $ 767 million
1966: $ 3.9 billion
1986: $ 64.7 billion
1997: $ 193.6 billion

Statistics Canada

MONETARY MILESTONES IN THE TWENTIETH CENTURY

1. 1908: A branch of the Royal Mint was established in Ottawa. For the first time Canada's official coinage was struck in Canada.

2. 1911: The last Dominion of Canada four-dollar notes were issued. They were replaced by Dominion of Canada five-dollar notes in 1912. Legislation was passed authorizing the striking of the silver dollar, Canada's first dollar coin, and two patterns for 1911 dollars were struck in silver.

3. 1912–1914: The mint struck the first decimal gold coins for general circulation. They were five-dollar and ten-dollar coins.

4. 1914: Canada went off the gold standard. This meant Canadian bank notes were no longer redeemable for gold.

5. 1920: The size of the cent was reduced from 25.4 mm to 19.05 mm.

6. 1922: The mint replaced the small, inconvenient silver five-cent piece with one made out of nickel. These quickly became known as "nickels."

7. 1931: The mint became the Royal Canadian Mint rather than a branch of the Royal Mint in England. The last twenty-five-cent note or "shinplaster" was issued for circulation.

8. 1935: On March 11, 1935, the Bank of Canada opened with a mandate to be the sole issuer of Canadian bank notes. The first issue of bank notes was unilingual English or French. The mint struck Canada's first silver dollar to

The introductions of loonies and twonies were two of the significant monetary events of the century. *Photo by Catherine Blake.*

commemorate King George V's silver jubilee and the Bank of Canada issued a $25 note to commemorate the silver jubilee.

9. 1937: Bank of Canada notes became bilingual.

10. 1968: The rising price of silver forced the mint to replace the 10-, 25-, 50-cent pieces and the dollar coin with coins made out of nickel.

11. 1989: The Bank of Canada issues the last one-dollar notes on June 30.

12. 1996: The two-dollar note is withdrawn and replaced on February 19 by a bi-metallic coin consisting of an outer ring made out of nickel and an inner core made of aluminum-bronze.

List prepared by J. Graham Esler, chief curator and head of the currency Museum, Bank of Canada.

Snapshot

Canada's Inflation Rate: Highs and Lows
Seven years when inflation was in double-digits:

1920: 16.1 percent
1981: 12.4
1951: 11.1
1982: 10.9
1974: 10.8
1975: 10.8
1980: 10.2

Eight years when inflation was less than 1 percent:

1953: -0.9 percent
1930: -0.7
1955: 0.0
1994: 0.2
1954: 0.5
1945: 0.7
1961: 0.8
1935: 0.9

Statistics Canada

TEN LARGEST CHARTERED BANKS IN 1901 (BY TOTAL ASSETS)

1. Canadian Bank of Commerce $70.5 million
2. Bank of British North America $36.1 million
3. Merchants' Bank of Canada $35.3 million
4. Dominion Bank $27.9 million
5. Bank of Nova Scotia $25.7 million
6. Imperial Bank of Canada $24.4 million
7. Molson's Bank $23.1 million
8. Bank of Toronto $21.8 million
9. Royal Bank of Canada $19.4 million
10. Bank of Hamilton $19.1 million

TEN LARGEST CHARTERED BANKS IN 1998 (BY TOTAL ASSETS)

1. Canadian Imperial Bank of Commerce $281.4 billion
2. Royal Bank of Canada $274.3 billion
3. Bank of Nova Scotia $233.5 billion
4. Bank of Montreal $222.5 billion
5. Toronto-Dominion Bank $181.8 billion
6. National Bank of Canada $ 70.6 billion
7. HSBC Canada $ 24.6 billion
8. Laurentian Bank of Canada $ 13.3 billion
9. Citibank (Canada) $ 9.1 billion
10. Deutsche Bank of Canada $ 7.9 billion

Snapshot

Telephones in Use in Canada:

1911:   303,000
1930: 1,403,000
1950: 2,917,000
1970: 9,750,000
1996: 17,781,000

Canadian Almanac

TICKER TAPE ... TEN EVENTS THAT AFFECTED CANADA'S STOCK MARKETS IN THE TWENTIETH CENTURY

1. 1929: The great crash occurred in North American financial markets, including those in Canada, in October. To this day it continues to have a psychological impact on investors.

2. 1930: The Smoot-Hawley tariff was enacted in the United States in June, killing international trade and greatly increasing the severity and length of the depression, as well as devastating Canada's financial markets.

3. 1933: The greatest statistical year ever saw North American markets skyrocket 54 percent.

4. 1946: World War II ended a year before and a massive baby boom begins. This generation of Canadians goes on to dramatically impact interest rates, inflation, stock markets, and every other commodity.

5. 1958: After decades of stocks yielding higher returns than bonds, the trend reversed. Markets finally acknowledged that bonds were a superior asset.

6. 1972: The federal government announced a budget deficit, which led to an enormous run up of debt. This in turn led to higher interest rates in Canada and a decade-long stagnation in the markets.

7. 1981: Ottawa announced a 19.5 percent savings bond rate, starting the greatest bull market for bonds in this century.

8. 1987: In October, the markets took a dive that was reminiscent of the 1929 crash. On October 19 alone, the Toronto Stock Exchange recorded an 11.13 percent loss, its largest ever drop in share prices. But governments had learned from previous crashes and managed this correction well.

9. 1989: The North American Free Trade Agreement came into effect, leading to a decade of prosperity and economic expansion in Canada and the United States and Canada's longest period of uninterrupted economic expansion since World War I.

10. 1998: The federal government balanced the books, leading to lower interest rates and setting the stage for future economic prosperity.

List prepared by David Cork, Associate Director, ScotiaMcLeod Inc. and author of The Pig and the Python: How to Prosper from the Aging Baby Boom.

TOP TEN TAX CHANGES OF THE TWENTIETH CENTURY

1. **First Federal Income Tax Introduced, 1917**: The Income War Tax Act, provided for the first federal direct tax on income in Canada. It was presented as a "temporary" measure to help finance World War I, but unsurprisingly, proved too good for the government to give up, even though the war it financed ended on November 11, 1918.

2. **Income Tax Becomes Law, 1949**: The Income Tax Act was enacted on June 30, 1948 and took effect for the 1949 and subsequent taxation years. After numerous amendments to the Income War Tax Act, the new act largely reworded and codified the former law with little change in actual policy.

3. **Registered Retirement Savings Plans Introduced, 1957**: RRSPs were unveiled so that Canadians who were either self-employed or did not belong to a benefit plan at their place of employment could put aside money for their retirement on a tax-deferred basis. At the end of the twentieth century, RRSPs were a multi-billion dollar industry, and despite some criticism in recent years, were still one of the few (and best) tax breaks available for so-called "ordinary Canadians."

4. **Arrival of the Canada Pension Plan, 1966**: Essentially a payroll tax that requires contributions from both employers and employees for a publicly financed retirement savings plan. The CPP has been mired in controversy in recent years due to serious concerns about its solvency, resulting in steep increases in the premiums that employers and employees must pay.

5. **Introduction of Capital Gains Tax, 1972**: Previously, only income from employment and investments was taxed in Canada. Effective January 1, 1972, a major tax reform resulted in a tax being levied on capital gains at a rate of 50 percent of the gain. Taxpayers were allowed two "tax-exempt" personal residences per family unit (reduced to one after 1981). Also, 1972 was the first year Revenue Canada started processing returns by computer, which meant new tax forms for all and the introduction of computerization to millions of Canadians.

6. **Tax Reform, 1985 to 1988**: This major overhaul of the tax system took effect for 1988. The number of federal tax rates was reduced from ten to three; many former tax deductions became non-refundable credits (only deducted against federal tax payable as opposed to being deducted from total income) and a "temporary" surtax, which lasted eleven years, was introduced. A $500,000 Capital Gains Exemption was introduced, and then pared down to $100,000, and the Minimum Tax plucked more from those who took advantage of

certain tax preferences. The measure that has proven to do the most long-term tax damage, especially to lower income earners, was the partial de-indexation of non-refundable credits.

7. **The Goods and Services Tax, 1991:** The GST took effect on January 1, with the intention of replacing the old Manufacturer's Sales Tax, which was hidden and open to abuse. The new national value-added tax was visible and supposedly more fairly administered; ironically its very visibility made it very easy for many people to hate it. Needless to say, it's not likely to disappear soon, given that it was expected to bring in more than $20 billion in revenue for the government in 1999.

8. **Radical Change in Claiming Tax Relief for Children, 1992:** This year was the last taxation year that Canadian families could claim a credit for their dependent children on their federal returns, although some provinces continue to have their own credits. Also, 1992 was the last year for the Child Tax Credit which was subsequently replaced with the Child Tax Benefit (since renamed the Canada Child Tax Benefit). The key difference at the time, was that the taxpayer calculated the Child Tax Credit right on his/her tax return, while the Child Tax Benefit was calculated in Ottawa and mailed to qualifying families monthly based on the level of family net income previously reported on the parents' tax returns.

9. **Common-Law Unions Recognized, 1993:** Effective for the 1993 and subsequent tax years, common-law unions began to be considered the equivalent of legal marriages for tax purposes. This was a response to court challenges that had argued that the tax system discriminated against legally married couples in favour of common-law ones. The provision cost single parents, who lived common law, their Equivalent-to-Spouse credits, and certain provincial refundable tax credits.

10. **The $100,000 Lifetime Capital Gains Exemption Abolished, 1994:** Paul Martin's first budget as finance minister on February 22 eliminated the capital gains deduction, except for qualified farm property and qualified small business corporation shares. Easily one of the most complex pieces of tax legislation ever introduced, the many Canadians who utilized the capital gains exemption that year also provided the government with a large database of information as to who owns what and where. Will an inheritance tax be the eventual result?

List prepared by Ken Baker, Manager, New Product Development, The Jacks Institute.

DOWN ON THE FARM ...
TEN SIGNIFICANT AGRICULTURAL EVENTS

Charles Saunders developed Marquis Wheat. *Photo courtesy of Agriculture and AgriFood Canada.*

1. **Development and Breeding of Marquis Wheat by Charles Saunders**: Breeding a rust resistant, high-yielding wheat enabled western Canada to become the breadbasket of the world.

2. **Massey-Harris Company Limited**: The development of farm mechanization was promoted both in Canada and around the world by Massey-Harris of Toronto, which in the 1950s became Massey-Ferguson Ltd.

3. **Potato Exports, Prince Edward Island**: The growing and export of disease-free seed potatoes from PEI has helped to improve the quantity and quality of potatoes around the world.

4. **McIntosh Apples**: The propagation of the McIntosh apple made Eastern Canada the source for quality apples all over the world. The McIntosh has parented many other notable varieties.

5. **World War II**: During the war, Canada was looked upon as the main source of food for the United Kingdom and Allied soldiers.

6. **Harvest Excursion**: During the early to mid-point of the twentieth century, when western Canada was in need of help to harvest immense crops, thousands of young men from eastern Canada headed west by train to help with the work.

7. **Foot and Mouth Disease**: The outbreak of this disease in Saskatchewan in 1952 resulted in the slaughter of thousands of animals but also set the stage for very rigorous regulations regarding the health of domestic livestock.

Canada's herd health programs are recognized around the world as being the most stringent anywhere.

8. **Artificial Insemination and Frozen Semen**: Canada is recognized worldwide for quality in dairy cattle. This high standard resulted because the dairy industry embraced artificial insemination, which made superior sires available to all in the dairy business.

9. **Canola**: The greatest change ever in crop planting came during the 1970s as a result of plant breeders developing a canola plant able to produce a more desirable oil for the food trade. As a result canola became a dominant crop on the Canadian prairies.

10. **Poultry**: Poultry production around the world has played a large part in feeding many nations. A world leader in poultry breeding was Shaver Poultry Breeding Farms of Cambridge, Ontario, where Don Shaver was a visionary in breeding strains of poultry that were both efficient and high-yield producers.

List prepared by Doug McDonell, Assistant General Manager, Royal Agricultural Winter Fair.

Snapshot

Annual Federal Income Taxes Paid by a Single Person with No Dependants:
(Does not include provincial income taxes)

	$ 30,000	$ 50,000	$100,000
1917	$ 2,520	$ 5,320	$ 14,820
1947	$ 12,564	$ 24,773	$ 59,323
1967	$ 10,520	$ 20,965	$ 50,855
1998	$ 5,527	$ 13,369	$ 37,350

Public Accounts of Canada; CCH Canada; Revenue Canada

TOP TEN AGRICULTURAL EXPORTS IN 1901*

1. Cheese
2. Pork, bacon, ham
3. Cattle
4. Wheat
5. Flour
6. Butter
7. Peas
8. Oats
9. Fruit
10. Eggs

TOP TEN AGRICULTURAL EXPORTS IN 1998

1. Wheat and meslin, which is a mix of wheat and rye
2. Live cattle
3. Rape or colza seeds (which come from the yellow-flowered plant of the same name)
4. Cuts of beef and beef carcasses
5. Crustaceans
6. Pork
7. Rape, colza, or mustard oil
8. Dried vegetables
9. Alcohol (by volume less than 80 percent), liqueurs, spirits
10. Fresh or chilled fish

Note: the definition of what consitutes an agricultural product may have changed over the years.

THE TEN LARGEST MERGERS/ACQUISITIONS IN THE TWENTIETH CENTURY INVOLVING CANADIAN COMPANIES*

(ranked by size of merger in billions of dollars)

1. Seagram Company Limited, Montreal, acquires Polygram NV of the Netherlands, May 1998. Value: $15 billion.

2. Nova Corporation and TransCanada Pipelines Limited, both of Calgary, merge, January 1998. At the same time, Nova's chemical division was spun off into a public company and distributed to shareholders of the merged company. Value: $14 billion.

3. E.I. DuPont de Nemours & Company, Wilmington, Delaware, buys back a stake in itself from Seagram Company Limited, May 1998. Value: $12.2 billion.

4. Northern Telecom Limited, Brampton, Ontario, purchases Bay Networks Incorporated, Santa Clara, California, May 1998. Value: $ 9.8 billion.

5. Seagram Company Limited acquires MCA Inc. Chicago, from Matsushita Electric Industrial Company Limited, Tokyo, April 1995. Value: $7.77 billion.

6. HSN Incorporated, St. Petersburg, Florida, acquires the U.S. television assets of Seagram Company Limited, October 1997. Value: $5.6 billion.

7. Amoco Corporation, Chicago, Illinois, acquires Dome Petroleum Limited, Calgary, April 1987. Value: $5.2 billion.

8. Imperial Oil Limited, Toronto, acquires Texaco Canada Incorporated, Calgary, January 1989. Value: $4.92 billion.

9. PepsiCo Incorporated, New York, acquires Tropicana Products Incorporated, Delaware, from Seagram Company Limited, July 1998: Value $4.9 billion.

10. Thomson Corporation, Toronto, acquires West Publishing Company, Eagan, Minnesota, February 1996. Value: $4.6 billion.

* Based on date transactions were announced.
List prepared with the assistance of Crosbie & Company Incorporated.

TOP CROWN CORPORATIONS IN CANADA IN 1998
(ranked by revenue in billions of dollars)

1.	Ontario Hydro, Toronto	$8.97
2.	Hydro-Québec, Montreal	$8.81
3.	Canada Post Corporation, Ottawa	$5.06
4.	The Canadian Wheat Board, Winnipeg	$4.68
5.	LotoQuébec, Montreal	$2.83
6.	British Columbia Hydro and Power Authority, Vancouver	$2.53
7.	Ontario Lottery Corporation, Toronto	$2.17
8.	Liquor Control Board of Ontario, Toronto	$2.16
9.	Toronto HydroElectric Commission, Toronto, Ontario	$1.85
10.	Workers' Compensation Board of Quebec, Quebec City	$1.79
11.	New Brunswick Power Corporation, Fredericton	$1.14
12.	Société des alcools du Québec, Montreal	$1.13

Canada Post headquarters in Ottawa.
Photo by Randy Ray.

HEAVYWEIGHTS ... CANADA'S TWELVE LARGEST CORPORATIONS
(Ranked by revenue in billions of dollars, year ending December 1998)

1.	General Motors of Canada, Oshawa, Ontario	$31.76
2.	BCE Incorporated, Montreal, Quebec	$27.45
3.	Ford Motor Company of Canada, Oakville, Ontario	$26.47
4.	Nortel Networks Corporation, Brampton, Ontario	$26.07
5.	Chrysler Canada Limited, Windsor, Ontario	$20.71
6.	TransCanada Pipelines Limited, Calgary, Alberta	$17.23
7.	Power Corporation of Canada, Montreal, Quebec	$15.06
8.	George Weston Limited, Toronto, Ontario	$14.73
9.	The Seagram Company Limited, Montreal*	$13.43
10.	Alcan Aluminum, Montreal, Quebec	$11.55
11.	Bombardier Incorporated, Montreal, Quebec**	$11.50
12.	Canadian Pacific Limited, Calgary, Alberta	$10.15

* Year ending June 1998
** Year ending January 1999

Snapshot

Stamp Prices
(The cost to mail a one ounce letter)

1910: 2 cents

1930: 2 cents

1950: 4 cents

1970: 6 cents

1999: 46 cents

Canada Post Corporation

CANADA'S LARGEST FOREIGN-CONTROLLED COMPANIES
(ranked by 1998 revenue)

	% Foreign ownership	Parent	Country
1. General Motors of Canada Limited $31.76 billion	100	General Motors	U.S.
2. Ford Motor Company of Canada $26.46 billion	100	Ford Motor Co.	U.S.
3. Chrysler Canada Limited $20.71 billion	100	Chrysler	U.S.
4. IBM Canada Limited $8.7 billion	100	IBM	U.S.
5. Imperial Oil Limited $7.81 billion	82	Exxon 70%	U.S.
6. Sears Canada Incorporated $4.96 million	55	Sears Roebuck	U.S.
7. Honda Canada Incorporated $4.81 million	100	Honda	Japan
8. Canada Safeway Limited $4.8 billion	100	Safeway	U.S.
9. Shell Canada Limited $4.5 billion	80	Shell 78%	Netherlands
10. Carghill Limited $3.81 billion	100	Carghill	U.S.
11. Mitsui & Company (Canada) Limited. $3.79 billion	100	Mitsui	Japan
12. Canadian Ultramar Company $3.66 billion	100	Ultramar Diamond Shamrock	U.S.

Snapshot

Foreign Investment in Canada:

1926: $ 1.7 billion
1946: $ 2.9 billion
1966: $ 19.5 billion
1986: $ 95.0 billion
1997: $ 187.5 billion

Statistics Canada

SHOP 'TIL YOU DROP ...
SEVEN SIGNIFICANT SHOPPING CENTRES IN CANADA

1. **Park Royal Shopping Centre**: Opened in West Vancouver in 1950, it was the first suburban shopping mall in Canada. The mall now has both a north side (the original mall) and a south side (construction on it began in the 1960s).

2. **Wellington Square**: Built in 1960 in London, Ontario, it was Canada and North America's first downtown mall. It was later transformed into Galleria, a larger downtown mall.

3. **Place Ville Marie**: The shopping mall running below this office tower in Montreal gained renown for being the first underground mall in Canada when it was built in 1962. Other such malls have been built since, notably under a stretch of office buildings in Toronto's core, but Montreal's is believed to be the largest in Canada.

4. **Yorkdale Shopping Centre**: Opened in 1966, this mall just off Highway 401 in Toronto was the world's largest in the late 1960s.

5. **Square One**: When this mall was built in Mississauga in 1973, it was a key component in creating a city centre, the first time in Canada where a shopping centre helped define a community core.

6. **The Eaton Centre**: Built in downtown Toronto in the 1970s, it represented a new thrust in downtown redevelopment, changing the face of Yonge Street and retailing in Canada's then second largest city.

7. **West Edmonton Mall**: One of the most famous malls in the world, this huge complex's first phase was opened in 1981 in Alberta's capital. When completed, it sprawled across 483,000 square metres and was the world's largest for many years. It still had more retail square footage than any other mall in 1999, as well as such attractions as an ice rink, a casino, and an indoor water park.

Environment & Nature

WHEN IT RAINS, IT POURS ...
TEN MOST SIGNIFICANT WEATHER EVENTS

Canadian army personnel clear debris after Hurricane Hazel in 1954. *Photo courtesy of National Archives of Canada: Gordon Jolley PA174539.*

1. **Ice Storm '98**: January 4 to 9, 1998. The most destructive and disruptive storm in Canadian history dropped close to one hundred millimetres of freezing rain in some areas of central and eastern Canada, affecting nearly 20 percent of Canada's population, mainly in Montreal and areas around Ottawa.

2. **Canada's longest and deadliest heat wave**: July 5 to 17, 1936. Seven hundred and eighty Canadians died when temperatures exceeded 42° Celsius from Alberta to southern Ontario.

3. **Hurricane Hazel**: October 15, 1954, Toronto. Canada's worst inland storm, with 178 millimetres of rain. Eighty-three people died, entire streets in west Toronto were destroyed and many bridges were washed out in the Humber River Valley in Toronto and the Holland Marsh area north of the city.

4. **Red River Flood**: May 7 to 21, 1950. More than 100,000 people were evacuated and losses exceeded $550 million (1991 dollars), compared to $450 million (1998 dollars) in the 1997 flood in the same region.

5. **Saguenay Flood**: July 18 to 21, 1996. Canada's first billion-dollar disaster resulted in 10 deaths and 1,718 houses and 900 cottages destroyed or damaged when the Saguenay River in Saguenay, Quebec, flooded.

6. **Worst blizzard in Canadian history**: January 30 to February 8, 1947. A ten-day storm buried towns and trains in the southern prairies.

7. **Edmonton's "Black Friday" tornado**: July 31, 1987. This severe twister killed twenty-seven people.

8. **Calgary hailstorm**: September 7, 1991. There were 116,000 insurance claims and damage exceeded $340 million.

9. **Ocean drilling rig *Ocean Ranger* sinks**: February 15, 1982. Eighty-four people died in the world's second worst disaster in offshore drilling when an intense Atlantic storm from the Gulf of Mexico battered the rig with five-storey high waves and hurricane-force winds that reached 168 kilometres per hour.

10. **Snag, Yukon Territory**: February 3, 1947. Canada's record cold temperature was set when the mercury plunged to -63° C, solidifying Canada's reputation as a cold weather country.

List prepared by David Phillips, Senior Climatologist, Environment Canada.

Fabulous Fact

In the summer, an average of one tornado every five days is reported in Canada, compared to five tornadoes every day in the United States.

SHAKE, RATTLE, AND ROLL ...
TEN MAJOR CANADIAN EARTHQUAKES
(in order of magnitude)

1. 1949: Magnitude 8.1 on the Richter Scale. Off the Queen Charlotte Islands in British Columbia. Canada's largest earthquake in the twentieth century. The shaking was so severe on the islands that cows were knocked off their feet and people could not stand, but the value of the damage was not high because of the sparse population. Felt over a wide area of western North America.

2. 1970: Magnitude 7.4. Offshore, south of the Queen Charlotte Islands. Widely felt but no damage.

3. 1933: Magnitude 7.3. Baffin Bay. Largest earthquake known to have occurred north of the Arctic Circle.

4. 1946: Magnitude 7.3. Central Vancouver Island. Canada's largest on-land earthquake in the twentieth century. Extensive property damage along the east coast of Vancouver Island; 75 percent of the chimneys were knocked down in the closest communities of Courtenay, Cumberland, and Union Bay. One person was drowned and one died of a heart attack. The earthquake was felt from Oregon to Alaska and east to the Rocky Mountains.

5. 1929: Magnitude 7.2. Atlantic Ocean, south of Newfoundland. Most serious loss of life in any recorded Canadian earthquake. Felt over a wide area of eastern North America, the earthquake caused a large underwater landslide which broke twelve trans-Atlantic telegraph cables and generated a tsunami (tidal wave). Twenty-seven people were drowned and much damage was caused by the five-metre high wave along the Burin Peninsula. A two-storey house was swept into the sea in southern Newfoundland.

6. 1918: Magnitude 7. Near the west coast of Vancouver Island. The earthquake occurred just after midnight on December 6 and awakened people all over Vancouver Island and in the greater Vancouver area. Damage was light due to the very sparse population in the epicentral area. Estevan lighthouse and a wharf in Ucluelet were damaged.

7. 1985: Magnitude 6.9. Nahanni region, Northwest Territories. Widely felt in the Northwest Territories, Alberta, and British Columbia. A smaller event (magnitude 6.6) that occurred in the same area two months earlier triggered an immense rock avalanche containing five to seven million cubic metres of rock.

8. 1925: Magnitude 6.2. Charlevoix-Kamouraska region, Quebec. Felt over most of Quebec, the Maritimes, southern Ontario, and parts of northeastern United States. There was considerable damage in the epicentral region, and on both shores of the St. Lawrence River, with churches in Saint Urbain and Rivière-Ouelle severely damaged. Buildings were damaged in the lower-town area of Quebec City and also in Shawinigan, about 250 kilometres from the epicentre.

9. 1988: Magnitude 5.9. Saguenay region, Quebec. Felt to a one-thousand-kilometre radius from the epicentre. The earthquake occurred in the Laurentian Fauna Reserve some 40 kilometres south of Chicoutimi. It caused several tens of millions of dollars in damage, with damage reported as far away as the city hall in Montreal, about 350 kilometres from the epicentre.

10. 1944: Magnitude 5.8. Eastern Ontario-New York border. Widely felt. Although the earthquake was of relatively low magnitude, it caused considerable damage in Cornwall, Ontario and Massena, New York. Damage totalled $2 million.

List prepared by the National Earthquake Hazards Program, Geological Survey of Canada, Natural Resources Canada.

ELEVEN SIGNIFICANT METEORITE STRIKES

1. **Abee, Alberta**: A single stone weighing about 110 kilograms fell June 9, 1952 at 11:05 p.m., and was found on June 14, 1952, nearly two metres deep in a seventy-five centimetre hole. The rock's mineralogy and composition suggested it originated near the sun and may have come from Mercury.

2. **Annaheim, Saskatchewan**: Possibly fell January 21, 1914, when there was a spectacular fireball. Found July 30, 1916. It is an iron meteorite weighing 11.84 kilograms, with textbook "regmaglypts" or thumbprint-like depressions on its surface caused by atmospheric melting.

3. **Bruderheim, Alberta**: A shower of more than five hundred stony meteorites, some as small as peas, which fell March 4, 1960, at 1:06 a.m. It is the biggest Canadian meteorite fall, with more than three hundred kilograms recovered from snowy fields.

4. **Catherwood, Saskatchewan**: A single rusted stony meteorite weighing four kilograms was found in 1964 or 1965 and recognized as a meteorite in 1971. It contains shocked veins with high pressure minerals probably formed by impact or collision in space.

5. **Dresden, Ontario**: Several pieces of this stony meteorite fell July 11, 1939 at 8:56 p.m. after a spectacular fireball moved south over Georgian Bay. The largest fragment, weighing about forty kilograms, was found July 12, in a vertical hole 1.5 metres deep in a beet field. Sold by the farmer to an oil prospector for four dollars, it is now at the University of Western Ontario.

6. **Innisfree, Alberta**: About four kilograms of this stony meteorite fell February 5, 1977 at 7:17 p.m. The first two-kilogram piece was recovered February 17. The fall of the meteorite was recorded on special cameras and the data was used to find the pieces and to calculate an orbit that showed it came from the Asteroid Belt, only the third such calculation from a fall.

7. **West of Peace River, Alberta**: Pieces of this stony meteorite, totalling forty-six kilograms, fell March 31, 1963, at 4:35 a.m., accompanying a noisy and brilliant fireball. Quick action by scientists from the University of Alberta in compiling eyewitness reports led to the recovery of nine fragments weighing between .36 kilograms and 16.6 kilograms.

8. **St-Robert-de-Sorel, Quebec**: Just after 8 p.m. on June 14, 1994, a shower of stony meteorites fell on this village. Curious cows alerted Stéphane Fortier to

Stéphane Fortier holds piece of a meteorite found near Montreal in 1994. *Photo courtesy of Geological Survey of Canada.*

the first 2.3-kilogram piece minutes later. Analytical work started within three days. In all, more than twenty kilograms have been recovered. The first piece was bought by the National Meteorite Collection of Canada for $10,000 (Cdn). The largest 6.5-kilogram piece, the biggest meteorite from Quebec, was donated to the national collection as a cultural property gift.

9. **Shelburne, Ontario**: Hundreds of witnesses reported a fireball on the evening of August 13, 1904. Two stones of 12.6 kilograms and 6.0 kilograms were recovered. The smaller one fell near a house and penetrated about sixty centimetres into the ground, carrying with it a large burdock leaf, which was still green and uncharred when dug up.

10. **Springwater, Saskatchewan**: Three separate masses weighing 38.6, 18.6, and 10.5 kilograms were recognized in the summer of 1931. Slices of this "pallasite" stony-iron reveal yellow-brown gemmy olivine (peridot) crystals in an iron matrix. Famous in collections throughout the world, only a small amount of it remains in Canada thanks to the famous American meteorite hunter, H.H. Nininger.

11. **Doon Valley Golf Course near Kitchener, Ontario**: A single stony meteorite weighing 203 grams narrowly missed hitting a golfer on the sixth tee just after 8:30 a.m., July 12, 1998. Identified at the University of Toronto, it was purchased on October 1, 1998. The finder got a year's worth of free golf as part of his reward.

List prepared by Dr. Richard K. Herd, Curator, National Meteorite Collection of Canada, Geological Survey of Canada, Natural Resources Canada.

SPECIES DECLARED EXTINCT IN CANADA IN THE TWENTIETH CENTURY

1. **Passenger Pigeon**: Saskatchewan, Manitoba, New Brunswick, Nova Scotia, Ontario, Prince Edward Island, Quebec, 1914.

2. **Woodland Caribou**: Queen Charlotte Islands, British Columbia, 1920s.

3. **Eelgrass Limpet**: Newfoundland, Nova Scotia, Quebec, 1929.

4. **Deepwater Cisco**: Ontario, 1952.

5. **Blue Walleye**: Ontario, 1965.

6. **Longjaw Cisco**: Ontario, 1975.

7. **Banff Longnose Dace**: Alberta, 1986.

List prepared by the Committee on the Status of Endangered Wildlife in Canada.

RUTH GRIER'S ENVIRONMENTAL MILESTONES OF THE TWENTIETH CENTURY

1. 1909: The Boundary Waters Treaty between Canada and the U.S. created the International Joint Commission. The IJC's first investigation of pollution in the Great Lakes was in 1912. Its research and advocacy led to the Great Lakes Water Quality Agreement in 1972.

2. 1917: The Migratory Birds Convention Act was enacted. This implemented the Treaty for International Protection of Migratory Birds which was signed by Canada and the U.S. in 1916. It was the first international treaty for the conservation of wildlife.

3. 1935: The Prairie Farm Rehabilitation Act was enacted. Under this legislation federal and provincial governments joined to rehabilitate agricultural land and improve community life in the drought-stricken prairies.

4. 1970: Mercury pollution of the English-Wabigoon River system in Northern Ontario and the destruction of the native community's fishery and way of life drew attention to the damaging effects of industrial discharges and forced the Ontario government to order an end to mercury emissions.

5. 1971: Opening of the first CANDU nuclear power reactor at Ontario Hydro's Pickering plant just east of Toronto began years of controversy over the use of nuclear power. The problem of how to dispose of radioactive waste is still unsolved.

6. 1971: Greenpeace was founded by anti-nuclear activists in Vancouver and quickly became a national and international movement in the fight for a clean environment. Ontario's Pollution Probe had been founded in 1969 and environmental groups mushroomed in the 1970s and 1980s and mounted effective campaigns to raise awareness and change public policy towards protecting the environment.

7. 1975: The James Bay and Northern Quebec agreement on hydro-electric development was signed by the governments of Canada and Quebec, Quebec Hydro, and the Cree and Inuit nations. The agreement dealt with future development over a huge area and was the first such negotiation with First Nations.

8. 1977: The Berger Report on the proposed Mackenzie Valley Pipeline was released. The importance of the Berger Inquiry was not just the conclusion that a ten-year moratorium be placed on pipeline development but also the

way Justice Berger travelled throughout the north listening to the concerns of native peoples and the innovative concept of providing public funding to ensure intervenors a voice in the process.

9. 1979: An epidemic of spruce budworm in Nova Scotia led to widespread protest against the spraying of pesticides. The provincial government was forced to move to Bacillus thuringiensis, an organic substitute for synthetic pesticide which has since become widely used.

10. 1982: The City of Kitchener, Ontario, introduced a blue box into which householders could place paper, glass, and cans for recycling. The Blue Box has become widely used in Canada in response to widespread public demands for better management of waste and for opportunities for individual action.

11. 1985: The Acid Rain Agreement was signed, committing Canada and the seven eastern provinces to reduce sulphur dioxide emissions. The signing ended a successful campaign by the Canadian Coalition Against Acid Rain which had effectively lobbied the Canadian and U.S. governments and drawn attention to the acidification of lakes in Ontario and Quebec.

12. 1987: South Moresby Island became a national park. The struggle to stop logging in British Columbia's temperate rain forests did not end with this victory. In the 1980s and 1990s, the Carmanah and Stein valleys, Clayoquot Sound, and the Great Bear rainforest saw environmentalists, loggers, First Nations, and governments repeatedly clash over the future of forests.

List prepared by Ruth Grier, who was Ontario Environment Minister, 1990 to 1993.

TEN KEY ENVIRONMENTAL EVENTS IN CANADA FROM A LEGAL PERSPECTIVE

1. The Boundary Waters Treaty which established the International Joint Commission in 1909: Using the treaty, the six-member commission prevents or resolves disputes between Canada and the United States involving air and water pollution.

2. The development, use, and banishment of destructive polychlorinated biphenyls (PCBs) imported into Canada for use in light ballasts, capacitors, and transformers: Significant public attention was focused on PCBs in the late 1980s after a spill of the deadly material onto the Trans-Canada Highway in Ontario and a significant fire involving PCBs and solvents in Quebec. PCB destruction technology was first developed in Ontario, Alberta, and Quebec.

3. The use of environmental assessments in the 1980s and 1990s for new projects, and particularly for the establishment and development of major developments, such as waste disposal sites, water diversion, and hydro-electric projects: Environmental assessments have had a checkered past, but have had a major impact on the development of projects, both public and private, in Canada. Significant issues such as intervenor funding, social and economic policies, and aboriginal claims have resulted in extensive hearings lasting many years.

4. The November 10, 1979, train derailment in Mississauga, Ontario: Twenty-four of 106 eastbound cars derailed, including a tanker carrying chlorine, triggering the evacuation of 220,000 people. The incident ultimately led to the development of the federal Transportation of Dangerous Goods Act and a series of important regulations. It also assisted in the development of a model for emergency evacuations used around the world.

5. Development of the blue box program in Kitchener, Ontario, in 1982.

The blue box recycling program has played a key role in making Canada's environment better. *Photo by Catherine Blake.*

6. The Montreal Protocol on Substances that Deplete the Ozone Layer: After being ratified by twenty-nine countries and the European Economic Commission, which represented approximately 82 percent of world consumption of ozone-depleting substances, the protocol came into force on January 1, 1989. In 1999, 165 countries were parties to the Convention and the Protocol, which had been amended four times in a continuing bid to reduce and eventually eliminate emissions of man-made ozone-depleting substances.

7. The imposition of personal liability for environmental damage: This issue was highlighted when charges were laid against shoemaker Thomas Bata for events which occurred in 1988 and 1989. He was charged with failing to take reasonable care in preventing unlawful discharge. Although Bata was acquitted, the case sent shock waves through boardrooms across Canada and has been partly the impetus in Canada for increased corporate environmental management, such as environmental auditing and formal written environmental management systems.

8. The "death" of the fisheries, both in Atlantic Canada and British Columbia in the 1980s and 1990s: For some, this crisis illustrated the need to act regionally and globally to protect resources and be skeptical of government resource policies.

9. The North American Free Trade Agreement (NAFTA) and the companion North American Agreement for Environmental Cooperation (NAAEC) in 1994: The Commission for Environmental Cooperation (CEC) was created under the NAAEC. The CEC's members include Canada, Mexico, and the United States. Their mandate is to address regional environmental concerns, help prevent potential trade in environmental conflicts, and promote effective enforcement of environmental law.

10. The identification and remediation of contaminated property, particularly in the 1980s and 1990s: It has sparked a number of issues and developments, including the recognition of significant risks associated with sites such as the Sydney, Nova Scotia tar ponds, Hamilton Harbour, and Vancouver's Expo '86 site; the development of new techniques to identify contaminants at extremely low levels and the development and use of risk assessment.

List prepared by Len Griffiths and Roger Cotton, environmental specialists and partners at Toronto law firm Tory Tory DesLauriers & Binnington.

FIFTEEN LARGEST OIL DISCOVERIES

	Oil Field	Year of Discovery	Reserves (millions of barrels)
1.	Pembina, Alberta	1953	3374
2.	Swan Hills, Alberta	1957	943
3.	Redwater, Alberta	1948	811
4.	Rainbow, Alberta	1965	723
5.	Hibernia, Grand Banks, Newfoundland	1979	671
6.	Bonnie Glen, Alberta	1952	534
7.	Judy Creek, Alberta	1959	466
8.	Swan Hills South, Alberta	1957	425
9.	Nipisi, Alberta	1965	392
10.	Mitsue, Alberta	1964	384
11.	Leduc-Woodbend, Alberta	1947	383
12.	Wizard Lakes, Alberta	1951	365
13.	Terra Nova, Grand Banks, Newfoundland	1984	341
14.	Willesden Green, Alberta	1956	336
15.	Weyburn, Saskatchewan	1953	331

List prepared by N.J. McMillan, Senior Research Scientist, Geological Survey of Canada.

ALL THAT GLITTERS ...
TEN KEY MINERAL DISCOVERIES

1. 1903: Discovery of silver, with accompanying cobalt and nickel, at Cobalt, Ontario. Ontario rapidly became one of the world's leading silver producing districts, yielding more than 18,000 metric tonnes of silver between 1903 and 1989, when the last mine closed.

2. 1909: Discovery of the large Hollinger, McIntyre, and Dome gold deposits in the Porcupine District of Ontario (now the city of Timmins). The Porcupine has been Canada's all-time largest gold producing district, and has yielded some 2,200 metric tonnes (seventy million troy ounces) of gold.

3. 1911: First discoveries of gold ore along the "Golden Mile" at Kirkland Lake, Ontario, which has yielded some 780 metric tonnes (twenty-five million troy ounces) of gold from several mines. This makes Kirkland Lake Canada's second most important gold district. Production continues from the one remaining mine (Macassa).

4. 1943: Discovery of some fifty billion tonnes of potash, during drilling of an oil well, in southern Saskatchewan. This discovery has made Canada the world's leading producer of potash, which is used as fertilizer.

5. 1954: Commencement of production of iron ore from the "Labrador Trough" on the Quebec-Labrador boundary, Canada's leading iron-ore producing region.

6. 1956: Discovery of the Thompson nickel deposit in Manitoba. The Thompson Nickel Belt has yielded nickel from six mines and is Canada's second most important nickel mining area.

7. 1963: Discovery of the world-class Kidd Creek orebody at Timmins, Ontario. With its 150 million tonnes of copper-zinc-silver ore, formed by volcanic action on the former ocean floor, Kidd Creek is one of the world's largest orebodies of its type.

8. 1968: Discovery of the Rabbit Lake uranium deposit in Saskatchewan's Precambrian Athabasca Basin, the first of many uranium orebodies found in the Basin, which has become the world's most important uranium mining area.

9. 1972: Discovery of a five hundred million tonne-plus zinc-lead deposit at Howard's Pass, on the Yukon-Northwest Territories boundary. Although this deposit has not yet been mined because of its remote location, it is likely the world's largest zinc-lead deposit.

10. 1992: Discovery of Canada's first diamond orebody, at Lac de Gras, Northwest Territories, where production began in October 1998. With production from this mine and others expected in the Northwest Territories, Canada will become one of the world's important diamond-producing nations.

List prepared by Donald A. Cranstone, Senior Mineral Economist, Minerals and Metals Sector, Natural Resources Canada.

Fabulous Fact

Between two and five billion years ago pieces of the earth's crust butted together in northern Ontario with a force that created a mountain range as tall as the Rocky Mountains in Western Canada. This area, which runs from the Ontario-Quebec border north of Lake Superior to the Manitoba-Ontario border, contains some of the world's richest gold, silver, copper, and zinc mines.

DON'T YOU DARE ... TEN ENVIRONMENTAL NO-NOS IN RECENT TIMES

1. Throwing old newspapers or metal and plastic containers out with the trash.

2. Burning garbage.

3. Using aerosol hair spray and deodorants fuelled by CFCs.

4. Tossing litter out the car window.

5. Pouring used motor oil down a drain or into street sewers.

6. Using leaded gas in vehicles.

7. Clearcutting forests.

8. Drinking from styrofoam cups.

9. Using PCBs in transformers.

10. Smoking cigarettes indoors or in a vehicle.

FOUR OF THE WORST FOREST FIRES IN CANADA* IN THE TWENTIETH CENTURY

Location	Year	Lives Lost	Buildings Destroyed	Area Burned (km²)
1. Hailebury, Ont.	1922	44	6000	5000
2. Matheson, Ont.	1916	244	500	2000
3. Porcupine, Ont.	1911	73	1000	2000
4. Baudette, Ont.	1910	42	500	1000

*No information for historical fires available from western Canada

List prepared by Natural Resources Canada.

CANADA'S KEEPERS OF THE ENVIRONMENT IN THE TWENTIETH CENTURY

1. **Elizabeth May**: Originally a Nova Scotia environmental activist and, in 1999, executive director of the Ottawa-based Sierra Club of Canada, she was a policy advisor with Environment Canada who went on to co-ordinate efforts that saved the South Moresby forests on the Queen Charlotte Islands. She told the story in the book *Paradise Won*. May's 1998 book, *At the Cutting Edge: The Crisis in Canada's Forests*, warned that the country's trees could suffer the same fate as the Atlantic cod.

2. **Bob Hunter and Paul Watson**: Co-founders in Vancouver in 1971 of Greenpeace, the world's largest environmental group, with operations in more than twenty-five countries. Hunter and Watson were among twelve people who sailed a rickety fishing boat to Alaska's Amchitka Island in an attempt to stop a U.S. underground nuclear bomb test. They later branched out to help stop the baby seal hunt off Canada's east coast.

3. **Monte Hummel**: Hummel was a member of the group of right-thinking University of Toronto students who founded one of Canada's most highly regarded environmental groups, Pollution Probe, in 1969. He was also in on the ground floor of the influential Canadian Coalition on Acid Rain. Since 1978, Hummel, who holds Master's degrees in philosophy and forestry, has been president of the World Wildlife Fund/Canada, one of the biggest conservation groups in the country.

4. **Michael Keating:** He built a reputation as Canada's finest environmental journalist when he pushed the acid rain issue onto the front pages of *The Globe and Mail*, where he worked as a reporter from 1979 to 1988. He was awarded a United Nations environmental citation for his work. An influential opinion maker as an environmental consultant, he has written several books including *To the Last Drop: Canada and the World's Water Crisis*, and the indispensable *Covering the Environment: A Handbook on Environmental Journalism*.

5. **Daniel Green**: Quebec's most outspoken environmentalist, he joined the fledgling Montreal-based Societé Pour Vaincre la Pollution (Society to Vanquish Pollution) as a biological science college student in 1973. As head of the society, he has taken on and conquered numerous provincial institutions like Hydro-Quebec and major industries responsible for hazardous waste sites and the dumping of pollution into the St. Lawrence River.

6. **Ric Careless**: As the executive director of B.C. Spaces for Nature, he led the campaign that influenced the British Columbia government's decision to turn

the one-million-hectare Tatshenshini region in the remote northern end of the province into a park in 1993. He has received B.C.'s environmentalist of the year award, the Order of British Columbia, and was the American Rivers conservation group's Outstanding River Conservationist in 1993.

7. **Margherita Howe**: One of the first ladies of the Canadian environmental movement, she was 58 when she started Operation Clean in 1979. The group's aim was to battle the industrial chemical poisons flowing into the Niagara River and out to Lake Ontario, and spurred cleanup efforts on both sides of the Canadian and U.S. border to stop toxic waste from getting into the water.

8. **Firoz Rasul**: Chairman and chief executive officer of Ballard Power Systems Inc. of Vancouver, which has developed a revolutionary fuel cell for vehicle engines that converts hydrogen into electricity, leaving pure water as its only emission. Started in 1982, Ballard is working with several automakers to produce pollution-free vehicles that one day may operate without smog-producing gasoline.

9. **Adele Hurley and Michael Perley**: Both were environmental researchers in Toronto before opening shop in Washington D.C. in 1981 as lobbyists for the Canadian Coalition on Acid Rain. Nine years later they were on hand when the U.S. Congress approved an acid rain cleanup program. The American capital had seen nothing like it from north of the border since the British set fire to the White House during the War of 1812. They convinced the Americans that acid rain was hurting the U.S. as much as Canada.

10. **Pierre Beland**: He is senior research scientist with the St. Lawrence National Institute of Ecotoxicology and world-renowned expert on beluga whales. He has the unusual combination of scientific objectivity and the literary passion of an evocative writer. He is the author *of Beluga: A Farewell to Whales*, the most compelling book on the plight of the pure white and highly intelligent mammal that he discovered was being killed off by pollution in the St. Lawrence River. Since 1982, Beland has been determined to save these creatures.

11. **Sir George Gibbons**: In 1906, this British negotiator recognized the need to protect the Great Lakes-St. Lawrence River system and other waterways that traverse the border between Canada and the U.S. He hatched the idea of a Boundary Waters Treaty, which in 1909 was signed by the two countries, later leading to the creation of the International Joint Commission, the bilateral agency that has evolved into an environmental advocate.

List prepared by Brian McAndrew, environmental reporter at The Toronto Star.

CANADA'S TEN LARGEST ISLANDS

1.	Baffin Island	507,451 sq. km.
2.	Victoria Island	217,291
3.	Ellesmere Island	196,236
4.	Newfoundland Island	108,860
5.	Banks Island	70,028
6.	Devon Island	55,247
7.	Axel Heiberg Island	43,178
8.	Melville Island	42,149
9.	Southampton Island	41,214
10.	Prince of Wales Island	33,339

CANADA'S TEN HIGHEST MOUNTAINS
(all are in the Yukon)

1.	Mt. Logan	5,959 metres
2.	Mt. St. Elias	5,489
3.	Mt. Lucania	5,226
4.	King Peak	5,173
5.	Mt. Steele	5,067
6.	Mt. Wood	4,838
7.	Mt. Vancouver	4,785
8.	Mt. Fairweather	4,663
9.	Mt. Macaulay	4,663
10.	Mt. Slaggard	4,663

History

EIGHT DARK DAYS IN CANADA ... AND A BLOODY ONE

1. **June 21, 1919 — Bloody Saturday**: So named when police charged a demonstration of strikers during the Winnipeg General Strike, killing two strikers and wounding twenty others.

2. **October 24, 1929 — Black Thursday**: The Toronto Stock Exchange and other markets in North America take a dive, the first signal of what is to come five days later.

3. **October 29, 1929 — Black Tuesday**: Prices on Canadian stock markets crash, along with those on Wall Street and around the world. Experts say the Canadian economy was more seriously damaged than the American one. In the months of October and November the TSE lost 29 percent of its value.

4. **February 20, 1959 — Black Friday**: The Conservative government of John Diefenbaker cancelled the Avro Arrow supersonic jet aircraft project, throwing 14,000 employees out of work.

5. **June 1, 1966 - Black Friday**: So named by Conservative Member of Parliament Thomas Bell after a bill to provide an $80 million loan to U.S-owned Trans-Canada PipeLines was approved in the House of Commons.

6. **September 27, 1980 — Black Tuesday**: Term given to this day, which saw the simultaneous closure of daily newspapers *The Ottawa Journal* and *The Winnipeg Tribune*.

7. **July 31, 1987 - Black Friday**: A dark weather day in Edmonton when a severe twister killed twenty-seven people.

8. **October 19, 1987 - Black Monday**: Aptly named after the Toronto Stock Exchange dropped 11.13 percent, the greatest one-day drop in share prices in its history.

9. **October 27, 1997 — Grey Monday**: The Toronto Stock Exchange 300 index lost 6.17 percent of its value.

TWELVE PASSINGS ... THE END OF AN ERA IN CANADA

1. **The *Bluenose***: Canada's most famous ship was sold in 1942 to a West Indies trading company. Four years later it was wrecked off the coast of Hawaii.

2. *Montreal Herald*: After 146 years, the newspaper stopped publication in October 1957.

3. **Studebaker**: In March 1966, the automaker announced it would stop building cars in Hamilton, Ontario.

4. **Saturday Mail Delivery**: Eliminated by Canada Post on February 1, 1969.

5. **Royal Canadian Mounted Police Dogs**: The RCMP announced on March 4, 1969, that its remaining dog teams would be replaced by snowmobiles.

6. **The Eaton's Catalogue**: In January of 1976, the department store stopped printing its catalogue, which had been a mainstay in Canadian homes since 1884, and in August 1999 the company declared bankruptcy and announced the closure of its stores.

7. **East Coast Rail Service**: In the summers of 1988 and 1989, Prince Edward Island and Newfoundland lost their railways.

8. **United Kingdom Authority**: At the request of Canada, the Parliament of the United Kingdom enacted the Constituton Act in 1982, patriating the Canadian constitution and ending all remaining UK control over Canada.

9. **Stanley Knowles**: The MP for Winnipeg North Centre didn't run for office in the 1984 election, after holding a seat in the House of Commons for thirty-eight years with the Co-operative Commonwealth Federation and the New Democratic Party. Knowles sat in the Commons longer than any other MP in the twentieth century and was known for his mastery of Commons rules of procedure.

10. **Front Page Challenge**: The popular CBC show, which featured a panel of celebrities who tried to guess the identity of people in the headlines, was last seen in the spring of 1995. The show first aired in June 1957.

11. **Red Cross Blood Collection**: On the heels of the 1980s tainted blood scandal, the Canadian Red Cross sold the blood supply system to the newly created Canadian Blood Services in September 1998. The Red Cross had been in charge of blood collection for more than forty years.

12. **Wayne Gretzky**: In 1999, after twenty years in the National Hockey League with the Edmonton Oilers, Los Angeles Kings, St. Louis Blues, and New York Rangers, The Great One announced his retirement. His last game in a Canadian arena was at the Corel Centre, in Kanata, Ontario, on April 15, 1999. His final game in the NHL was three days later at Madison Square Garden in New York.

Wayne Gretzky waves to Ottawa fans after playing his last game in Canada.
Photo courtesy of the **Ottawa Citizen.**

CANADIAN FIRSTS ... 1900 to 1950

1. The first symphony orchestra in Canada began at Quebec City: 1902.

2. The first dial telephones came into use at Sydney Mines, Nova Scotia: 1907.

3. The first Canadian service station was set up in Vancouver: 1908.

4. John Alexander Douglas McCurdy flew the Silver Dart at Baddeck, Nova Scotia in the first powered flight in Canada: 1909.

5. The first parachute jump in Canada was made by Charles Saunders at Vancouver: 1912.

6. Thomas Wilby became the first person to drive across Canada in a fifty-two-day trip between Halifax and Victoria: 1912.

7. Canada's first feature film, *Evangeline,* premiered in Halifax: 1913.

8. First radio transmission of music took place between Montreal and the Chateau Laurier Hotel in Ottawa: 1918.

9. First exhibition of the Group of Seven, Art Gallery of Toronto: 1920.

10. The first service of the United Church took place: 1925.

11. The Dionne quintuplets were born, the first surviving quintuplets in Canada and the world: 1934.

12. The Canadian Film Board documentary *Churchill's Island* was the first Canadian film to win an Academy Award: 1941.

13. The Co-operative Commonwealth Federation won the Saskatchewan provincial election to become the first socialist provincial government in Canada: 1944.

14. Canadian families received their first family allowance payments: 1945.

15. Canada's first drive-in movie theatre opened in the Hamilton area: 1946.

CANADIAN FIRSTS ... 1950 to 2000

1. CBFT, Canada's first television station, began transmitting in Montreal: 1952.

2. The Yonge Street subway opened, the first underground public transit system in Canada: 1954.

3. Seven-year-old Roger Woodward became the first person to fall accidentally over Niagara's Horseshoe Falls and survive: 1960.

4. The first non-North American car assembly plant in the country, built by Volvo, opened in Dartmouth, Nova Scotia: 1963.

5. Canada's new Maple Leaf flag was flown for the first time on Parliament Hill: 1965.

6. Free tuition was announced for all first-year students at Memorial University in Newfoundland, the first such tuition-break in Canada: 1965.

7. The Cat's Whiskers, Canada's first strip bar, opened in Vancouver: 1966.

8. Dr. Pierre Grondin of the Montreal Heart Institute performed Canada's first heart transplant operation: 1968.

9. Prime Minister Pierre Trudeau marries Margaret Sinclair in North Vancouver, becoming the first prime minister to marry while in office: 1971.

10. Canada's first astronauts were chosen, including Marc Garneau, Canada's first man in space and Roberta Bondar, Canada's first woman in space: 1983.

11. Pope John Paul II made the first papal visit to Canada: 1984.

12. The Canadian people received the Nansen Medal from the United Nations for helping refugees around the world, marking the first time an entire nation received the award: 1986.

13. New Democratic Party Member of Parliament Svend Robinson was the first MP to publicly declare his homosexuality: 1988.

14. Heather Erxleben became the first female combat soldier in the Canadian Armed Forces: 1989.

15. Gillian Guess of Vancouver was the first juror in North America and the Commonwealth to be tried for consorting sexually with an accused: 1995.

HEAD FOR THE HILLS …
TEN WORST KILLER DISASTERS
(ranked by number of fatalities)

1. **Spanish Influenza Outbreak**: Between 1918 and 1925 this virus infection affected all regions of the country, killing more than 50,000 Canadians.

2. **Halifax Explosion**: On December 6, 1917 the French munitions ship *Mont Blanc* collided with the Belgian relief ship *Imo* in Halifax Harbour causing an explosion that killed more than 1,600 people and seriously injured 9,000 more. Six thousand people were left homeless and property damage was estimated at $50 million.

Damage caused by the Halifax explosion. *Photo courtesy of National Archives of Canada: C19953.*

3. **St. Lawrence River Collision**: On May 29, 1914, 1,012 people died when Canadian Pacific steamer *Empress of Ireland* collided with the Norwegian ship *Storstad* in the Gulf of St. Lawrence. It was the worst maritime disaster in Canadian history.

4. **Matheson Fire**: A devastating forest fire broke out in this town northwest of North Bay, Ontario, on July 29, 1916, taking the lives of between 200 and 250 men, women, and children and destroying six towns, including Matheson and Cochrane. Property damage was estimated at more than $2 million.

5. **Hillcrest Explosion**: A dust explosion at a coal mine in Hillcrest, Alberta, on June 19, 1914, killed 189 miners.

6. *Noronic* **Fire**: On September 14, 1949, the *Noronic*, the largest Canadian passenger ship on the Great Lakes, was destroyed by fire at Toronto, claiming 118 lives.

7. **Newfoundland Fire**: During a dance at the Knight's of Columbus Hotel in St. John's, Newfoundland, on December 12, 1942, a fire killed ninety-nine people.

8. **Quebec Bridge Collapse**: Part of the Quebec Bridge in Quebec City collapsed on August 29, 1907, killing seventy-five workers and injuring eleven others.

9. **Frank Slide**: On April 29, 1903, at 4:10 a.m. seventy million tons of limestone from Turtle Mountain crashed onto the town of Frank, Alberta, and a nearby valley, killing at least seventy people. It was Canada's most destructive landslide.

10. **Train Derailment in Spanish River, Ontario**: On January 21, 1910, a Canadian Pacific Railways passenger train en route to Minneapolis hit a bridge causing the back half of the train to leave the tracks. Sixty-three people died and twenty others were injured.

Fabulous Fact

The Mississauga train derailment of 1979 garnered international headlines when 220,000 persons were evacuated after poisonous chemicals were spilled. Miraculously no one was killed.

THE TEN WORST AIR CRASHES IN CANADIAN AIRSPACE

Location	Airline	Date	Deaths
1. Gander, Nfld.	Arrow Air	Dec. 12, 1985	256
2. Peggy's Cove, N.S.	Swissair	Sept. 2, 1998	229
3. Ste. Therese de Blainville, Que.	Trans-Canada Airlines	Nov. 29, 1963	118
4. Toronto, Ont.	Air Canada	July 5, 1970	109
5. Issodun, Que.	Central Airways	Nov. 11, 1957	79
6. Chilliwack, B.C.	Trans-Canada Airlines	Dec. 9, 1956	62
7. 100 Mile House, B.C.	CP Air	July 8, 1965	52
8. Cranbrook, B.C.	Pacific Western Airlines	Feb. 11, 1978	43
9. Gander, Nfld.	Czechoslovakia State Airlines	Sept. 5, 1967	37
10. Moose Jaw, Sask.	Trans-Canada Airlines	April 8, 1954	34

List prepared with the assistance of the Canadian Aviation Safety Board.

THE FIVE WORST AIR CRASHES INVOLVING CANADA BUT OUTSIDE CANADIAN AIRSPACE

	Location	Airline	Date	Deaths
1.	Cork, Ireland	Air India	June 23, 1985	329
2.	Djeddah, Saudi Arabia	Nationair	July 11, 1991	261
3.	Tokyo, Japan	CP Air	March 4, 1966	64
4.	Cincinnati, Ohio	Air Canada	June 2, 1983	23
5.	Gulf of Thailand	Okanagan Helicopters	April 30, 1982	13

List prepared with the assistance of the Canadian Aviation Safety Board.

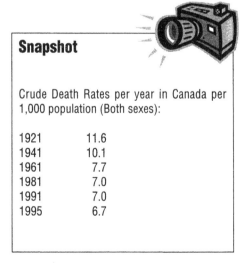

Snapshot

Crude Death Rates per year in Canada per 1,000 population (Both sexes):

1921	11.6
1941	10.1
1961	7.7
1981	7.0
1991	7.0
1995	6.7

TEN EVENTS WITH SIGNIFICANT IMPACT ON THE LIVES OF CANADIAN WOMEN

1. **World War I**: Women's contributions to the war effort between 1914 and 1918, particularly by filling the jobs of men who enlisted, gave them access to many new fields of employment. Their efforts also helped most women win provincial and federal enfranchisement, although victory was gradual and not complete until 1960 when Native women won the vote.

2. **Agnes Macphail elected to the House of Commons, 1921**: Macphail, a champion of justice issues, including women's rights, during her long political career, became a role model for the women who followed her in politics.

3. **The Persons Case**: In 1929, five women from Alberta (Emily Murphy, Nellie McClung, Louise McKinney, Irene Parlby, and Henrietta Muir Edwards) appealed the Supreme Court of Canada's decision that women were not qualified persons within the meaning of the British North America Act. The Judicial Committee of the Privy Council of the House of Lords in England, at that time Canada's final court of appeal, confirmed women as persons before the law, opening up many opportunities for full participation as citizens, including judgeships and the Senate.

4. **The Birth Control Pill became Generally Available in Canada, 1961**: The introduction of Bill C-150 in 1969 decriminalized the promotion, sale, and provision of contraception information, and legalized abortion under certain circumstances. Until that time, advocates of family planning and legal access to safe methods of birth control and abortion faced public harassment, prosecution, and imprisonment.

5. **Royal Commission on the Status of Women, 1967**: The commission travelled across Canada for four years, listening to women's concerns. Its 1970 landmark report established the first benchmarks of equality for Canadian women. Some of its 167 recommendations to help eliminate gender inequality included paid maternity leave, fair employment practices, and changes to the Indian Act so aboriginal women did not lose their status when they married non-status men. The report inspired the creation of a number of women's groups that worked to implement these changes, including the National Action Committee on the Status of Women.

6. **Passage of a comprehensive divorce law by the federal government, 1968**: All provincial enactments were repealed and divorce became more readily available by broadening the grounds, enabling many women who had been abused or abandoned to file for divorce. Issues of custody and support were also included in the law.

7. **Murdoch v Murdoch, 1974:** Irene Murdoch left her husband in 1968 after a violent assault. In a legal battle all the way to the Supreme Court of Canada, Murdoch claimed she was entitled to one-half interest in the farm properties owned in her husband's name because of her contribution of money and labour. The Supreme Court did not agree, upholding the lower court award of $200 per month in alimony. A public outcry followed the decision, resulting in a series of major changes in legislation.

8. **Canadian Charter of Rights and Freedoms, 1982:** Section 15 provides that individuals are equal before and under the law and cannot be discriminated against on the basis of "race, national or ethnic origin, colour, religion, sex, age or mental or physical disability." A few months before Section 15 came into effect in April 1985, the Women's Legal Education and Action Fund (LEAF) was formed. One of the primary objectives of the group is to achieve equality for women before and under the law "by means of litigation using the guarantees of the Charter." LEAF devotes its resources to the direct sponsorship of cases, and education and lobbying.

9. **The killing of fourteen young women by a gunman at École Polytechnique in Montreal, 1989:** The killer, who committed suicide at the scene, left a note blaming women and feminists for "ruining his life." This terrible tragedy sent shock waves across the country, focusing attention on the prevalence of violence against women. The federal government proclaimed December 6 a National Day of Remembrance and Action on Violence Against Women.

10. **The Supreme Court of Canada unanimously affirmed that "no means no":** In its 1999 ruling in R. v. Ewanchuk, the court said the idea of "implied consent" to sexual assault does not exist in Canadian law. The decision sent a strong message that consent to sexual activity must be voluntary and communicated. It cannot be given by third party, or motivated by fear or abuse of authority.

List prepared by Pat Staton, former co-ordinator of the Centre for Women's Studies at the Ontario Institute for Studies in Education/University of Toronto and a founding member of the Ontario Women's History Network.

FOURTEEN THINGS BANNED IN CANADA IN THE TWENTIETH CENTURY

1. **Sunday Shopping:** In 1906, the Tenth Parliament of Canada passed the Lord's Day Act, which also forbade working on Sunday, most Sunday transportation, and entertainment on the Sabbath for which a fee was charged. Seventy-nine years later the Supreme Court of Canada ruled the act unconstitutional and shopping on Sundays became a way of life in most parts of Canada.

2. **The Death Penalty:** In December 1967, federal legislation abolished the death penalty for murder, except when police officers or prison guards are the victims.

3. **Discrimination:** A section of the Charter of Rights and Freedoms was signed into law on April 17, 1985, banning discrimination on the basis of sex, age, colour, religion, race, national or ethnic origin, and physical or mental handicaps.

4. **Smoking on Airplanes:** In 1986, Air Canada became first North American carrier to ban smoking from its flights following the 1971 introduction of no-smoking sections on its aircraft.

5. *Pretty Baby*: The Ontario Board of Censors made headlines in 1978 by banning *Pretty Baby*, Louis Malle's controversial film about prostitution in turn-of-the-century New Orleans that starred Brooke Shields and Susan Sarandon.

6. **"Stay Awhile":** Some Toronto radio stations refused to play this 1971 hit by Montreal-based group The Bells because they believed the song, about a woman coming into a man's bedroom and undressing, was too risqué.

7. **Firecrackers:** Outlawed by the federal government on September 27, 1972, for safety reasons.

8. **The World Football League:** In April 1974, Liberal cabinet minister Marc Lalonde introduced legislation designed to prevent teams from the upstart World Football League from playing in Canada. Although the bill never became law, it caused the Toronto Northmen to move to Memphis, Tennessee, where they operated as the Southmen.

9. *Penthouse* **Magazine:** On grounds of indecency, a federal court upheld the censure of the May 1977 issue of the American men's magazine by customs officials.

10. **English on Signs**: The Quebec government outlawed English on public signs in the province in 1981. The law was struck down in 1988 by the Supreme Court of Canada but reinstalled by Quebec in the same year using the notwithstanding clause in the Charter of Rights and Freedoms.

11. **Prostitutes and Traffic**: In December 1985, Royal Assent was given to a federal bill which aimed to prohibit prostitutes from stopping motor vehicles, interrupting pedestrian or vehicular traffic, and making any other public attempts to solicit customers. The bill also prevented customers from propositioning hookers in public places.

12. **Leaded Gasoline**: After years of debate, the federal government banned the use of leaded gas in motor vehicles effective December 1, 1990. Research had linked lead to health problems, mainly in children.

13. **Cod Fishing**: In 1992, the federal Department of Fisheries and Oceans banned fishing for northern cod off the east coast of Canada after stocks of the fish were severely depleted by overfishing.

14. **The Little Sisters Bookstore and Emporium**: Canada Customs made a habit of seizing and detaining books, videos, and other materials intended for the Vancouver-based bookstore that caters to gays and lesbians. But with the support of many prominent Canadian and international writers and authors, the bookstore successfully challenged Canada Customs. In 1996, the British Columbia Supreme Court ordered the customs department to take the store off its "lookout list" and to pay legal costs.

Snapshot

Canadians Involved In Principle Fishing Operations

1901: 79,370

1951: 65,391

1971: 58,845

1991: 47,600

1998: 33,800

TEN SIGNIFICANT NON-BUSINESS MERGERS/AMALGAMATIONS

1. **United Church of Canada**: Formed when the Methodist Church, the Presbyterian Church of Canada, and the Congregational Churches of Canada united, June 10, 1925, in Toronto.

2. **Progressive Conservative Party**: The result of the 1942 marriage of members of the Conservative Party and the Progressive Party under leader John Bracken of Manitoba.

3. **Newfoundland joins the Dominion of Canada**: March 31, 1949.

4. **Hamilton Tiger-Cats**: Formed when the Hamilton Tigers joined with the Hamilton Wildcats, 1950.

5. **Canadian Labour Congress**: Born when the Trades and Labour Congress of Canada and the Canadian Congress of Labour merged, April 23–27, 1956.

6. **Canadian Armed Forces**: Formed when the Royal Canadian Navy, the Royal Canadian Air Force, and the Canadian Army united, February 1, 1968.

7. **Parti Québécois**: Two separatist organizations, Mouvement Souverainet-Association and Rassemblent pour l'Independence National, united to form the party made famous by René Lévesque, October 12–15, 1968.

8. **Thunder Bay, Ontario**: The new city resulted from the joining of Port Arthur and Fort William, January 1, 1970.

9. **World Hockey Association/National Hockey League**: Four remaining WHA teams, Hartford, Winnipeg, Quebec, and Edmonton, joined the NHL, 1979.

10. **Toronto the Big**: Despite rejection by 76 percent of those who voted in plebiscites, the megacity of Toronto was born when the regional Metro Toronto government and the cities of Scarborough, Toronto, York, East York, North York, and Etobicoke amalgamated, January 1, 1998.

CASH AND CROOKS ... FIVE NOTABLE CANADIAN SCAMS

1. **The Bre-X Stock Swindle:** Bre-X Minerals of Calgary, led by founder and chairman David Walsh, claimed to have found the richest gold mine in history in a Borneo jungle. Company officials estimated there were 71 million ounces of gold in the mine, news that sent the stock from a value of pennies a share in 1995 to a high of $280 a share in 1997. But in May 1997 it was revealed that there was no gold at the site, share prices plummeted, and Bre-X went down as one of the biggest hoaxes in financial history.

2. **The Albert Walker Frauds:** Walker, who in 1999 was serving a life sentence for the murder of an acquaintance in Britain, faces thirty-seven fraud-related charges in Canada after farmers, store employees, and bookkeepers were bilked for more than $3.2 million. The frauds are alleged to have occurred between 1986 and 1990 while Walker was operating a financial services company in southwestern Ontario.

3. **Julius Melnitzer's White Collar Crimes:** Melnitzer, a high profile, high-spending London, Ontario, lawyer pleaded guilty in 1992 to defrauding a handful of Canadian banks, friends, and business associates of a whopping $67 million. He was sentenced to nine years in jail, ordered to pay $20 million in compensation, and was disbarred by the Law Society of Upper Canada. Melnitzer was parolled after serving 2 1/2 years.

4. **Brian Molony's Bank Fraud:** While an assistant bank manager at the Canadian Imperial Bank of Commerce in Toronto, Molony executed what was up to that point the largest single-handed bank fraud in Canadian history — $10.2 million to fuel his obsession with gambling. He was arrested in 1982, pleaded guilty to fraud, and was sentenced to six years in prison.

5. **Viola MacMillan's Windfall Scam:** Following the 1964 discovery of a $2-billion copper-silver-zinc orebody near Timmins, Ontario, rumours swirled that the minerals extended under land owned by Windfall Oils and Mines, a company owned by MacMillan, who at the time was president of the Prospectors and Developers Association. This sent the stock from thirty cents a share to more than one dollar, and eventually to $5.70. As was the case with Bre-X, the company collapsed when it was revealed MacMillan's property was worthless. In 1966, she was handed a nine-month sentence for fraud. Nevertheless, MacMillan was inducted into the Canadian Mining Hall of Fame and a mineral gallery at the Museum of Nature in Ottawa bears her name.

List prepared by Ottawa writer Mark Bourrie.

THIRTEEN SIGNIFICANT INVENTIONS

1. **Pablum**: In 1930 at Toronto's Hospital for Sick Children, Dr. Alan Brown, with the assistance of research doctors Theodore Drake and Fred Tisdall, invented the nutritious baby cereal that would become the first semi-solid food tasted by millions of infants.

2. **Radio broadcasting**: In 1906 Reginald Aubrey Fessenden of Quebec made the first public broadcast of music and voice. Earlier he had orchestrated the first two-way voice transmission by radio.

3. **Snowmobile**: Armand Bombardier of Valcourt, Quebec, developed this unique snow machine in 1926. His vehicles were used wherever heavy loads were carried over difficult terrain. In the 1950s he pioneered the development of small, light snow vehicles for winter sports.

4. **Marquis Wheat**: In 1904, Charles Saunders, a native of London, Ontario, developed this superior strain of wheat at the Central Experimental Farm in Ottawa. It matured earlier than other varieties, produced larger crops and resisted the cold and strong winds. The wheat is given credit for bringing prosperity to Canada's prairies.

5. **The Anti-Gravity Suit**: In the late 1930s and early 1940s, Dr. Wilbur Franks of Weston, Ontario, developed the G-Suit, which allowed fighter pilots to carry out high-speed manoeuvres without blacking out. Used by Allied pilots from 1942 onwards, it led to the development of modern day astronauts' suits.

Wilbur Franks' flying suit prevented pilots from blacking out. *Photo courtesy of National Archives of Canada: PA63866.*

6. **Trivial Pursuit:** Invented in Montreal in 1979 by journalists Chris Haney and Scott Abbott, (with help from Haney's brother John and buddy Ed Werner) this game, which tests players' knowledge of movies, sports, history, and other trivial information, generated $1 billion in sales in 1984 and by the mid-nineties had sold more than sixty million copies, making it by far the most popular board game in the world.

7. **Variable-Pitch Propeller:** Devised by Wallace Rupert Turnbull of Saint John, New Brunswick in the 1920s, this propeller made it possible for aircraft to get off the ground and carry larger payloads economically to distant destinations.

8. **Paint Roller:** Norman Breakley revolutionized the paint and decorating industry in 1940 with the invention of the paint roller, which helped introduce the era of do-it-yourself home decorating.

9. **Farm combine:** In 1938, Thomas Carroll built the first experimental model of the self-propelled combine in a Massey-Harris factory in Toronto. It revolutionized wheat farming in Canada by saving time, money, and backbreaking work.

10. **Slicklicker:** This device, which consisted of an inflatable plastic boom, conveyor belts, a skirt, and a small motor, could lift up to 43,000 gallons of spilled oil per twenty-four-hour period off water fouled by spills. It was invented by Richard Sewell, a chemist with the Department of National Defence in Ottawa.

11. **Zipper:** First developed by an American, the zipper was improved upon and patented in Canada in the early 1900s by Swedish-born inventor Gideon Sundback, who in 1925 was president of the Lightning Fasterner Company of St. Catharines, Ontario.

12. **Heart Pacemaker:** Invented in 1950 in a National Research Council laboratory in Ottawa by Winnipeg native John Hopps to keep the weak of heart alive and kicking.

13. **Cobalt Bombs:** In 1951, Atomic Energy of Canada pioneered the field of cancer treatment with its Eldorado Beam Therapy Unit to replace radium therapy. The first unit was used in the London Clinic of the Ontario Cancer Foundation.

ELEVEN LESSER-KNOWN INVENTIONS

1. **The Sanivan:** Rinaldo Boissonault holds a patent for this garbage collection vehicle which is used in many major cities to compress waste in the back of the vehicle, making collection quicker and more hygienic.

2. **Table Hockey Game:** Developed in 1931 in Toronto by Don Munro, Sr., who built it as a Christmas present for his children. It consisted of six players and two goalies made from wood and painted red and green. The games sold for between $4 and $5 apiece and were produced until 1955. Many versions of this Canadian innovation have been produced ever since.

3. **Analytic Plotter:** U.V. Helava, of the National Research Council in Ottawa, developed this device which could process photographs taken from satellites. Introduced in Ottawa in 1963, the Helava machine is a computer that uses mathematical principles to convert the photo images into lines on paper.

4. **Horse Race Starting Gate:** Philip McGinnis, a racetrack reporter from Huntingdon, Quebec, invented the starting gate at horse races in the early 1900s. Before his device arrived, races started with the throwing of a flag, causing arguments if jockeys and horses left early. McGinnis's starting gates could be found at almost every race track in North America until electric gates were invented.

5. **The Automatically Controlled Machine Tool:** E.W. Leaver and G.R. Mounce built the world's first automatically controlled machine tool in Toronto in 1947. It had the dexterity of the human arm, hand, and wrist. It equalled a skilled worker using a lathe, and could record the operation in its memory and repeat it. It was called Automatic Machine Control by Recorded Operation, or AMCRO.

6. **Lines on Roads:** J.D. Millar, an engineer with the Ontario department of transport, was the first to suggest that dotted white lines be painted on roads in 1930 as a way of making roads safer. The first lines appeared near the Ontario-Quebec border.

7. **Census Machine:** The idea was conceived in Canada by Larry Wilson but the hardware was manufactured in the United States. This machine helped speed up census results by automatically transferring information onto special cards. The 1951 census in Canada marked the first time such a system was used in the world.

8. Aircraft Engine: William Gibson built the first successful aircraft engine in Canada in Victoria in 1910. It produced fifty-five horsepower and was installed in the Gibson twin plane, the first plane in North America to use contrarotating propellers.

9. Engineered Yarn: In 1965, while working for the Department of National Defence, J.V. Weinberger and Col. H.A. Delcellier produced the world's first engineered yarn. Their concept involved the winding of one kind of fibre spirally around a continuous fibre of another type.

10. The Scoot: Developed on Georgian Bay in Ontario in 1947 by Malcolm Dion, this sled-like boat is driven by an air propeller and can travel over ice and water. It solved the problem of carting supplies between the mainland and islands in Georgian Bay in spring and late fall when ice stopped boats but couldn't support automobiles. It is now used extensively in the Florida Everglades under the name Swamp Buggy.

11. Bush Plane: Bob Noorduyn realized there was a need for a high-wing single-engine aircraft that could carry heavy loads and get in and out of small spaces. In 1934, in Montreal, he built the Norseman, the world's first bush plane which became the universal workhorse of the north. Nearly one thousand were built and most are still in use around the world.

Fabulous Fact

Patents are granted by the federal government to give inventors exclusive rights to protect their inventions for a twenty-five-year period. Each year the government receives about 25,000 applications for patent protection at the Canadian Intellectual Property Office in Hull, Quebec.

CONTROVERSIAL TWENTIETH-CENTURY LEGISLATION
(in chronological order)

1. **Military Service Act, 1917**: In response to the military and political pressures of World War I, Prime Minister Robert Borden introduced a system of compulsory military enlistment for all male British subjects between the ages of 20 and 45. The military value of the act remains unclear, but the political and social impact is undeniable as it sharply divided French and English Canadians and helped elect Borden's Union government in December 1917.

2. **Wartime Elections Act, 1917**: To ensure the election of pro-conscription Union candidates in the December 1917 general election, the Borden government passed this act to alter the federal franchise. It gave the vote to female relatives of men in the military, while it disenfranchised immigrants from enemy countries who had been naturalized since 1902. Although it allowed women to vote in a federal election for the first time, it also discriminated against non-British citizens.

3. **Criminal Code Amendment Act, 1919**: Section 98 of the Criminal Code was adopted in the aftermath of World War I in response to the perceived Communist threat to Canadian society. It was an extraordinary piece of legislation, not simply because of its broad definition of seditious activity, but also because it assumed guilt through association. Section 98 was used against the leaders of the 1919 Winnipeg General Strike and the Communist Party of Canada in the early 1930s.

4. **Indian Amendment Act, 1927**: As part of its decades-long effort to control the lives of aboriginal people, the federal government amended the Indian Act to make it illegal to raise funds to pursue land claims. The measure remained in effect until 1951.

5. **Defence of Canada Regulations order-in-council, 1942**: In the wake of the December 1941 Japanese attack on the American fleet at Pearl Harbor and the start of the Pacific War, the Canadian government forcibly removed all Japanese persons, including Canadian citizens, from a 100-mile wide defence zone along British Columbia's coast. The evacuation was authorized under the 1939 Defence of Canada Regulations.

6. **National Flag of Canada, Imperial Order in Council, 1965**: The lengthy debate over Canada's national flag came to a head in 1964. One side, led by former prime minister John Diefenbaker, saw the Canadian Red Ensign as

representative of Canada's "glorious" British and Imperial past. The other side, headed by Prime Minister Lester Pearson, pushed for a distinctive new flag that represented Canada's international independence and united, it hoped, French-speaking, English-speaking, non-British, and non-French Canadians. The red Maple Leaf which first flew over Parliament on February 15, 1965, became a highly recognizable Canadian symbol.

7. **Criminal Law Amendment Act, 1968–69**: After several attempts in the 1960s at changing the abortion law, the federal Liberal government finally amended the Criminal Code in June 1969, permitting the establishment of therapeutic abortion committees in hospitals. This allowed for approval of abortions if the continuation of the pregnancy endangered the life or health of the pregnant woman. This change did not end the debate as pro-life supporters sought complete repeal of the new law, while pro-choice advocates saw abortion as a private matter to be decided by the individual women involved.

8. **Official Languages Act, 1969**: Prime Minister Pierre Elliott Trudeau's government passed this act in response to the recommendations of the Royal Commission on Bilingualism and Biculturalism. The legislation endeavoured to create bilingual federal institutions and increase official minority-language education and government services for Francophone communities outside of Quebec by making generous grants to participating provinces. Although initially supported by the three main political parties, the act has had its opponents, particularly during times of economic recession and financial restraint.

9. **Canada Act, 1982**: Since the 1920s, Canadian provincial and federal politicians had attempted to agree upon an amending formula and to bring home Canada's constitution (the British North America Act, 1867, and all of its amended forms were British laws). Finally, after much political wrangling in the 1960s and 1970s, the federal government, led by Prime Minister Pierre Trudeau, achieved an agreement with all provinces, except Quebec. The modified legislation, which included a constitutional amending formula and an entrenched Charter of Rights and Freedom, was approved by the British Parliament in March 1982. Passage of the Canada Act did not end the constitutional debate as politicians and others attempted throughout the 1980s and 1990s to create conditions that would make it possible for Quebec to sign the 1982 Constitution Act.

10. **Canada-United States Free Trade Agreement Implementation Act, 1988**: In 1988, the Progressive Conservative party reversed its longstanding opposition to free trade with the United States and pushed an agreement

through Parliament by limiting debate. Supporters of the pact argued that it would guarantee continued Canadian access to American markets, while critics argued that it would eliminate Canadian jobs and, more importantly, jeopardize Canadian sovereignty.

List prepared by Dave De Brou and Bill Waiser, editors, Documenting Canada: A History of Modern Canada in Documents.

TOP TEN LEGAL EVENTS

1. **Statute of Westminster, 1931:** Although the Dominion of Canada was created by the British North America Act in 1867, and given a considerable measure of self-government, Canada remained a British colony, subordinate to the enactments of the British Parliament. Much of the remaining vestiges of colonial status were removed by the Statute of Westminster, which adopted the principle that Canada was equal to the United Kingdom, and permitted future British Acts to extend to Canada only with Canada's consent.

2. **Abolition of appeals to the Privy Council, 1949:** Canada abolished appeals from the Supreme Court of Canada to the Privy Council in the United Kingdom, which had consistently interpreted the constitution in favour of the provinces. This ensured that all further development of Canadian constitutional law, which affects the very nature of Canadian federalism, was exclusively in Canadian hands.

3. **Constitution Act, 1982:** At the request of Canada, the Parliament of the United Kingdom enacted this act, which patriated the Canadian constitution, bringing to an end all remaining authority of the Parliament of the United Kingdom over Canada. The Constitution Act also created the Canadian Charter of Rights and Freedoms, Canada's first entrenched bill of rights.

4. **The Supreme Court gives a broad scope to the Charter of Rights, 1982–1986:** In the earliest Charter of Rights cases to reach the Supreme Court of Canada, the court clearly signalled that, unlike the 1960 "Diefenbaker" Bill of Rights, the rights protected by the Charter would be interpreted generously, to give effect to their purposes (Hunter v. Southam, 1984); that even cabinet decisions, such as a decision to allow missile tests in Canada, are subject to Charter scrutiny by the courts (Operation Dismantle v. the Queen, 1985); and that the government would have to meet a high standard in order to justify any law limiting a Charter right (The Queen v. Oakes, 1986).

5. **The Alberta Press Case, 1938:** In the earliest of several cases where the Supreme Court was able to protect civil liberties before the enactment of the Charter of Rights, an Alberta law requiring newspapers to give the provincial government a right of reply to criticism of its policies was struck down.

6. **Roncarelli v. Duplessis, 1959:** In this case, the Supreme Court of Canada held Quebec Premier Duplessis personally liable for ordering the cancellation of Roncarelli's restaurant liquor licence because the restauranteur provided bail money to Jehovah's Witnesses arrested for distributing religious literature.

The court's decision affirmed that the acts of even the highest government officials must be authorized by law.

7. **"Persons Case," 1929**: In Edwards v. the Attorney General of Canada, the Privy Council gave the constitution a "large and liberal interpretation," and concluded that women are "persons," and as a result, can be appointed to the Senate.

8. **The Divorce Act, 1968**: With this act, Parliament enacted the first uniform, Canada-wide set of rules governing divorce. These replaced a regime where divorce was generally only available, if at all, on grounds of adultery, with a new regime where divorce could be granted on the basis of "matrimonial offences" and marriage breakdown.

9. **Human Rights Codes, 1960s**: Beginning with Ontario in 1962, all Canadian provinces have enacted human rights codes which prohibit discriminatory practices by landlords and employers on grounds such as race, religion, nationality, sex, and age, and create commissions to investigate and boards to adjudicate complaints.

10. **Morgentaler v. the Queen, 1988**: In this case, the Supreme Court struck down Canada's Criminal Code prohibition of abortions other than those approved by hospital therapeutic abortion committees. The court reasoned that because the approval requirement restricted access to the procedure, caused delays in treatment, and increased the risk to health, there was an infringement of the mother's Charter right to liberty and security of the person.

List prepared by The Honourable Mr. Justice Michael Dambrot, Ontario Superior Court of Justice.

CANADA AT WAR ... TWELVE IMPORTANT BATTLES INVOLVING CANADIANS

1. **Paardeberg:** The first battle and first victory for Canadians on foreign soil in the twentieth century took place in February 1900 during the Boer War. Fighting alongside the British, the Canadians played a key role in what has been described as a turning point in that war.

2. **Second Battle of Ypres:** Canadian soldiers survived the first major gas attack in modern war and helped hold off an attack by German soldiers in April 1915.

3. **Vimy Ridge:** Arguably Canadian soldiers' finest hour. The four divisions involved in the fighting in April 1917 captured an enemy position many thought was impregnable.

Action during the Battle of Vimy Ridge. *Photo courtesy of National Archives of Canada: PA1187.*

4. **Moreuil Wood:** The Canadian Cavalry Brigade slowed down a German offensive in the spring of 1918. A decisive German victory here could well have prolonged the war for many more months.

5. **The Battle of the Atlantic:** Throughout World War II, it was crucial to get supplies to Britain. The Royal Canadian Navy and Canadian merchant sailors overcame fierce storms, German submarines, and heavy losses to transport the much-needed supplies across the ocean to Allied soldiers.

6. **The Battle of Britain**: Hundreds of Canadians took part in this key battle in the summer of 1940 and helped destroy much of the German Luftwaffe. This key battle prevented the Germans from conquering Britain.

7. **The Battle of Hong Kong**: Some two thousand mostly unseasoned Canadian troops valiantly fought off the Japanese for more than two weeks before surrendering in December 1941. More than a third were killed and wounded; the rest suffered horrible conditions in prison camps.

8. **Dieppe**: Considered by some to be a dress rehearsal for D-Day, Dieppe proved disastrous for Canadians. Almost five thousand Canadian troops took part in an almost suicidal raid on France in August 1942, where they came under heavy fire from German troops. More than nine hundred were killed and almost two thousand taken prisoner.

9. **The Battle of Ortona**: The December 1943 battle against elite German paratroopers saw Canadians involved in one of the toughest clashes in the Italian campaign of World War II. The Canadian victory helped take the sting out of the defeat at Dieppe a year earlier.

10. **D-Day**: Some fifteen thousand Canadians took part in the largest invasion in the world on June 6, 1944. Along with British and American soldiers, they turned the tide of World War II. The Canadians were the first troops to reach their planned objective.

11. **Battle of the Scheldt**: Canadian soldiers battled through coastal towns of France and Belgium in late 1944 removing the Germans. There were more than six thousand Canadian casualties, but they succeeded in freeing the port of Antwerp and opening a supply route for Allies to make a final onslaught against the Nazis.

12. **Kap'yong**: In April 1951 in the Korean War, Canadian soldiers prevented the Chinese from occupying Seoul, and for their action received the United States Presidential Distinguished Unit Citation for gallantry and heroism under fire.

TOP TEN MILITARY EVENTS IN CANADA IN THE TWENTIETH CENTURY

1. **Canada's Declaration of War, September 10, 1939**: The declaration, made after a full Parliamentary debate, came one week after Britain declared war. It confirmed Canada's status as an independent actor on the world stage, both to the mother country and to most Canadians. Canada's immense contribution to victory during World War II transformed the country economically, socially, politically, militarily, and diplomatically.

2. **The Battle of Vimy Ridge, 1917**: The Canadian Corps' capture of Vimy Ridge in April 1917 marked not only the first major victory for the Canadian Corps in World War I, but the first significant allied advance on the Western Front. The Canadian Corps came of age at Vimy. So too did Canada.

3. **The Ogdensburg Agreement, 1940**: On August 18, 1940, US President Franklin Delano Roosevelt and Canadian Prime Minister William Lyon Mackenzie King signed an agreement in Ogdensburg, New York, establishing the Permanent Joint Board on Defence (PJBD). A device for ensuring executive co-ordination of continental defence planning during the dark days at the start of World War II, the PJBD marked a historic shift in Canada's foreign and defence policy relations away from the United Kingdom and toward the United States.

4. **The Return of Canadian Troops to Europe**: The return of Canadian troops to Europe in 1951 under the aegis of the North Atlantic Treaty Organization, formed in 1949, marked the start of a half-century commitment to European defence, a commitment which largely dictated the nature of Canadian international security policy and defence organization in the decades since.

5. **The Military Service Act, 1917**: Extremely heavy Canadian casualties and a sharp decline in voluntary enlistment during World War I led Ottawa in 1917 to introduce compulsory military service, a controversial measure. French-Canadian opposition and English-Canadian support sparked a bitter linguistic and national unity crisis.

6. **The Suez Crisis, 1956**: The international crisis generated by the Israeli, French, and British attack on Egypt in 1956 led Lester B. Pearson, Canada's secretary of state for External Affairs, to propose to the United Nations that an international peacekeeping force be employed to monitor a ceasefire and permit belligerents to disengage. This marked the birth of international peacekeeping, netted Pearson a Nobel Peace Prize, and has remained a self-proclaimed Canadian vocation ever since.

7. **Creation of the Royal Canadian Navy, 1910:** As a result of a naval arms race in Europe, many English Canadians pressured Ottawa to contribute financially to Britain's Royal Navy. French Canada opposed this as a dangerous affront to Canadian autonomy. The result was the creation of a separate Canadian navy, a controversial compromise but also an important step on the road to Canadian military autonomy.

8. **The Hundred Days, 1918:** Beginning on August 8 and concluding on November 11, 1918, the Canadian Corps scored a series of brilliant but costly victories over German forces on the Western Front leading directly to German capitulation. It remains the greatest series of battlefield successes in Canadian military history.

9. **Unification, or the Canadian Forces Reorganization Act, 1968:** The unification of Canada's air, land, and sea services into the single-service Canadian Forces under Liberal defence minister Paul Hellyer sought to reduce costs, streamline organization, and free money for capital equipment projects. Individual service identities have since re-emerged, but the Canadian military remains officially a single-service force.

10. **Canadian Forces ordered to remove employment restrictions based on sex, except for submarine duty, 1989:** Women's long struggle for equality in Canada's military received a substantial boost in 1989 when a human rights tribunal ordered the Department of National Defence to lift restrictions on the employment of women in combat. A ten-year review later determined that the department had failed to implement fully the tribunal's rulings, but the legal basis provided by the decision helped clear the way for women's integration into all aspects of Canadian military life.

List prepared with the assistance of the Canadian War Museum.

THIRTEEN MISCONCEPTIONS ABOUT CANADA'S ABORIGINAL PEOPLES

1. **The history of North America began with the arrival of Europeans.** Fact: Long before the first lost European reached the shores of the New World there were many different indigenous nations living in various regions of what we now know as Canada. Each had its own customs, political structure, language, and spiritual beliefs, as well as highly developed trade and economic systems.

2. **The terms "Aboriginal" and "Native" are used to define one homogeneous group of people in Canada.** Fact: "Aboriginal," "Native," and "Indigenous" are used as general terms to collectively describe three different cultural groups known as the "Inuit," "Métis," and "First Nations." Each group has its own unique historical background, culture, and political goals.

3. **First Nations are the only peoples to have special rights and benefits above other Canadians.** Fact: First Nation peoples enjoy the same fundamental benefits as all other Canadians, including Child Tax Benefits, Old Age Security, and Employment Insurance. Where Constitutionally protected Aboriginal rights exist, First Nations do have priority over others. One example is the right to hunt and fish for subsistence, but these rights are subject to regulation.

4. **First Nations peoples are better off than most Canadians.** Fact: Although the United Nations ranked Canada as the number one place in the world to live, a comparison of First Nations on reserve ranked 47th after Panama and before Poland. It is clear that many First Nations do not enjoy even basic standards most Canadians take for granted.

5. **There has been no progress on First Nations issues in the last decade because of their dependency on the government.** Fact: Significant progress has been made by working in partnership with First Nations leaders on a number of fronts. About 16,700 homes have been built and 17,400 renovated in the past five years in First Nations communities. A federal Procurement Policy was implemented in 1996 to help Aboriginal businesses gain access to federal government contracts.

6. **If the government of Canada abolishes the Indian Act, every citizen will be treated equally.** Fact: This is false because the Indian Act covers some, but not all facets of First Nations peoples' lives. The majority of rights are found in treaties and existing Aboriginal and treaty rights are protected under S.35 of the Canadian Constitution.

7. **All Aboriginal peoples do not pay tax.** Fact: Inuit, Métis, and non-status Indians are required to pay tax. Sections 87 and 90 of the Indian Act say income earned by registered Indians working for companies situated on reserves is exempted from federal and provincial income tax. Generally, First Nation individuals working for companies located off reserve pay income tax.

8. **All First Nations communities are incapable of administering their own finances.** Fact: Every First Nation council in Canada is required to submit an annual audit each year before receiving funding from the federal government. Over the years First Nations have significantly improved their financial management systems and timeliness in reporting: 61 percent submit their audits within 120 days.

9. **Because of the remote location of many First Nations communities, economic development is non-existent on reserves and there are few businesses owned by First Nations.** Fact: Recent statistics from Industry Canada revealed there are more than 20,000 Aboriginal businesses in Canada active in every sector of the economy, many located in First Nations communities where they have brought increased employment as a result of joint business ventures with non-Aboriginal companies.

10. **All First Nations communities face living conditions similar to Third World countries.** Fact: No two communities are the same. Differences in geographic location, (urban, rural, and isolated) combined with access to economic development makes it possible for some First Nations communities to enjoy a better standard of living than other Canadians.

11. **First Nations are not ready for self-government.** Fact: The Haudenosaunee (Six Nations Confederacy) existed since the beginning of their history as distinct people with their own laws and customs, territories, political organization, and economy. Benjamin Franklin and Thomas Jefferson, the founding fathers of the U.S., were so impressed with the Six Nations Confederacy's Great Law of Peace that they used it as a model for the United States Constitution.

12. **All Aboriginal people receive free housing and post-secondary education.** Fact: Métis and non-Status Indians do not receive free housing or education assistance. Housing and education are important legal benefits of some treaties for Treaty First Nations. Under the federal government's on-reserve housing policy, Status Indians obtain funds through their band councils, to build or renovate homes on reserves. In many cases these loans are repaid over a number of years. Low-income non-Aboriginal families in various regions of Canada seeking housing assistance from governments may also receive

assistance through various federal and provincial government programs. Department of Indian Affairs and Northern Development provides elementary and post-secondary education assistance to Inuit and Status Indians to help improve their standard of living.

13. **First Nations land claims are settled by government based on political guilt over past injustices committed against them.** Fact: Land claims are based on government's outstanding legal obligations to the original inhabitants of this land. Settlements are based on the basic principle of British common law that there can be no confiscation of land without compensation.

List prepared by Assembly of First Nations.

WHO SAYS CANADIANS ARE DULL? ...
TEN UNUSUAL FACTS ABOUT CANADA IN THE TWENTIETH CENTURY

1. **Canada Wins an Olympic Gold Medal ... in Soccer:** Though known more as a country that specializes in hockey, Canada won gold in soccer at the 1904 Olympics in St. Louis. A team from Galt, Ontario, defeated the Americans for gold at an Olympics where there was little European representation.

2. **A Hockey Player Charged with Murder:** In 1907, Charles Masson of the Ottawa Vics of the Federal Amateur Hockey League, was slapped with a murder charge after Cornwall player Owen McCourt died in hospital in March 1907, less than a day after being hit over the head by a stick during a melee. Masson was acquitted when witnesses claimed another player delivered the fatal blow.

3. **Parliament is Held in a Museum:** After the Centre Block of Parliament Hill burned to the ground on February 3, 1916, MPs and Senators conducted the nation's business in a museum not far from the Hill. Senators did their work in the former hall of invertebrate fossils. No kidding!

4. **Canada's Plan to Invade the United States:** Canada's director of military operations and intelligence in the 1920s drafted a plan called Defence Scheme Number 1 that called for the Canadian army to invade certain cities in the U.S. Fortunately, no one took him or his plan seriously.

5. **A Canadian was Prime Minister of Britain:** Andrew Bonar Law of New Brunswick moved to Britain and became an MP in 1900. He eventually became leader of the Conservatives and then prime minister in 1922. He held the post for 209 days before resigning because of bad health.

6. **Canadians are Responsible for Such Americana as the Oscars, the Hardy Boys, and the Fuller Brush Company:** The honours go to Louis B. Mayer, who grew up in New Brunswick and came up with the idea of the Academy Awards in the 1920s; Leslie McFarlane, of Haileybury, Ontario, who wrote the first twenty books in the Hardy Boys series under the name Franklin W. Dixon; and Alfred Fuller of Nova Scotia, who began selling brushes in 1906 and founded the company that bears his name seven years later.

7. **A Canadian Woman was the World's First Professional Television Performer:** Joan Miller of Nelson, British Columbia, was the star of the first TV show, produced by the BBC in November 1936. As the "Picture Page Girl" Miller was paid £12.10 per week.

8. **Beatlemania has Canadian Roots:** Former Ottawa music journalist Sandy Gardiner coined the term "Beatlemania" in a newspaper article in 1963. Capitol Records later used it as the title of the first Beatles album released in Canada.

9. **Use of the Name Parliament Hill for Commercial Purposes is a No-No:** Since 1972, the words "Parliament Hill," when used together, have been protected in legislation. Use them to earn money, by starting a business named Parliament Hill Internet Service, for instance, and you could have the feds banging on your door asking for a name change. You could also face a fine and a jail term.

10. **A Canadian Dollar is Valued at More Than $1 Million:** In 1998, a 1911 silver dollar was purchased for more than $1 million by an American coin collector. The coin attained such a high value because only two were made, both as patterns for a set of coins which were cancelled by the federal government of the day. The other silver dollar is on display at the Bank of Canada Currency Museum in Ottawa.

The 1911 Silver Dollar: Canada's first million-dollar coin.
Photo courtesy of National Currency Collection, Bank of Canada, James Zagon.

STOP THE PRESSES … CANADA'S TOP NEWS STORIES: 1900 TO 1950
(in chronological order)

1. Marconi transmits first wireless message from North America to Europe from a transmitting station at Glace Bay, Nova Scotia: 1902.

2. Saskatchewan and Alberta join Confederation: 1905.

3. The *Titanic* sinks off the coast of Newfoundland, taking more than 1,500 lives: 1912.

4. More than 1,000 people die when the Canadian Pacific steamer *Empress of Ireland* collides with a Norwegian ship in the Gulf of St. Lawrence: 1914.

5. Canada enters World War I: 1914.

6. Fire destroys the Centre Block at Parliament Hill: 1916.

7. The Halifax Explosion kills more than 1,600 people: 1917.

8. Canadian Troops capture Vimy Ridge, the first significant allied advance on the Western Front: 1917.

9. The Winnipeg General Strike, the most famous general strike in Canadian history: 1919.

10. Canadian stock markets crash along with American markets: 1929.

11. Canada and the United States agree to build the St. Lawrence Seaway: 1932.

12. The Dionne Quintuplets are born in Callandar, Ontario: 1934.

13. Canada declares war on Germany: 1939.

14. Oil is struck near Leduc, Alberta, starting the Alberta oil boom: 1947.

15. Newfoundland joins Confederation: 1949.

CANADA'S TOP NEWS STORIES: 1950 TO 2000
(in chronological order)

1. A coal mine explosion at Springhill, Nova Scotia, kills seventy-four miners: 1958.

2. *The Toronto Star* tracks down Gerda Munsinger, a German immigrant and prostitute who had an affair with Pierre Sévigny, Canada's Associate Minister of Defence: 1966.

3. Canada celebrates its one-hundredth birthday. Events include the opening of Expo '67 in Montreal and Parliament Hill celebrations attended by Queen Elizabeth and Prince Phillip: 1967.

4. The FLQ crisis in Quebec: 1970.

5. Approximately 220,000 people in Mississauga, Ontario, are evacuated when twenty-four rail cars carrying dangerous materials are derailed. It is the largest single movement of people in Canada in peacetime: 1979.

6. Ken Taylor, Canada's ambassador to Iran, helps a group of Americans leave Iran: 1980.

7. The Terry Fox cross-Canada Marathon of Hope raises money for cancer research: 1980.

8. Defeat of separatists in Quebec referendums: 1980 and 1995.

9. Clifford Olson's string of murders: 1981.

10. Patriation of the Constitution and creation of the Charter of Rights: 1982.

11. Massacre of fourteen women at Montreal's École Polytechnique: 1989.

12. The Paul Bernardo murder trial: 1995.

13. Collapse of Bre-X Minerals of Calgary: 1997.

14. The Manitoba Flood: 1997.

15. The eastern Canada ice storm: 1998.

BOB WHITE'S TOP TEN LABOUR EVENTS

Crowds gather during the Winnipeg General Strike.
Photo courtesy of National Archives of Canada:
PA163001.

1. 1914: Workmen's Compensation Act, Ontario. Its formation established a program, later copied across Canada, for compensating injured workers without the need to sue.

2. 1919: Winnipeg General Strike. Workers shut down the city for six weeks in solidarity with skilled workers in the building and metal trades.

3. 1935: On to Ottawa Trek. The biggest depression protest against unemployment. It moved the social safety net onto the political agenda.

4. 1945: Rand Formula. The Windsor Ford of Canada strike settlement included a ruling that all workers in a bargaining unit should pay dues. This gave financial security to unions.

5. 1956: Canadian Labour Congress. Formed when the Canadian Congress of Labour merged with the Trades and Labour Congress of Canada to create a single house of labour.

6. 1961: New Democratic Party. Labour was a founding partner of the political party that would carry its views into the political arena.

7. 1963/1967/1976: Formation of the Canadian Union of Public Employees, the Public Service Alliance of Canada, and the National Union of Provincial Government Employees. This public sector union "Big 3'" was an important new wave of unionization, especially for women.

8. 1972: Quebec Common Front. Public sector unions staged the biggest general strike in Canadian history, involving all three major labour bodies in Quebec. More than 200,000 workers were involved.

9. 1976: October 14 Day of Protest. Organized by the Canadian Labour Congress to oppose wage controls, it was Canada's first national general strike and saw more than one million workers leave their jobs for a day.

10. 1983: B.C. Operation Solidarity. Labour joined with other groups such as women, students, and anti-poverty groups to protest against a right-wing government. It was a sign of alliances to follow in the battle against issues such as free trade, health care cuts, and unemployment insurance benefits.

List prepared by Robert White, former president, Canadian Labour Congress.

SOLIDARITY FOREVER ...
TOP TEN VICTORIES FOR WORKERS IN THE FEDERAL PUBLIC SERVICE

1. **Clerical and Regulatory (CR) Workers' strike, 1980:** The two-week work stoppage resulted in paid maternity leave and family leave provisions. It was the Public Service Alliance of Canada's largest strike at that time and proved to be a turning point for the union. The role of unionized women would never be the same and has continued to grow ever since.

2. **Indexation of Pensions, 1970s:** The value and indexation of pension funds were ensured by the contribution of a percentage of members' salaries matched with the employer's contribution.

3. **Free Collective Bargaining in the Federal Public Service, mid-1960s:** The minority Liberal government of Lester Pearson yielded to widespread pressure and recognized the right to collective bargaining by introducing the Public Service Staff Relations Act.

4. **Political Rights:** Until 1988, federal public service workers were forbidden to take part in political activities during elections but could vote. In 1991, the Supreme Court of Canada upheld a 1988 Federal Court of Appeal decision that struck down restrictions and confirmed they had no force and effect for the vast majority of federal workers with the exception of deputy department heads.

5. **Negotiation of a Master Collective Agreement, 1986:** A first master collective agreement was negotiated to replace bargaining for twenty-seven individual Treasury Board bargaining units represented by PSAC.

6. **Public Service Alliance of Canada National Strike, 1991:** By far, the largest national strike ever conducted by a single union in Canada. It involved members inside and outside of Canada, including those in embassies around the world. The back-to-work legislation signalled the end of free collective bargaining in the federal public service as subsequent governments renewed the freeze on bargaining, wages, and working conditions until 1997.

7. **Negotiation of Workforce Adjustment Directive:** Although members were forced back to work with legislation by the Conservative government to end the 1991 strike, PSAC was able to negotiate iron-clad job security provisions for its members.

8. **Establishment of Joint Adjustment Committees, 1996:** These committees avoided the layoffs of thousands of government workers during the massive

downsizing program launched by the federal government. They facilitated job exchanges between people who wanted to retire and those who didn't want to leave the workforce.

9. **Election of PSAC Members in the House of Commons, 1997**: For the first time, voters sent PSAC members to the Commons. They were Angela Vautour (Beausejour-Petitcodiac) and Louise Hardy (Yukon), both representing the New Democratic Party.

10. **Political Action Helps Defeat Tory Government, 1993**: PSAC members worked hard in targeted ridings across the country during the 1993 election campaign to provide information about the Tories' track record and to urge members in ridings not to support the Conservatives. This collective action was launched at PSAC's 1991 triennial convention where delegates voted to defeat the government.

List prepared by Daryl T. Bean, National President, Public Service Alliance of Canada.

TEN YEARS WITH THE HIGHEST IMMIGRATION TO CANADA

1. 1913   400,870 immigrants arrived

2. 1912   375,756

3. 1911   331,288

4. 1910   286,839

5. 1957   282,164

6. 1907   272,409

7. 1993   255,935

8. 1992   253,345

9. 1991   232,020

10. 1996   226,074

Fabulous Fact

Toronto and Vancouver are Canada's immigration hotbeds: In the late 1990s, 21 percent of Torontonians were immigrants who arrived between 1981 and 1996, while 19 percent of Vancouver residents were people from outside the country who landed during the same period. By contrast, just 9 percent of Calgarians and 8 percent of Montrealers were immigrants who arrived after 1981.

Miscellaneous

STRANGE TALES ...
TWELVE CANADIAN MYSTERIES

Artist Tom Thomson in Algonquin Park where he drowned mysteriously. *Photo courtesy of* ***National Archives of Canada: PA125406.***

1. **The Death of Tom Thomson: Foul play or not?** The thirty-nine-year-old Canadian landscape painter was in perfect health when he drowned in Canoe Lake in Algonquin Park on July 8, 1917, while fishing for trout from a canoe. His body was discovered eight days later with a gash on the right side of his head and fishing line wrapped around one of his ankles. There was no water in his lungs and his canoe was never recovered.

2. **Crop Circles: Fields of Schemes?** As recently as in August 1998, large circles appeared on grain fields in Saskatchewan. Observers say crops such as durum wheat were flattened close to the ground in a counter-clockwise manner. A witness described one of the circles as "donut shaped," and noted that three others couldn't be made "any more perfectly." Some say visitors from outer space are the likely culprits but similar markings in England were proven to be part of an elaborate hoax.

3. **The Phantom Train: Who's Railroading Whom?** The Phantom Train of Wellington was first seen crossing a bridge outside the village of Wellington, west of Summerside, Prince Edward Island, in December 1885 but numerous sightings have been reported in the twentieth century. Islanders and visitors report seeing a railroad engine, cars, and passengers, generally during December evenings — even though a train is not scheduled to pass by at that time.

4. Ogopogo: Strange Creature or Apparition? Described as Canada's Loch Ness monster, this legendary creature of the deep is said to live in Okanagan Lake in British Columbia, where modern-day sightings have been reported since the 1930s. Ogopogo apparently resembles a prehistoric creature with a small head and a long neck. It was first captured on film in 1968 in a movie that showed serpent-like movements across the surface of the lake.

5. Klaatu: Hip or Hype? Toronto-based band Klaatu made international headlines in 1977 when critics claimed it was the Beatles reunited. Band members Terry Draper, John Woloschuk, and Dee Long, who had purposely tried to sound like the Fab Four on some songs, managed to keep their identities secret for some time, which only fueled the rumours. For their efforts Klaatu was named "Hype of the Year" by *Rolling Stone Magazine*.

6. The Lac Champlain Sea Serpent: Steam Yacht or Monster? Although Lac Champlain is mainly in New York State and Vermont, this twenty-foot-long horned serpent, first seen in the 1600s by French explorer Samuel de Champlain and nicknamed "Champ," has been sighted by Canadians. One couple described the beast as having a head "as large as a flour barrel ... of irregular shape" and with eyes of "greenish tinge." They also noted that it made a noise that "sounded like the paddle wheels of a steam yacht."

7. The Great Northeast Blackout: Short Circuit or Cover Up? On November 9, 1965, thirty million people in the northeastern region of Canada and the United States were plunged into blackness by a power outage. The official investigation blamed the malfunction of equipment near Niagara Falls, Ontario, for causing a sudden surge of power. Some commentators point out that the reason for the surge was never divulged; others say UFOs were sighted in the vicinity of hydro installations at the time of the blackout.

8. Our Lady of Marmora: Down on the Farm with the Mother of God? In June 1991, Shelagh and John Greensides arranged the Stations of the Cross on their hobby farm near the village of Marmora, Ontario. Shortly after, in the presence of about two hundred people, the sun is said to have changed colour, spun about, pulsated, moved toward earth and returned to its normal position. Since that day people say they have seen and received messages from Mary, the mother of God. Some say they have seen angels at the Greensides' farm.

9. Oak Island: A Money Pit? Legend has it that this island in Nova Scotia's Mahone Bay, is the repository of untold wealth in the form of buried treasure — although no one seems to know how the booty got there and no valuables have ever been found. Nevertheless, many treasure-seekers, including several since 1900, have gone looking. In the process, thousands of dollars have been invested and at least half a dozen lives have been lost.

10. Sasquatch: Great Ape, or Figment of Many Imaginations? Sightings of this nomadic and solitary creature have been reported in various areas of British Columbia, including near the communities of Chilliwack, Terrace, and Agassiz, and on Vancouver Island. In 1996 a Sasquatch forum was held in Harrison Hot Springs, British Columbia to study what has been described as "the continent's most misunderstood large mammal."

11. Ghost of the Arctic Sea: Who's on the Bridge? The Hudson Bay Company operated the 1,300-ton fur ship S.S. *Baychimo* on the Beaufort Sea for ten years until 1931, when it was caught in ice and its captain and crew abandoned ship. When a storm loosened the ice, the ship drifted away. It was later boarded when it got trapped in ice again and the furs were removed, but the ship again broke free. In the 1950s, the *Baychimo* was spotted on several occasions, drifting aimlessly about the Beaufort Sea, still seaworthy and still crewless. Experts say derelict ships are usually destroyed by sea ice within two years.

12. The Flatrock Fires: Too Hot to Handle? Over a two-week period in December 1950, a series of fires broke out for no apparent reason at the home of Mike Parsons in Flatrock, Newfoundland. The fires occurred in a dictionary, a sack of sugar, in a box of religious material, under the eaves of the house, and in the floorboards. The mysterious fires were small and easily extinguished but the attorney-general would not comment on an RCMP investigation into the incidents.

DIDN'T YOU USED TO BE ...
TWELVE SIGNIFICANT NAME CHANGES IN THE TWENTIETH CENTURY

1. *Busy Man's Magazine* to *Maclean's* magazine: March 1911.

2. Royal North-West Mounted Police to Royal Canadian Mounted Police: February 1, 1920.

3. Toronto St. Pats to Toronto Maple Leafs: 1927.

4. Labatt Pilsener to Labatt Blue: 1952.

5. Co-operative Commonwealth Federation to New Democratic Party: August 1961.

6. Chad Allan and the Expressions to The Guess Who: 1964–65.

7. Trans-Canada Airlines to Air Canada: January 1, 1965.

8. Ontario's Highway 401 to Macdonald-Cartier Freeway: 1965.

9. Legislative Council in Quebec to National Assembly of Quebec: December 13, 1968.

10. Dominion Day to Canada Day: October 26, 1982.

11. Canadian Football League Montreal Alouettes to Montreal Concorde in 1982 and back to Montreal Alouettes in 1986.

12. Frobisher Bay to Iqaluit: January 1, 1987.

NEW KIDS ON THE BLOCK IN THE TWENTIETH CENTURY

1. Canada Dry Ginger Ale first bottled: December 1907.

2. The National Hockey League formed: November 26, 1917.

3. Daylight Savings Time first used: March 18, 1918.

4. Canada's first nuclear reactor goes into operation: September 5, 1945.

5. Canada Savings Bonds introduced: October 1946.

6. Thanksgiving declared a holiday: January 31, 1957.

7. Social Insurance Numbers put into use: April 1964.

8. First colour television broadcast by CBC: August 1966.

9. Canada gets its first major league baseball franchise: Montreal Expos, May 27, 1968.

10. Use of breathalyzer tests for suspected impaired drivers: December 1, 1969.

11. Canada's highway signs converted to metric (except in Quebec and Nova Scotia): September 6, 1977.

12. Daily activities in the House of Commons aired live on television, making Canada the first country to broadcast the complete proceedings of its legislature: October 17, 1977.

13. "O Canada" proclaimed Canada's national anthem: July 1, 1980.

14. The National Post newspaper launched: October 27, 1998.

15. Nunavut, Canada's newest territory, officially created (out of the Northwest Territories): April 1, 1999.

TWELVE THINGS MANY CANADIANS NEVER REALLY UNDERSTOOD IN THE TWENTIETH CENTURY

1. The federal Goods and Services Tax, better known as the GST.

2. Why Wayne Gretzky was traded to the Los Angeles Kings in August 1988.

3. The federal income tax system.

4. Separation from Canada by Quebec, or any other province that raises the idea of leaving the federation.

5. Bank service charges.

6. Voter turnout in municipal elections, which is often as low as 30 percent, even though local government has the most direct effect on our daily lives.

7. Wildly fluctuating gasoline prices.

8. The Meech Lake Accord.

9. Why your airfare cost $699 but the person in the seat beside you paid $369.

10. The metric system, particularly among people born before 1970.

11. Why a letter can take five days to get from one Ottawa address to another, for example, but two days or less to go from Ottawa to Vancouver.

12. Canada's falling dollar. We live in one of the most prosperous countries in the world, yet our buck continues to tank against other currencies.

When it comes to filling up, sometimes it costs more, sometimes less. *Photo by Randy Ray.*

TEN GREAT THINGS ABOUT CANADA ... A VIEW FROM THE OTHER SIDE

1. **Three-Way Calling:** I can talk to both my sisters at the same time, just by dialing *71.

2. **Cheap Parking:** In many cities in Canada, an hour of parking can cost less than $2. In New York and other large U.S. cities, you'll pay $20 (U.S.) and wait 45 minutes to retrieve your car from a parking garage. Finding parking on the streets of Manhattan is the Impossible Dream.

3. **Easy Commuting:** In most Canadian cities commuting time is measured in minutes. In most major American cities it's measured in hours.

4. **Road Rage:** With lighter traffic than is the norm in U.S. centres, it is a term that is rarely used in Canada.

5. **Airports with Parking Close to the Terminal:** In many parts of Canada your trip doesn't start until you get to the plane. In large American cities getting to the aircraft can be a long and expensive ordeal. (See items 2 and 3 above.)

6. **Six-Month Subsidized Maternity Leave and Subsidized University Tuition:** In Canada, you're actually encouraged to spend time with your children and become educated.

7. **Dinner at a Reasonable Cost:** Canadians can pay $30 to $50 and receive a lovely meal. In big U.S. cities, you'll pay twice the price.

8. **More Commercial-Free Children's Television:** In the U.S. parents have no choice but to tune into PBS (which is often very good); in Canada there are public stations, such as TVOntario, in addition to PBS.

9. **Ability to Manage in Times of Disaster:** Perhaps because of the very difficult climate, Canadians seem to cope better in tough times, such as the 1998 ice storm when thousands pitched in to help neighbours, even strangers. More impressive is what Canadians consider to be a disaster. Two inches of snow closes airports, roads, and schools in New York, yet Canadians have little trouble coping with twenty-five inches of the white stuff.

10. **Immigration policy**: Canadians can sponsor the immigration of highly qualified and trained nannies. In the U.S. it is exceedingly difficult to find well-trained nannies (Zoe Baird, a nominee for U.S. attorney general, once hired someone illegally because she couldn't find anyone who was qualified.)

List prepared by Wendy Myers, a lawyer and former New Yorker who has lived in Boston, Washington, and London and now lives in Ottawa.

Snapshot

Annual Birth Rates:

Year	Births per 1,000 women	Babies Born
1921	29.3	264,879
1941	27.3	263,993
1961	34.1	475,700
1981	17.8	371,346
1990	15.3	405,486*
1995	12.8	378,011
1997	12.1	364,765

* figure adjusted due to undercounts

Statistics Canada

TEN THINGS CANADIANS SHOULD BE PROUD OF ...
FROM AN AMERICAN'S POINT OF VIEW

1. **Beautiful Scenery**: Of course, much of it is covered with snow half the time, but nevertheless, breathtaking.

2. **Weather**: Canada does NOT stop for snow but Canadians will, however, occasionally close their schools for hot, sunny days. Some Canadians are proud of how much snow and cold they get.

3. **Mountie Attire**: The second-best looking uniform in the world. (U.S. Marines' uniforms are first.) The requirement to get to be a Mountie is that you have to look as good as the uniform.

4. **Cottages**: It seems everyone has one, even those on government aid. Don't bother asking the question "What are you doing this summer?" Because the answer is "Going to the cottage."

5. **Hockey**: Many Canadians play, watch, read hockey. It's the social life for parents. It's what many Canadians have in common. Without hockey, Canada would be just be another very cold country with pretty scenery.

6. **Health Care**: Very good, and free. You do have to pay to get out of the parking lot, though. Good social services. All those taxes have to be going somewhere, so it might as well be toward a longer life.

7. **Boring**: Canada should be proud of this one. Even your scandals are boring. Quebec wanting to secede is boring. Maybe it's the cold and the fact that you guys are too numb to raise a ruckus.

8. **Humour**: Canadians are funny. We in the United States know this because many of your comedians and actors end up in the United States.

9. **Grocery Shopping**: Those conveyor belts that take the groceries out are so cool. I wish the U.S. had them.

10. **Lack of Crime**: To feel safe in a major city in Canada is the norm. The United States could take some lessons from Canada.

List prepared by Susan Roe, a resident of San Clemente, California. She has lived in three other countries, including Canada, where she resided in Ottawa from 1993 until 1995.

TEN BIGGEST CITIES BY POPULATION IN 1901

1.	Montreal	266,826
2.	Toronto	207,971
3.	Quebec City	68,834
4.	Ottawa	59,902
5.	Hamilton	52,550
6.	Winnipeg	42,336
7.	Halifax	40,787
8.	Saint John	40,711
9.	London	37,983
10.	Vancouver	26,196

TEN BIGGEST CITIES BY POPULATION IN 1996
(Census Metropolitan Area — includes suburbs and bedroom communities)

1.	Toronto	4.26 million
2.	Montreal	3.36 million
3.	Vancouver	1.83 million
4.	Ottawa-Hull	1.01 million
5.	Edmonton	862,597
6.	Calgary	821,628
7.	Quebec City	671,889
8.	Winnipeg	667,360
9.	Hamilton	624,360
10.	London	398,616

City of Vancouver skyline. *Photo courtesy of Tourism Vancouver.*

WHAT WE BELONG TO ... TWELVE OF CANADA'S LARGEST ORGANIZATIONS BY MEMBERSHIP IN 1998*

Organization	Members
1. Canadian Automobile Association	3,984,420**
2. Canadian Labour Congress	2,200,000
3. Young Men's Christian Association (YMCA)	1,500,000
4. Royal Canadian Legion	533,000
5. Canadian Hockey Association	508,000
6. Canadian Federation of Students	400,000
7. Young Women's Christian Association (YWCA)	400,000
8. Canadian Soccer Association	337,319
9. Liberal Party of Canada	325,000
10. Royal Canadian Golf Association	250,000
11. Canadian Wildlife Federation	250,000
12. Royal Canadian Geographical Society	238,000

** Includes all eleven CAA clubs in Canada.

Canadian Labour Congress headquarters in Ottawa. *Photo by Andrew Ray.*

BEHIND BARS ...
TEN MOST COMMON CRIMINAL OFFENCES IN 1921*
(in order)

1. Theft
2. Burglary
3. Assault and battery
4. Keeping bawdy houses
5. False pretenses
6. Fraud and conspiracy to defraud
7. Aggravated assault
8. Feloniously receiving stolen goods
9. Rape and other crimes against decency
10. Assault on a police officer

* By number of charges

TEN MOST COMMON CRIMINAL OFFENCES IN 1991*
(in order)

1. Theft under $1,000
2. Breaking and Entering
3. Assault (not sexual)
4. Theft of motor vehicles
5. Frauds
6. Theft over $1,000
7. Drug offences
8. Possession of stolen goods
9. Robbery
10. Sexual assault

* Excluding provincial statutes
and municipal bylaws

Snapshot

Suicides in Canada

1950: 1,067
1970: 2,413
1990: 3,379
1995: 3,970

Statistics Canada.

WE'RE BACK! ...
TEN GREAT CANADIAN COMEBACKS

1. **The Great Lakes:** In the late 1960s and early 1970s Lake Erie was declared dead and lakes Ontario, Superior, Huron, and Michigan were on their way to becoming ecological wastelands. But since Canada and the U.S. signed the Great Lakes Water Quality Agreement in 1972, the lakes have returned to better health, as evidenced by the return of many species of fish and wildlife.

2. **The 1941–42 Toronto Maple Leafs:** After losing the first three games to the Detroit Red Wings in the 1942 Stanley Cup Final, the Leafs under coach Hap Day roared back with four straight wins to capture the cup, the only team in NHL history to accomplish such a feat.

3. **Chrysler Canada:** On May 10, 1980, the federal and Ontario governments provided $200 million in loan guarantees as part of a Canada-U.S. government restructuring program which saved the automaker from bankruptcy and salvaged more than 12,000 Canadian jobs.

4. **Pierre Trudeau:** After stepping down as Liberal leader in November 1979, Trudeau returned and on February 8, 1980 led the Liberals to a majority election victory, winning 146 seats.

5. **Silken Laumann:** The Canadian rower was the reigning world singles champion and the overwhelming favourite to win gold at the 1992 Olympics in Barcelona until her boat was accidentally hit by a German rowing pair prior to the Games, seriously injuring her right leg. Doctors said she would not compete in the Olympics but she recovered and won a bronze medal.

Moe Closs helped engineer Chrysler's comeback in Canada. *Photo courtesy of Chrysler Canada.*

6. **Tall beer bottles:** Long-necked bottles were popular with beer drinkers until 1962 when the "stubby" bottle arrived. But between 1982 and 1984, stubbies were phased out and tall bottles were reintroduced, mainly for aesthetic reasons.

7. **John Fraser:** He resigned as Fisheries Minister on September 23, 1985, after releasing more than one million cans of tuna that were declared unfit for human consumption. On October 1, 1986, he was again an influential figure, being elected Speaker of the House of Commons.

8. **The Whooping Crane:** In 1900 there were approximately 1,350 birds in Canada, but by 1951 only fifteen remained because of hunting practices, destruction of prairie breeding habitats, and egg and specimen collection. By 1999, the population had rebounded to more than 250 birds, thanks to strong preservation methods and a captive breeding program.

9. **Margot Kidder:** In 1996, the Yellowknife-born actress who is best known for her role as Lois Lane in the Superman movies was found in a state of mental distress in a Los Angeles backyard. In late 1997, after successful treatment for manic depression, she was back in business, having completed eight acting projects, including parts in a sitcom, a stage production, and a film.

10. **Sunday Shopping:** At the turn of the century, commerce on the Sabbath was banned in most provinces and in 1906 the federal government also ruled it a no-no, by passing the Lord's Day Act. But on April 24, 1985, the Supreme Court of Canada ruled the act was unconstitutional and Canadians could again shop-till-they-drop on Sundays, in most parts of Canada.

The whooping crane: Among the comebacks of the century. *Photo by Dalton Muir courtesy of Canadian Wildlife Service.*

NOT SO FOND MEMORIES ... NINE GREAT CANADIAN BUSTS

1. **The Olympic Stadium, Montreal:** Without a doubt, one of the century's biggest screwups. The Big O (or more appropriately, the Big Owe), had problems from the start, including a flawed design, poor workmanship, and a $52 million retractable roof that was not installed in time for the 1976 Summer Olympics. In subsequent years, roofs have been damaged by weather and by workmen; on other occasions pieces of the outside walls and a fifty-five-ton beam crashed to the ground. And if that's not enough, the initial $120 million price tag will have ballooned to close to $3 billion by the time the debt is paid off in 2006.

2. **John Turner and the National Leaders' Debate:** In a televised set-to with Brian Mulroney during the 1984 federal election campaign, it was widely acknowledged that Turner's handling of the patronage issue helped blow the election for the Liberals. A debilitating blow to the Grits' campaign was delivered when Mulroney suggested Turner, as incoming prime minister, should have reversed several eleventh-hour appointments approved by retiring prime minister Pierre Trudeau. Turner's meek reply was: "I had no option." Forty-one days later, Mulroney's Conservatives won the election with a huge majority and Turner was out of office after a mere eighty days.

3. **The Bricklin:** A U.S.-designed sportscar built in New Brunswick in 1974 and 1975 by American promoter Malcolm Bricklin. Only 2,857 were sold because the car was plagued by a high sticker price and technical problems with its unique "gullwing" doors. The company fell into receivership, owing the provincial government $23 million.

4. **Mirabel International Airport:** Known as Montreal's other white elephant (right behind the Big O), Mirabel opened in 1975 but was soon a dud because its use was based on faulty assumptions about air traffic, it was too far from Montreal, and it was poorly designed. In the fall of 1997, the multi-billion-dollar facility was relegated to a cargo and charter terminal after all regularly scheduled international flights were consolidated at Dorval Airport in Montreal.

5. **Pickering Airport:** Known as the international airport that never got built, plans were announced in 1973 and scrapped in September 1975 after fierce opposition from area residents. Over the years, with the federal government still the owner of 7,530 hectares of land it expropriated for the airport, a few villages have become ghost towns, nineteenth-century farm houses have fallen into disrepair and many buildings have deteriorated into firetraps. In 1997, Ottawa spent $3.5 million, mostly to maintain buildings on the site.

6. **Conservative Budget, 1979**: On December 13, Prime Minister Joe Clark's government fell on a 139 to 133 vote of non-confidence in the House of Commons on John Crosbie's budget, which contained a large fuel tax increase designed to satisfy Alberta oil magnates at the expense of Ontario energy consumers. Clark's embarrassing defeat allowed the Liberals under Pierre Trudeau to make a comeback two months later.

7. **Canadian Football League Expansion to the U.S.**: In 1992, the CFL announced plans to expand south of the border and in 1993, the Sacramento Gold Miners became the first U.S. team to play in the league. Several other American teams were added the next year, and expansion did produce an exciting Grey Cup in 1994. But dogged by poor attendance and huge financial losses, the move to the U.S. ended in failure. By 1996 all American franchises had disappeared.

8. **Film Tax Shelters**: From the late 1970s to the early 1980s, the federal government encouraged more films to be shot in Canada by providing financial incentives to the domestic film industry through tax benefits and the Capital Cost Allowance program. The result was a massive increase in the amount invested in Canadian production but most of the films were pale imitations of American movies and only a handful did well at the box office. With few exceptions, most were also critically panned.

9. **The Ross Rifle**: In 1903, after Great Britain nixed Canada's request for a British-made rifle during the South African War, Canada began producing its own weapon, known as the Mark 1 Ross rifle. But the rifle turned out to be a dud. It was delivered two years late, various problems caused it to be recalled, and in the first years of World War I a later version of the rifle was seen as unsuitable because it was too heavy, too long, and would often jam. In 1916, the Ross rifle was withdrawn from service at a cost of $2 million to Canadian taxpayers, and Canada's troops were re-armed with the same brand of rifle the British had refused to supply earlier.

TEN FAMOUS DUOS

1. **Frederick Banting and Charles Best**: Co-discoverers of insulin in 1922 for the treatment of diabetes. Banting was awarded the Nobel Prize, Medicine, in 1923 and gave half his share to Best, who was an American.

2. **Johnny Wayne and Frank Shuster**: Canada's most popular comedy duo whose wide-ranging skits won them international fame. Despite their popularity in the U.S., they remained in Canada.

Wayne and Shuster: One of Canada's dynamic duos. *Photo courtesy of National Archives of Canada: PA152117.*

3. **Ian and Sylvia**: Popular folk duo formed in 1959. Wrote hit songs such as "Four Strong Winds" and "You Were On My Mind," which became major hits for many other artists.

4. **Bob and Doug McKenzie**: This toque-bearing, parka-wearing pair of Canuck dimwits were known as the McKenzie Brothers and found fleeting stardom in the 1980s on the comedy show SCTV, and in the movie *Strange Brew*. In real life they were Rick Moranis and Dave Thomas.

5. **Barbara Wagner and Robert Paul**: Other duos have been more popular but only Wagner and Paul have won Olympic gold for Canada in pairs skating. Between 1956 and 1960 they also won four world championships, two North American titles, and five Canadian senior pairs championships.

6. **Eaton's and Simpson's:** Though the two major department stories had their beginnings in the nineteenth century, it was in the twentieth century that competition between them heated up Canada-wide. For much of the century you couldn't think of one store without thinking of the other.

7. **Allan Hamel and Michele Finney:** Hamel and Finney were co-hosts on *Razzle Dazzle*, a pre-*Sesame Street* CBC kids' variety show that aired from 1961 to 1967. Finney was later replaced by Trudy Young.

8. **Harvey Kirck and Lloyd Robertson:** They weren't the first two-person news anchors in Canada and other duos outlasted them, but they are more widely remembered because their nightly newscast on the CTV network was seen from coast to coast. They were paired from 1976 to 1984.

9. **Rusty the Rooster and Jerome the Giraffe:** The harp-playing rooster and sarcastic giraffe were pals with the Friendly Giant on the TV show of the same name, which aired from 1958 to 1985.

10. **Danny Gallivan and Dick Irvin:** The two provided play-by-play and colour commentary for the Montreal Canadiens games on "Hockey Night in Canada" for seventeen years from the 1960s through to the early eighties.

Fabulous Fact

Wayne and Shuster appeared a record sixty-seven times on the popular Ed Sullivan Show television program of the 1950s, 60s, and 70s.

MOST POPULAR BABY NAMES IN CANADA: 1950 to 1998

1950		1970	
Boys	*Girls*	*Boys*	*Girls*
Robert	Linda	Michael	Lisa
David	Patricia	David	Michelle
John	Barbara	Robert	Jennifer
James	Susan	Jason	Tracy
William	Sharon	James	Tammy
Richard	Margaret	Christopher	Karen
Kenneth	Donna	John	Nicole
Donald	Judith	Richard	Christine
Ronald	Carol	Kevin	Shannon
Douglas	Sandra	Mark	Susan

1988		1998	
Boys	*Girls*	*Boys*	*Girls*
Michael	Amanda	Matthew	Emily
Matthew	Jessica	Joshua	Sarah
Christopher	Sarah	Nicholas	Taylor
Andrew	Ashley	Brandon	Jessica
David	Stephanie	Tyler	Samantha
Kyle	Jennifer	Jordan	Ashley
Daniel	Nicole	Michael	Megan
Ryan	Melissa	Jacob	Nicole
Justin	Samantha	Alexander	Emma
Joshua	Laura	Kyle	Hannah

Snapshot

Infant Deaths per year, under one year of age

1921:	27,051
1941:	16,117
1961:	12,940
1981:	3,562
1991:	2,573
1995:	2,321

Statistics Canada

WINNIE, WILLY, AND THE GANG ... TWELVE FAMOUS CANADIAN ANIMALS
(in alphabetical order)

1. **Big Ben**: A popular show-jumping horse and international equestrian winner for many years.

2. **Clyde**: The Stratford, Ontario, swan captured national attention in 1994 when he left his mate Bonnie (swans normally mate for life) and took up with Jezebel.

3. **Elisha**: The popular flamingo gained attention in November 1997, when she was spotted wading in the Ottawa River after she bolted from her home in Connecticut. A lengthy rescue campaign by the Wild Bird Care Centre led to her being brought back to her U.S. preserve in mid-December. She later left her original mate, then stole another male by reportedly beating up his mate.

4. **Hammy Hamster**: A TV star since 1959, Hammy's exploits have been seen in thirty-four countries around the world.

5. **The Littlest Hobo**: London, the German Shepherd, was a TV icon in the 1960s series and later in new 1980s episodes.

6. **Northern Dancer**: The greatest racehorse and sire in Canadian history. Winner of the Kentucky Derby, The Preakness, and the Queen's Plate.

7. **Pat**: Mackenzie King's Irish terrier was a favourite companion of the quirky prime minister and was known to sing along with King when he played piano.

8. **Skana**: The most famous killer whale at the Vancouver Public Aquarium arrived in 1967 and created a splash for more than seven million visitors over thirteen years. Skana helped change public opinion about killer whales from one of fear and distrust to one of protection for these intelligent animals.

9. **Slippery Seal**: The sea lion of London, Ontario's Storybook Gardens who made headlines in 1958 with his daring escape down the Thames River. He was later captured in Lake Erie near Sandusky, Ohio, and was the subject of a documentary and stage play.

10. **Starbuck**: Canada's top bull, who died in September 1998, sired about 200,000 dairy cows and an equal number of bulls during his nineteen years at the Artificial Insemination Centre of Quebec. Starbuck earned an estimated

$25 million during his life, and even after his death his frozen semen was selling for $250 a dose.

11. **Wiarton Willie:** The furry forecasting groundhog who every February 2 looked for his shadow to predict how long winter will last. In 1999, he garnered national attention when his handlers announced on Groundhog Day that Willie had been found dead a few days earlier.

12. **Winnie the Pooh:** The real Winnie was a bear cub from White River, Ontario, who was named for the city of Winnipeg. He became a fixture at the London Zoo and inspired the stories by A. A. Milne.

UNLUCKY THIRTEEN ... A DOZEN AND ONE BAD YEARS
FOR CANADIAN SMOKERS

1. 1908: Parliament passed the Tobacco Restraint Act prohibiting the sale of tobacco to persons under 16, and prohibiting them from purchasing or possessing tobacco.

2. 1961: The Canadian Medical Association concluded that cigarette smoking causes lung cancer.

3. 1971: Tobacco companies announced that effective in 1972 they would voluntarily place a warning on cigarette packages and would not advertise cigarettes on radio or television.

4. 1976: The City of Ottawa passed the first municipal by-law in Canada restricting smoking in certain public places. The by-law took effect in 1977.

5. 1986: Vancouver passed a by-law restricting smoking in the workplace. Quebec adopted a law restricting smoking in some workplaces and public places. Air Canada became the first North American carrier to introduce entirely smoke-free flights.

6. 1987: The Northwest Territories banned smoking in all government workplaces. In subsequent years, many provincial governments would do likewise.

7. 1988: Parliament passed the Non-smokers' Health Act restricting smoking in federally regulated workplaces and public places. The Tobacco Products Control Act was also passed banning tobacco advertising.

8. 1989: Smoking was banned on all domestic air flights and prohibited on interprovincial bus travel. An Ontario law restricted smoking in private and public workplaces.

9. 1990: A Manitoba law set 18 as the minimum smoking age and restricted smoking in public places.

10. 1991: Federal tobacco taxes were increased by six dollars a carton.

11. 1994: British Columbia, Ontario, New Brunswick, Nova Scotia, and Newfoundland laws prohibiting the sale of tobacco to persons under 19 came into force. Ontario and Nova Scotia banned cigarette-vending machines outright. Ontario banned the sale of tobacco in pharmacies. Newfoundland

restricted smoking in workplaces and public places. Smoking was banned on all international flights of Canadian air carriers. McDonald's announced all of its company-owned restaurants in North America would be smoke free.

12. 1996: Vancouver banned smoking in restaurants.

13. 1999: Smoking was banned in restaurants and bars in British Columbia's Capital Region, which includes Victoria.

List prepared by Rob Cunningham, author of Smoke & Mirrors: The Canadian Tobacco War.

The introduction of no smoking in public places in 1976 made that year one of the bad years for smokers in the twentieth century. *Photo by Mark Kearney.*

Snapshot

How Long We Live: Life Expectancy of Canadians at Birth

Born In	Life Expectancy (Men)	Life Expectancy (Women)
1920–1922	58.8	60.6
1940–1942	63.0	66.3
1960–1962	68.4	74.3
1990–1992	74.6	80.9

Statistics Canada

EIGHT LEADING CAUSES OF DEATH IN 1923
(in order)

1. Diseases of the heart
2. Pneumonia
3. Diseases of early infancy
4. Cancer
5. Tuberculosis
6. Violent deaths (excluding suicide)
7. Influenza
8. Diseases of the arteries

EIGHT LEADING CAUSES OF DEATH IN 1954
(in order)

1. Arteriorsclerotic and degenerative heart disease
2. Cancer
3. Vascular lesions affecting central nervous system
4. Accidents (other than motor vehicle)
5. Pneumonia
6. Hypertension with heart disease
7. Diseases peculiar to early infancy and immaturity (not including birth injuries and infections of the newborn)
8. Birth injuries

EIGHT LEADING CAUSES OF DEATH IN 1995
(in order)

1. Cancer
2. Heart disease
3. Cerebrovascular disease
4. Chronic obstructive pulmonary disease
5. Accidents and adverse effects
6. Pneumonia and influenza
7. Diabetes
8. Suicide

GHOSTS AND GOBLINS ... CANADA'S TOP TEN HAUNTED LOCATIONS

1. **The Maritimes**: Phantom ships/ghost ships/Flying Dutchmen: the terms are synonymous and the phenomena are an important component to the folklore of Canada's Maritime provinces. These retrocognitive images are often so detailed that witnesses throughout the twentieth century are still able to identify not only the long-ago sunken ship but, in some cases, even see what's happening on board.

2. **Oak Island, Nova Scotia**: This is the haunted site of treasure buried in the eighteenth century. Despite the enormous amounts of money, technology, and time spent trying to uncover the fortune, only disappointment, poverty, and unexplained deaths have resulted. The ghostly guardians of the cache have been the victors, despite concerted efforts by many determined souls over the last fifty years.

3. **Kingsmere in Quebec**: The summer residence of Canada's longest-serving prime minister, William Lyon Mackenzie King, was the venue for many ghostly visitations during King's lifetime. He and his friends frequently, and successfully, conducted seances during which they summoned numerous spirits into their midst. Since his death in 1950, King's ghost has been seen there. The spirit reportedly conversed with journalist Percy J. Philip in June of 1954, at the property the deceased had so loved in life.

4. **The Hockey Hall of Fame**: Situated in a century-and-a-half-old Bank of Montreal building in downtown Toronto, it is haunted by the ghost of a former teller at the bank who killed herself during the early 1950s in response to an unrequited love affair. Her presence has been seen and felt amid the displays of hockey history as recently as the mid-1990s.

"He Shoots ... He's Scared?" It's said that the ghost of a former teller haunts the Hockey Hall of Fame, which is located in what used to be a Bank of Montreal building. *Photo by Mark Kearney.*

5. **Grand Theatre in London, Ontario:** Staff at the theatre are extremely fond of their resident ghost — Ambrose Small, the theatre's original owner. Small disappeared in December 1919 under suspicious circumstances and has never been seen since — alive, that is. His ghost continues to make regular appearances at his favourite theatre.

6. **The Hotel Fort Garry:** The Winnipeg hotel, which opened in December 1913, is home to several ethereal residents. The ghost of a woman wearing a formal gown has been reported by a guest. Employees once caught a glimpse of a male apparition enjoying a meal in the hotel's dining room, long after the room was closed for the day. Moments later the image vaporized.

7. **The Moose Head Inn at Kenosee Lake in Saskatchewan:** A much-investigated and well-documented ghost is frequently heard walking around the place. He has grabbed a worker's hand, borrowed small items, and caused plumbing and electrical fixtures to turn on and off independently. This ghostly activity continues today.

8. **Banff Springs Hotel:** Legend has it that this Alberta hotel is home to several ghosts. The manifestation of a dancing bride is said to be seen, even today, at the base of the stairs where she apparently fell to her death. A long-deceased bellman reportedly helped guests with their luggage a few years ago.

9. **Doris Gravlin's ghost:** It's only seen for a few weeks in the spring and so has been dubbed "The April Ghost." However, she's also known as B.C.'s most famous ghost. Since she died in 1936, Doris's image, wearing a number of different outfits, is seen on the fairways of the Victoria Golf Course in Victoria, British Columbia. Every spring ghost-hunters gather in hopes of catching a glimpse.

10. **The ghost town of Barkerville, British Columbia:** Even though many of the buildings currently standing are modern-day re-constructions, ghosts continue to be both seen and felt there. The most poignant of the resident spectres is the ghost of an unidentified woman seen at a second-floor window of Madame Fannie Bendixon's Saloon.

List prepared by Barbara Smith, author of Ghost Stories of Alberta.

ON THE BRINK OF DISAPPEARING ... CANADA'S CHANGING LANDSCAPE

The lighthouse: a disappearing breed in Canada. *Photo courtesy of National Archives of Canada: PA148158.*

1. **Lighthouses**: In 1900 there were eight hundred staffed light stations. In 1999, only fifty-two remained, largely because of fiscal cutbacks and the rise of technology on shore and on vessels.

2. **Elm Trees**: There were three million elms in Canada in 1945. Near the end of 1999 there were 700,000. Dutch Elm disease was the culprit.

3. **Primary Grain Elevators**: In 1933, there were 5,757 elevators in Canada but by late 1999, less than one thousand were still standing as a result of the grain industry's bid to increase efficiency. Some of the postcard-pretty wooden elevators have been replaced with computerized concrete monstrosities with eight times the holding capacity.

Grain elevators: not what they used to be on the Prairies. *Photo courtesy of Agriculture and AgriFood Canada.*

4. **Canadian Forces Bases:** There were approximately 140 active military bases across Canada when World War II ended in 1945. In 1999, only twenty-one remained thanks to an easing of the threat of war and federal government belt-tightening.

5. **Door-to-Door Milk Delivery:** Ninety-five percent of milk consumed at home arrived by delivery vehicles until the 1960s, when supermarkets began selling three-quart jugs at bargain prices. In 1999, door-to-door delivery was reduced to a trickle and accounted for less than 1 percent of milk purchased.

6. **Cabooses:** They were once on the tail end of every freight train in Canada where they served as mobile offices, parts centres, and lookouts for sparks and mechanical problems that could start fires or cause derailments. Today, cabooses are found on only a handful of trains, usually in remote areas. Their demise was sealed by the arrival in 1990 of Train Information Braking Systems, which feed information between the end of a train, the locomotive, trackside monitors, and centralized dispatch centres.

7. **Income-producing Farms:** In 1901 there were 543,000 farms. As Canada's rural population grew, the number swelled to 623,087 in 1951. Today, only 274,955 remain as rising costs and falling incomes have seen many farms amalgamate with larger operations.

8. **Pre-recorded Cassettes:** In 1985, cassette sales in Canada peaked at 41 million units. In 1998, with compact disc sales on the rise, music lovers purchased only 8.4 million cassettes.

9. **One- and Two-dollar Bills:** At the peak, between 1986 and 1995, there were 335.7 million one-dollar bills and 245.7 million two-dollar bills in circulation. But with the arrival of the "loonie" in 1987 and the "twonie" in 1996, ones and twos have all but disappeared from pockets and billfolds. Although there were 160 million one-dollar bills and 116 million two-dollar bills outstanding in 1999, only a few thousand remained in circulation because most have been destroyed or squirrelled away in currency collections.

10. **Banking at the Wickets:** Until the early 1970s, tellers were involved every time Canadians undertook a routine banking transaction, such as withdrawing and depositing money, making bill payments, and transferring funds between accounts. But as the century drew to a close, the use of automated teller machines, debit cards, and telephone and computer banking was on the rise and tellers were handling only 20 percent of everyday banking.

WHERE ARE YOU FROM?
IMMIGRATION BY NATIONALITY IN 1925

1.	British	53,178
2.	American	15,914
3.	Russian	5,411
4.	Finnish	4,261
5.	Hebrew, Russian	2,946
6.	Polish	2,734
7.	Norwegian	2,550
8.	Italian	2,349
9.	German	2,215
10.	Swedish	2,138

IMMIGRATION BY COUNTRY OF LAST PERMANENT RESIDENCE IN 1955

1.	U.K.	29,382
2.	Italy	19,139
3.	Germany	17,630
4.	U.S.	10,395
5.	Netherlands	6,759
6.	Austria	2,871
7.	France	2,869
8.	Greece	2,856
9.	China	1,918
10.	Belgium	1,751

IMMIGRATION BY COUNTRY OF LAST PERMANENT RESIDENCE IN 1989

1.	Hong Kong	19,904
2.	Poland	15,979
3.	Philippines	11,385
4.	Vietnam	9,403
5.	India	8,817
6.	Britain	8,417
7.	Portugal	8,185
8.	U.S.	6,924
9.	Lebanon	6,172
10.	China	4,426

BIG, BIG JOBS ...
TWELVE OF CANADA'S MOST SIGNIFICANT TWENTIETH-CENTURY
CONSTRUCTION PROJECTS

1. **CN Tower, Toronto:** The 553-metre tower soars over downtown Toronto and is the world's tallest building and free-standing structure. It was built by Canadian National (CN), which wanted to demonstrate the strength of Canadian industry by constructing a structure taller than any other. It opened on June 26, 1976, at a cost of $63 million. The American Society of Civil Engineers has classified the tower as one of the Seven Wonders of the Modern World.

2. **Distant Early Warning (DEW) Line and Mid-Canada Lines of Radar Stations:** Built in the early 1950s and stretching from the western end of the Aleutian Islands to Baffin Island and the Greenland Icecap, these enabled Canadian contractors to gain experience in major Northern construction projects in the Arctic and Sub-Arctic regions, often on isolated sites far from supply sources, where challenges included weather, the short construction season, blackflies, and mosquitoes.

3. **St. Lawrence Seaway and Power Project:** Opened in 1959, this engineering feat facilitated marine trade to and from Canada's industrial heartland by enabling deep-draft ocean vessels to navigate 15,285 kilometres of waterways, including the Great Lakes. In addition, the Barnhardt Island Power Dam, located half in Canada and half in the United States, provided a showcase and classic "laboratory" test of comparative construction methods.

4. **Confederation Bridge:** The 12.9-kilometre span joins Borden-Carleton, Prince Edward Island and Cape Jourimain, New Brunswick, as the longest bridge over ice-covered waters in the world. It opened on May 31, 1997, at a cost of $1 billion.

5. **Trans-Canada Highway:** Started in 1950 and completed in 1970, the 7,821-kilometre roadway cost more than $1 billion. It ranks with the transcontinental railroad as one of Canada's most important transportation projects.

6. **West Edmonton Mall:** The world's largest shopping and entertainment centre was built in four phases in 1981, 1983, 1985, and 1998. It cost $1.2 billion to build and includes six major department stores, nineteen movie theatres, a chapel, a hotel, an indoor lake with submarine rides, and a National Hockey League-size ice rink. The mall covers an area equivalent to 104 Canadian football fields and has been called the "Eighth Wonder of the World."

Construction of the Trans-Canada Highway. *Photo courtesy of National Archives of Canada: PA111479.*

7. Manicouagan 5 Hydro-Electric Power Project, Quebec: On the Manicouagan River, 210 kilometres north of Baie-Comeau, Manic 5 is an example of how Canadians could mobilize huge teams of workers and equipment to build massive dams and power projects in the Canadian wilderness. This project, which includes the Daniel Johnson Dam, a power station, and a two-thousand-square-kilometre reservoir, was started in 1959 and completed in 1968 at a cost of $600 million. It feeds power to Quebec, Ontario, the Maritime Provinces, and the Northeastern United States.

8. Replacement of the Centre Block of the Parliament Buildings, Ottawa: Canada's best-known building was destroyed by fire on February 3, 1916 and over the four years that followed, was rebuilt at a cost of about $12 million. The new building reopened in early 1920, longer, wider, and a storey higher than its predecessor.

The rebuilt Centre Block at Parliament Hill: a milestone in Canadian construction history.
Photo by Andrew Ray.

9. **Sun Life Building, Montreal**: Originally built as a six-storey structure in 1913, this building in Dominion Square was expanded in 1923 and again in 1929 when its height was increased to twenty-six storeys, making it the highest tower in the British Empire during the 1930s and 1940s. It is considered an architectural achievement to have maintained the consistent appearance of one building throughout all phases of expansion.

10. **Hibernia Project, Newfoundland**: After six years of design, engineering and construction, the mammoth Hibernia oil production platform was towed offshore and installed 315 kilometres southeast of St. John's in 1997. At 224 metres tall and weighing 1.2 million tonnes, the platform is the first of its kind in the world. It can withstand the impact of a six-million tonne iceberg.

11. **Synthetic Rubber Plant, Sarnia, Ontario**: Polymer Corporation Limited was formed in 1942 when western nations were cut off from all sources of natural rubber during World War II. It took fourteen months to build a $50-million plant, which became the forerunner of many large-scale petro-chemical plants and refineries. It was a war effort that has been described as second in scope only to the Manhattan Project to build the atomic bomb. The company name was changed to Polysar in 1973.

12. **TransCanada Pipeline**: On October 10, 1958 the last weld was completed on this 2,290-kilometre, $375 million line, which took twenty-eight months to build and ran from Burstall, Saskatchewan to Kapuskasing, Ontario. It was a huge twentieth century achievement, similar to the building of the transcontinental railway in the nineteenth century. In 1999, the Canadian main line, which is operated by TransCanada PipeLines Ltd, ran from Burstall to the Quebec/Vermont border and could deliver more than nine billion cubic feet of natural gas per day.

List prepared with the assistance of Don Chutter, retired general manager of the Canadian Construction Association.

HOME BASE: SEVEN NOTABLE CANADIAN RESIDENCES

1. **Casa Loma, Toronto**: Built between 1911 and 1914 by millionaire financier, industrialist, and military officer Sir Henry Pellatt, this eccentric stone mansion has been a jewel for much of its history. When occupied by Pellatt, it had its own telephone exchange with fifty-nine telephones, fifteen bathrooms, five thousand electric lights, a kitchen range large enough to roast an entire ox, and a pipe organ that cost $75,000. The castle cost $3.5 million dollars to build and Pellatt spent another $1.5 million on furnishings. When Pellatt's personal fortune was lost in the 1920s, the home was taken over by the city. In 1937, the Kiwanis Clubs of Toronto took over and restored the building, which is now a popular Toronto tourist attraction.

2. **The Cowpland Home, Rockliffe, Ontario**: Built by Michael Cowpland, chairman and CEO of Ottawa-based Corel Corp., and his wife Marlen, this $9.6-million futuristic, copper-coloured mansion has attracted occasional crowds of gawkers in Ottawa's ritzy Rockcliffe neighbourhood since it was built in 1994. That could be because of its sheer size — 20,000 square feet — or because passersby aren't sure if it's a house or some kind of low-rise office complex tucked into a residential area. It consists of three major sections clad in a continuous glaze of glass that reflect tinted and fractured images of the neighbourhood.

The Cowpland home has turned many a head.
Photo by Randy Ray

3. **The Hollies, Vancouver, British Columbia**: This stately white-and-yellow, 15,487-square-foot mansion on a two-acre lot in the pricey Shaughnessy area has been called Vancouver's most prestigious address. It was built in 1912 for Pacific Great Eastern Railway mogul George MacDonald and in mid-1999 was on the market for $11.88 million, making it Vancouver's most expensive residence at the time. Its owner was believed to be a shipping magnate from Japan who didn't live in the place but every Christmas spent tens of thousands of dollars to decorate it for a single night's entertainment for three hundred of his closest friends.

4. **Coste House, Calgary**: Built in 1913 in southwest Calgary, this home was a symbol of the success achieved by Eugene Coste, who is known as the father of Canada's natural gas industry and the founder of the Canadian Western Natural Gas, Light, Heat, and Power Company. It's a twenty-eight-room brick and sandstone Tudor-style home on a one-hectare lot in Calgary's prestigious Mount Royal neighbourhood. The house faced demolition after World War II but was saved and until the late 1950s served as the Allied Arts Centre. It has been a private residence since 1960 and in 1999 was owned by Robert Lamond, owner of a Calgary oil company. It is valued at approximately $2.5 million.

5. **The Risley Residence, Chester, Nova Scotia**: This palatial mansion, believed to be worth about $10 million, sits on Lobster Point, next to the Chester Golf Course, and with a view of Mahone Bay. It's owned by John Risley, president of Clearwater Fine Foods Inc., who estimates the interior square footage of his English country-style home at between 30,000 and 40,000 square feet. It was built between 1995 and 1998 on a 250-acre parcel of land and has both indoor and outdoor swimming pools, where Risley is said to swim laps with his two golden retrievers.

6. **Casa Mia, Vancouver, British Columbia**: In the spring of 1999, this historic 1930s Spanish-style mansion in the Southlands neighbourhood was on the market for $20 million but the vendor, believed to be a Japanese investor, thought better and reduced the price to a mere $10 million. It was built for brewmaster and distiller George C. Reifel and in the late 1980s underwent a $4.5-million renovation that took three years to complete. The place sits on a 1.8-acre lot overlooking the Fraser River, has an outdoor swimming pool, nine fireplaces, fifteen bathrooms, a ballroom with a sprung dance floor, a recreation centre, a workshop, and a multi-car garage. A third-floor playroom includes murals hand-painted in the 1930s by artists from Walt Disney Studios. In 1999, property taxes were more than $26,000.

7. **The Stroll Residence, Montreal, Quebec:** This place, occupied by Lawrence Stroll, Montreal-born partner in menswear designer Tommy Hilfiger Corporation, was renovated in 1993–94, and in 1999, a swimming pool and four-car underground garage were being added. The Mediterranean-style mansion with its red terra cotta tile roof is located in prestigious Upper Westmount, on a very private lot with a view of the St. Lawrence River and downtown Montreal. Although its assessed value in 1999 was $4.6 million, real estate experts say it is worth more than $10 million. Property taxes in 1999 were $62,100.

Snapshot

Average Resale Value of Canadian Homes (sold on the Multiple Listing Service, in current dollars)

1980: $ 66,951
1985: $ 80,122
1990: $139,922
1995: $150,321
1997: $154,630
1998: $152,361

The Canadian Real Estate Association

CANADA'S TEN TALLEST OFFICE BUILDINGS IN 1950

	Building	Height	Storeys	Year Built
1.	Bank of Commerce, Toronto	145m	34	1931
2.	Royal York Hotel, Toronto	133m	26	1929
3.	Royal Bank, Montreal	121m	22	1928
4.	Sun Life Building, Montreal	119m	26	1925
5.	Aldred Building, Montreal	119m	25	1928
6.	Bank of Nova Scotia, Toronto	115m	27	1950
7.	Hotel Vancouver, Vancouver	107m	22	1940
8.	City Hall, Toronto	104m	-	1899
9.	Bell Telephone, Montreal	99m	22	1929
10.	Marine Building, Vancouver	98m	21	1930

CANADA'S TEN TALLEST OFFICE BUILDINGS IN 1999

	Building	Height	Storeys	Year Built
1.	First Canadian Place, Toronto	290m	72	1975
2.	Scotia Plaza, Toronto	275m	68	1988
3.	Canada Trust Tower, Toronto	263m	61	1989
4.	Commerce Court West, Toronto	239m	57	1972
5.	Toronto Dominion Centre, Toronto	226m	56	1967
6.	Bay-Wellington Tower, Toronto	215m	47	1991
7.	Petro-Canada Tower, Calgary	210m	52	1984
8.	1000 Rue de la Gauchetière, Montreal	204m	51	1991
9.	Banker's Hall, Calgary	197m	50	1989
10.	IBM Tower, Montreal	195m	47	1989

Lists prepared by Dylan Llewellyn, whose hobby is tracking tall buildings.

TEN MOST POPULAR RELIGIOUS DENOMINATIONS IN 1901
(based on what religion people identified themselves with)

1.	Roman Catholic	2.2 million
2.	Methodist	924,750
3.	Presbyterian	847,635
4.	Church of England	689,540
5.	Baptist	319,234
6.	Lutheran	94,110
7.	Mennonite	31,949
8.	Congregationalist	28,504
9.	Pagan	18,215
10.	Church of Christ, Disciples	17,250

TEN MOST POPULAR RELIGIOUS DENOMINATIONS IN 1951

1.	Roman Catholic	6 million
2.	United Church	2.8 million
3.	Church of England	2 million
4.	Presbyterian	781,747
5.	Baptist	519,585
6.	Lutheran	444,923
7.	Jewish	204,836
8.	Greek Catholic	191,051
9.	Ukrainian Catholic	190,831
10.	Greek Orthodox	172,271

TEN MOST POPULAR RELIGIOUS DENOMINATIONS IN 1991*

1.	Roman Catholic	12.2 million
2.	United Church	3.1 million
3.	Anglican	2.1 million
4.	Baptist	663,400
5.	Presbyterian	636,300
6.	Lutheran	636,200
7.	Pentecostal	436,400
8.	Eastern Orthodox	387,400
9.	Jewish	318,100
10.	Muslim	253,300

* Note that 3.3 million indicated they had no religious affiliation in 1991.

A, B, C, D ...
TWELVE CANADIANISMS BETTER KNOWN BY THEIR INITIALS

1. **GST**: Goods and Services Tax, a 7 percent tax paid at the cash register since January 1, 1991 when Brian Mulroney's Conservative government replaced the 13.5 percent federal manufacturer's tax.

2. **FLQ**: Le Front de Libération du Québec, a terrorist organization formed in Montreal in 1960 and dedicated to obtaining at any cost the independence of Quebec from the rest of Canada.

3. **CBC**: Canadian Broadcasting Corporation, founded originally in 1932 as the Canadian Radio Broadcasting Corporation, and in 1936 reorganized into the CBC, a Crown corporation, to establish a publicly owned radio network broadcasting in English and French.

4. **NDP**: New Democratic Party, founded in Ottawa in 1961 at a convention that united the Co-operative Commonwealth Federation, affiliated unions of the Canadian Labour Congress, and New Party clubs. The party dedicated itself to democratic socialism for Canada.

5. **CPR**: Canadian Pacific Railway, received its charter in the nineteenth century but for much of the twentieth century it was the predominant mode of long-haul travel in Canada.

6. **NAFTA**: North American Free Trade Agreement, negotiated by Canada, the United States, and Mexico in 1994 to remove bilateral tariffs and other trade restrictions. This new agreement followed the Canada-U.S. Free Trade Agreement, which was negotiated in 1989 after years of contentious debate.

7. **SIN**: Social Insurance Number, a nine-digit number in use since 1964 for unemployment insurance, pensions, income tax, and medical plans, among other things.

8. **CCM**: Canada Cycle and Motor Company Ltd. Since the company was formed in 1899 in Weston, Ontario, these letters have been found on bicycles, sports jerseys, and hockey and exercise equipment used by millions of Canadians.

9. **CANDU**: Canadian Deuterium Uranium reactors designed, developed and built by the Atomic Energy Board of Canada Ltd. and exported around the world.

10. **CUPW:** Canadian Union of Postal Workers, a militant union representing postal workers. Over the years CUPW has launched a handful of national strikes which have paralyzed Canada's postal system.

11. **CAA:** Canadian Automobile Association. The familiar sticker of this four-million-member organization has been spotted on millions of windshields and bumpers since it was formed in 1913 as an advocate for Canada's motoring and travelling public.

12. **INCO:** Short for International Nickel Company but now known as INCO Ltd., the company was formed in 1902 to take advantage of rich nickel deposits near Sudbury. Now the world's leading nickel producer.

Logo of the Canadian Automobile Association. *Photo by Andrew Ray.*

Snapshot

Therapeutic Abortions in Canada:

1970:	11,200
1975:	49,390
1980:	65,855
1985:	62,740
1990:	71,222
1995:	70,621

Statistics Canada

TEN LARGEST UNIVERSITIES BY STUDENT ENROLLMENT: 1901–02

1. University of Toronto (includes affiliates)   2,241 students
2. McGill University   1,041
3. Queen's University   774
4. Laval University (Quebec and Montreal)   769
5. Dalhousie University   345
6. University of Manitoba   300
7. Trinity University   156
8. McMaster University   135
9. University of New Brunswick   129
10. University of Western Ontario   127

TEN LARGEST UNIVERSITIES BY FULL-TIME ENROLLMENT: 1997–98

1. University of Toronto   38,782
2. University of Montreal   28,499
3. York University   28,321
4. University of Alberta   25,842
5. University of British Columbia   25,108
6. University of Western Ontario   21,467
7. McGill University   21,069
8. Laval University   20,475
9. University of Calgary   19,832
10. University of Waterloo   17,149

The University of Toronto was the largest university in Canada at the beginning of the twentieth century, and is still number one at the end. *Photo by Mark Kearney.*

WHAT FIFTEEN OUTSIDERS SAID ABOUT CANADA

1. "Believe me, the very name is an asset, and as years go on will become more and more of an asset. It has no duplicate in the world; it makes men ask questions." — Rudyard Kipling, in a 1910 letter that supported Albertans opposed to changing the name of their town from Medicine Hat to Progress.

2. "Great deeds are better than great sonnets, and Canada's call to her sons is a stirring one to action; for the poetry of actions exists just as does the poetry of words and the great deed that is accomplished is more glorious than the great sonnet." — Sir Arthur Conan Doyle, attempting to console Canadians on the lack of national literary expression, during a 1914 speech to the Canadian Club of Montreal.

3. "Down from Canada came tales of a wonderful beverage.... For years and years, visitors to Canada have come back with tales of a wonderful ginger ale. They described its exquisite flavour — they told of drinking it in the Houses of Parliament in Ottawa and in the Royal Canadian Yacht Club." — A 1921 newspaper advertisement written by American George Cecil which introduced Canada Dry, "The Champagne of Ginger Ales," to the American public.

4. "You in Canada should not be dependent either on the United States or on Great Britain. You should have your own films and exchange them with those of other countries. You can make them just as well in Toronto as in New York City." — D.W. Griffith, American pioneer director of silent films, in a speech to the Canadian Club in Toronto in 1925.

5. "I don't even know what street Canada is on." — Chicago Mobster Al Capone, 1931, when asked by a newspaper reporter if Canada was the main source of supply for his lucrative bootlegging operation.

6. "Before I left London, a friend of mine, with a great knowledge of this Dominion, gave me his views on various great cities, and when he came to Toronto he prefaced his remarks, I remember, by saying, 'here are two things they understand in Toronto — the British Empire and a good horse.'" — Governor General, the Earl of Bessborough, in a 1931 speech to the Canadian Club, Toronto.

7. "The Dominion of Canada is part of the sisterhood of the British Empire. I give you my assurance that the people of the United States will not stand idly by if domination of Canadian soil is threatened by any other empire. We can assure each other that this hemisphere, at least, shall remain a strong citadel

wherein civilization can flourish unimpaired." — U.S. President Franklin Delano Roosevelt, 1938, during a convocation address at Queen's University, Kingston, Ontario.

8. "In Canada, for example, there are 2.6 persons per square mile; in other countries perhaps, 16, 18, 20, or 26 persons. Well, no matter how stupidly one managed one's affairs in such a country, a decent living would still be possible." — Adolf Hitler, 1940, in a speech in Berlin.

9. "Canada and the United States have reached the point where we no longer think of each other as 'foreign' countries. We think of each other as friends, as peaceful and co-operative neighbours on a spacious and fruitful continent." — U.S. President Harry S. Truman, 1947, addressing a joint meeting of the Senate and the House of Commons.

10. "Montreal is the only place where a good French accent isn't a social asset." — Irish playwright Brendan Behan, 1960, as quoted in *The Wit of Brendan Behan* (1968).

11. "Vive le Québec! Vive le Québec libre! Vive le Canada français! Vive la France!" — French President Charles de Gaulle, in a 1967 speech at Montreal's city hall.

12. "You know what I think Oshawa needs? A good brothel." — Xavier Hollander, author and former madame, known as the Happy Hooker, 1973.

13. "Canada is so far away it hardly exists." — Argentine writer Jorge Luis Borges, 1974, during an interview in which he was asked, "What do you think of when you think of Canada?"

14. "Toronto ... is a kind of New York operated by the Swiss." — Peter Ustinov, in a 1987 interview with *The Globe and Mail*.

15. "When I'm in Canada, I feel like this is what the world should be like." — Actress Jane Fonda, 1987, quoted in *Saturday Night* magazine.

FIFTEEN OF CANADA'S MOST SIGNIFICANT MAN-MADE TWENTIETH CENTURY LANDMARKS

1. **Cabot Tower, St. John's, Newfoundland**: Completed in 1900 at the top of Signal Hill, it commemorates Queen Victoria's Diamond Jubilee and the 400th anniversary of John Cabot's voyage to the New World. The tower dominates St. John's harbour from a site that has been a natural lookout for as long as the region has been occupied.

Cabot Tower, St. John's, Newfoundland.
Photo courtesy of Parks Canada/Pam Coristine/1998.

2. **Confederation Bridge, Prince Edward Island/New Brunswick**: The 12.9-kilometre span joins Borden-Carleton, Prince Edward Island, and Cape Jourimain, New Brunswick. It opened on May 31, 1997, at a cost of $1 billion.

3. **Ste. Anne-de-Beaupre, Quebec**: The basilica was erected in 1923 to replace one that had burned down in 1922. It measures 129 metres long, 60.9 metres wide and 91.4 metres to the top of the twin steeple crosses. It's dedicated to the grandmother of Christ.

4. **The Cross on Mount Royal, Montreal, Quebec**: This thirty-metre high, illuminated cross was built in 1924 at the summit of the 250-metre "mountain" at the point where Paul de Chomedey de Maisonneuve, one of Montreal's founders, planted a cross in 1643.

5. **The Inco Super Stack, Sudbury, Ontario**: The 381-metre high smoke stack came into operation in 1972, shooting sulphur-containing emissions higher into the atmosphere and improving local air. It is the tallest stack in the world.

6. **The National War Memorial, Ottawa, Ontario**: In Confederation Square, less than a minute's walk from Parliament Hill (a landmark in its own right), the war memorial was erected to pay tribute to Canadians who fought in World War I. Every November 11 it's the site of a Remembrance Day ceremony to commemorate fallen Canadian soldiers.

7. **The CN Tower, Toronto, Ontario**: Described by some as an "exclamation mark" on the city's skyline, the world's tallest free-standing structure soars 553 metres above Toronto. It opened in 1976.

8. **Terry Fox Monument, near Thunder Bay, Ontario**: This larger-than-life bronze statue stands on the Trans-Canada Highway near the spot where the one-legged runner was forced to end his "Marathon of Hope" for cancer research on September 1, 1980.

9. **Golden Boy, Winnipeg, Manitoba**: Perched atop Manitoba's Legislative building, seventy-six metres from the ground, the figure of a running boy is the province's most recognized symbol. The five-tonne gilded bronze statue was hoisted into place in 1920.

10. **Saskatchewan Legislative Building, Regina, Saskatchewan**: Its thirty-three-metre tower and dome, completed in 1912, can be seen for miles around. The building is one of the primary attractions in Wascana Centre, which at 930 hectares, is said to be the world's largest urban park.

11. **The Calgary Tower, Calary, Alberta**: It is 191 metres high, and was built in 1968. Until it was surpassed by the 210-metre Petro Canada Centre in 1985, it was the tallest structure in the city. Nevertheless, it remains far more interesting to look at than any office tower.

12. **West Edmonton Mall, Edmonton, Alberta**: The world's largest shopping and entertainment centre was built between 1981 and 1998 at a cost of $1.2 billion and can't be missed during a visit to Edmonton, considering it covers an area equivalent to 104 Canadian football fields.

13. **Banff Springs Hotel, Banff, Alberta**: Rising out of the thick Alberta forest and nestled at the base of the Rocky Mountains 130 kilometres west of Calgary, it consists of a mix of French and Scottish baronial styles. It was built in 1928.

14. **Cairn at Craigellachie, British Columbia:** Erected in 1927, it marks the spot where, on November 7, 1885, the last spike of the Canadian Pacific Railway was driven by Donald Smith.

15. **The Lion's Gate Bridge, Vancouver, British Columbia:** Since 1939, this 450-metre long suspension bridge has linked the north shore to downtown Vancouver, spanning the First Narrows at the entrance to the Burrard Inlet. In rush hour the commute is frustratingly slow — but what the heck, the view is great.

Snapshot

Value of New Residential Construction

1926: $ 201 million

1956: $ 1.5 billion

1976: $ 10.8 billion

1996: $ 13.4 billion

Statistics Canada

HOT WHEELS ...
TEN HISTORIC CANADIAN-MADE CARS

1. The "LeRoy": The Good brothers, Milton and Nelson, founded their company in Berlin, Ontario (now Kitchener) in 1899 and produced the first true Canadian "production car" in 1902. Its name comes from the French "le roi" meaning "king." The first car built is on display at the Doon Heritage Crossroads museum in Kitchener.

2. The "Ivanhoe": A popular electric car made by the Canada Cycle and Motor Co. of Toronto beginning in 1903. This company, together with the National Cycle and Automobile Company of Hamilton, Ontario, which had been assembling steam cars since 1902, later became C.C.M.

3. The "Russell": Called the "thoroughly Canadian car" it was the last word in luxury from 1905 to 1915 and a very popular car before World War I. Based in Toronto, the Russell Motor Car Co. had branches in Hamilton, Montreal, Winnipeg, Calgary, Vancouver, and Melbourne, Australia. Its slogan was "Made up to a standard — not down to a price." After World War I, the company was bought out by Willys-Overland, which later introduced the famous "Jeep."

4. The "Tudhope": Produced in Orillia, Ontario by the Tudhope Carriage Co. Ltd. from 1906 to 1924. The car was built in a plant covering three city blocks. The first vehicle sold for $550 and had a top speed of twenty-five miles per hour. After the plant was destroyed by fire in 1909, the company began assembling a U.S. car known as the "Everitt." Two years later they were back to building their own cars with the slogan "The car ahead — Just one step ahead of the horse."

5. The "McLaughlin-Buick": Built by The McLaughlin Motor Company Ltd. of Oshawa, Ontario. In 1909, R.S. (Sam) McLaughlin joined with W.C. Durant in a fifteen-year contract to build McLaughlin bodies fitted with U.S. Buick engines. By 1914 they'd built 1,098 cars. The company merged with Chevrolet Motor Company of Canada to form General Motors of Canada Ltd. and continued production of McLaughlin-Buicks until the 1920s.

6. The "Superior": In 1910, wagon maker William English produced a car in Petrolia, Ontario, with an open steel body over a wood frame that could be converted into a truck. About sixty Superiors were built.

7. The "McKay": Built by the Nova Scotia Carriage and Motor Company of Amherst, Nova Scotia, between 1911 and 1914. The company produced about

one hundred cars, but had hoped to reach one thousand. Cars featured hand-buffed leather upholstery and an electric self starter. World War I and a shortage of operating capital cut off their supplies, and the firm folded.

8. **The "Peck"**: Electric cars produced by Peck Electric Ltd. of Toronto from 1911 to 1913. The company's slogan was "Keeps pecking."

9. **The "Briscoe"**: Produced by the Canadian Briscoe Motor Company Ltd. of Brockville, Ontario. The company began making cars in 1916, basing the design on a French automobile being assembled in the U.S.

10. **The "London Six"**: Between 1921 and 1925 almost one hundred of these cars were built by London Motors Ltd. in London, Ontario. The bodies were made of aluminum over a wood frame supplied to the company by a coffin maker.

List prepared with the assistance of automobile historian Tony Durham.

Fabulous Fact

The first persons to drive across Canada were Thomas Wilby and F.V. Haney in 1912. Although there were some portions of the country that didn't have roads, the two managed to complete the journey in fifty-two days.

Music

ONE HIT WONDERS (I) — SIXTEEN CANADIAN PERFORMERS WHO MADE IT ONTO BILLBOARD'S TOP 40 IN THE UNITED STATES ONLY ONCE: 1955 to 1974

1. **Gisele MacKenzie**, "Hard to Get": The Canadian star of TV's *Your Hit Parade* had her own number 4 hit in 1955.

2. **Priscilla Wright**, "The Man in the Raincoat": The young singer from London, Ontario, reached number 16 in 1955 with this ballad.

Priscilla Wright and friend in the singer's "Man in the Raincoat" era. *Photo courtesy of Priscilla Wright.* **Priscilla Wright still going strong in 1999. *Photo by Denise Grant.***

3. **Moe Koffman Quartette**: The catchy "Swingin' Shepherd Blues" propelled this Canadian music legend and his band to number 23 in 1958.

4. **Ronnie Hawkins**: His version of "Mary Lou" hit number 26 in 1959, but Hawkins would go on to have a bigger influence in Canada by working with hot, new talent for the next thirty-five years.

5. **Gale Garnett**, "We'll Sing in the Sunshine": This wistful Grammy-winning tune had actress/singer Garnett at number 4 in 1964.

6. **Lorne Greene,** "Ringo": The former news broadcaster in Canada and Pa Cartwright from *Bonanza* saw his spoken song about a gunfighter hit number one in 1964.

7. **Motherlode,** "When I Die": Released in 1969, this pop quartet's song, co-written by band members Steve Kennedy and William Smith, reached number 18. Other band members were Kenny Marco and Wayne Stone.

8. **Mashmakhan,** "As the Years Go By": Supposedly written in less than half an hour by keyboardist Pierre Senecal, this catchy tune by the Montreal group got to number 31 in 1970.

9. **Original Caste,** "One Tin Soldier": The song, used in the movie "Billy Jack," led this Canadian band to position 34 in 1970, but Chicago group Coven did even better with the song a year later, reaching number 26.

10. **R. Dean Taylor,** "Indiana Wants Me": Back in 1970, a lot of people also wanted Taylor's smash hit. It reached number 5 and stayed on the charts for thirteen weeks.

11. **Ocean:** The Scarborough, Ontario-based group was looking for a song that would get them higher paying gigs. "Put Your Hand in the Hand," written by Canadian Gene MacLellan, did much better, hitting number 2 in 1971.

12. **The Bells:** Their breathy ballad "Stay Awhile," penned by fellow Canadian Ken Tobias, made it to number 7 back in 1971. The Bells had other hits in Canada, but this was the only one on Billboard's Top 40.

13. **Ian Thomas:** Though he's written songs for others that made it onto Billboard's Top 40, and had many hits in Canada, "Painted Ladies" was the only song Thomas sang that made it. The song reached number 34 in 1973.

14. **Skylark,** "Wildflower": Though it hit number nine in 1973, this song is probably more notable for being the start of a successful career for band member David Foster, who went on to be a successful producer and multiple-Grammy winner.

15. **Terry Jacks,** "Seasons in the Sun": Although he also charted while with the Poppy Family, this was Jacks' only solo appearance on Billboard. It was number 1 for three weeks in 1974.

16. **Wednesday:** This Canadian group's version of "Last Kiss" reached number 34 in 1974.

ONE HIT WONDERS (II) — SIXTEEN CANADIAN PERFORMERS WHO MADE IT ONTO BILLBOARD'S TOP 40 IN THE UNITED STATES ONLY ONCE: 1975 to 1996

1. **Stonebolt**, "I Will Still Love You": A soothing ballad from this west coast band weighed in at number 29 in 1978.

2. **Nick Gilder**: He made it onto Billboard only once, but "Hot Child in the City" reached number 1 in 1978.

3. **Frank Mills**: Mills' bouncy piano instrumental "Music Box Dancer" climbed to number 3 in 1979.

4. **France Joli**: The young singer from Montreal made it to number 15 in 1979 with "Come to Me."

5. **Bruce Cockburn**: One of Canada's most respected singer-songwriters cracked the U.S. chart with "Wondering Where the Lions Are," topping out at the number 21 spot in 1980.

6. **Rush**: Primarily an album band with a huge following, "New World Man" was their only appearance in the Top 40. It reached number 21 in 1982.

7. **Cheri**: This Canadian duo just made it, reaching number 39 in 1982 with "Murphy's Law."

8 **Prism**: It came late in the band's career, but they slipped onto the Top 40 with "Don't Let Him Know," reaching position 39 in 1982.

9. **David Foster**: He's produced and composed many hits, but as a solo performer his only chart success was the "Love Theme From St. Elmo's Fire," which reached number 15 in 1985.

10. **Honeymoon Suite**: Their song "Feel it Again" climbed to number 34 in 1986.

112. **Glass Tiger**: This Canadian band hit it big with "Don't Forget Me (When I'm Gone)," which soared to number 2 in 1986.

12. **The Nylons**: Their strong harmonies made them a concert success around the world, but only "Kiss Him Goodbye," which got to number 12 in 1987, cracked Billboard's Top 40.

13. **Kon Kan:** The Toronto group hit number 15 in 1989 with "I Beg Your Pardon."

14. **The Jeff Healey Band:** "Angel Eyes" reached number 5 for this Toronto band in 1989.

15. **Tom Cochrane:** "Life is a Highway" was his biggest solo hit and reached number 6 in 1992.

16. **k.d. Lang:** The Alberta singer saw her "Constant Craving" reach number 38 in 1992.

Fabulous Fact

"Cover Girl," a cut from Prism's *All the Best* album was about sexy Vancouver-born model and Playboy Playmate Dorothy Stratten, who was murdered in 1980. Some saw the song as exploitative, but band member Lindsay Mitchell says, "It was just a song."

TOP TEN ALL-TIME JUNO AWARD WINNERS (AS OF 1999)

1. **Anne Murray:** 25 awards (includes one Hall of Fame award).

2. **Céline Dion:** 20 (includes two International Achievement awards).

3. **Bryan Adams:** 17 (includes one International Achievement award).

4. **Gordon Lightfoot:** 13 (includes one Hall of Fame award).

5. **Murray McLauchlan:** 10

6. **The Tragically Hip:** 9

7. **Alanis Morissette:** 9 (includes one International Achievement award).

8. **Montreal Symphony Orchestra:** 9

9. **Bruce Cockburn:** 8

10. **The Good Brothers:** 8

List provided by the Canadian Academy of Recording Arts and Sciences.

Music

ROCK GREATS ...
SEVEN CANADIANS IN THE ROCK AND ROLL HALL OF FAME

1–4. **The Band**: Four Canadians — Robbie Robertson, Rick Danko, Garth Hudson, and Richard Manuel, all from Ontario — were part of this popular and influential group, inducted into the Hall in 1994.

5. **Neil Young**: Inducted as a soloist in 1995, the singer-songwriter from Winnipeg was also a key member of Buffalo Springfield, who were inducted in 1997.

6. **Joni Mitchell**: The highly praised and successful musician from Alberta joined the Hall in 1997.

7. **Gene Cornish**: The Ottawa-born guitarist for the popular sixties group, The Young Rascals, was inducted along with his bandmates in 1997.

8–9. **Buffalo Springfield**: Besides Young, two other Canadians who were part of this important band of the late sixties, inducted into the Hall in 1997, were drummer Dewey Martin and bassist Bruce Palmer.

10. **Denny Doherty**: The smooth-voiced singer from Halifax was inducted along with fellow members of the Mamas and Papas in 1998.

TEN POPULAR SONGS WRITTEN BY CANADIANS: PRE-1950
(in chronological order)

1 and 2. **"Peg O' My Heart"** and **"I Didn't Raise My Boy to be a Soldier"**: The words to the 1913 hit "Peg O' My Heart" were by Alfred Bryan of Brantford, Ontario, who also gained fame two years later for penning the lyrics of "I Didn't Raise My Boy to be a Soldier," a popular World War I anti-war song.

3. **"The Darktown Strutters' Ball"**: Shelton Brooks of Amherstburg, Ontario, pursued his musical career in the U.S., and one of his most famous and popular songs was this one, written in 1917.

4. **"K-K-K Katy"**: Written by Geoffrey O'Hara of Chatham, Ontario, while he was living in Kingston, Ontario, during World War I. This song about a stuttering soldier was a hit throughout North America.

5. **"Mademoiselle from Armentières"**: The authorship of this 1918 song is disputed, but one of the possible co-writers was Gitz Ingraham Rice of New Glasgow, Nova Scotia.

6. **"Tumbling Tumbleweeds"**: Written by Bob Nolan of New Brunswick, who with Roy Rogers formed the singing group, The Sons of the Pioneers. This song was a hit for Gene Autry in 1935.

7. **"I'll Never Smile Again"**: Written by Toronto-native Ruth Lowe after the death of her husband, this song was recorded by Tommy Dorsey and Frank Sinatra and was a smash in the U.S. In 1940, it received the ASCAP award for Most Beautiful Song of the Year.

8 and 9. **"Seems Like Old Times"** and **"Boo-Hoo"**: Written by Carmen Lombardo (brother of Guy) of London, Ontario, and John Jacob Loeb in 1946, the nostalgic tune "Seems Like Old Times" was used by Arthur Godfrey as his radio theme and was later sung by Diane Keaton in the movie *Annie Hall*. Lombardo and Loeb had earlier collaborated with Edward Heyman to write the hit "Boo-Hoo," which topped the Hit Parade in the U.S. for seventeen weeks in 1937 and was apparently banned in Nazi Germany.

10. **"Far Away Places"**: Montrealer Alex Kramer wrote this with his wife Joan Whitney, and it became a fixture on the Hit Parade for nineteen weeks and a bestselling record for Bing Crosby in 1949.

MY SONG, YOUR HIT … TWELVE MODERN-ERA SONGS WRITTEN BY CANADIANS THAT WERE HITS FOR OTHERS

1. **"You Were On My Mind"**: Written by Sylvia Fricker (Tyson), this tune was a Top 10 hit for We Five in 1965.

2–3. **"Love Child"** and **"I'm Livin' in Shame"**: Though R. Dean Taylor is best known for his own hit "Indiana Wants Me," he also received a co-writing credit for these two smash hits by the Supremes in 1968 and 1969.

4. **"Both Sides Now"**: A 1968 Top 10 hit for Judy Collins that was penned by Joni Mitchell.

5. **"My Way"**: This Paul Anka tune became Frank Sinatra's signature song once "Ol' Blue Eyes" had a hit with it in 1969.

6. **"Good Morning Starshine"**: Co-written by Galt McDermot, this song from the Broadway musical "Hair" was a Top 10 hit for Oliver in 1969.

7. **"Until it's Time for You to Go"**: This Buffy Sainte-Marie song was a hit for Elvis Presley in 1972.

8. **"Calling Occupants of Interplanetary Craft"**: Written by Canadian group Klaatu, the Carpenters turned it into a hit in 1977.

9. **"Hold On"**: Ian Thomas had a hit with his own song first and then saw Santana crack the Top 10 with it in 1982.

10. **"St. Elmo's Fire"**: John Parr hit number 1 in 1985 with his recording of David Foster's tune.

11. **"Rhythm of My Heart"**: Rod Stewart's version of the Marc Jordan song was a number 5 hit in 1991.

12. **"Something to Talk About"**: Songwriter Shirley Eikhard was the creator behind this number 5 hit for Bonnie Raitt in 1991.

RICHARD PATTERSON'S TOP TEN CANADIAN ROCK VENUES

1. **Pineland Dance Pavilion, Ottawa:** Close to my heart because it was where my 1960s band The Esquires landed its first steady gig as house band, which eventually led to a loyal following of fans and a record contract with Capitol Records Canada.

2. **The Bonaventure Curling Club, Montreal (also known as Canadian Hopsville):** This curling-club-turned-teen-night-club featured three bands every night, from Montreal, Toronto, and Ottawa. Playing Hopsville provided support from the Montreal media, helped build a wider following, and offered the opportunity to meet other bands and pick up tips.

3. **The Hawk's Nest, Toronto:** If you were too young to play the licensed night clubs in Toronto, then this Yonge Street club, owned by "Rompin'" Ronnie Hawkins, was the place to be booked at. If you were an out-of-town band and were booked into The Hawk's Nest you had truly arrived on the Canadian music scene.

4. **The original Montreal Forum and Maple Leaf Gardens:** Although they were hockey rinks, both provided bands and their fans with some fantastic musical memories because of the acts that played in both, including The Rolling Stones, The Beach Boys, and The Dave Clark Five. The Forum and the Gardens gave many bands their first taste of playing to a large audience.

Many great bands have played at Toronto's Maple Leaf Gardens.

5. **The Esquire Club, Hanover, Ontario**: A wonderful example of a rural Ontario teen club on a highway close to other small towns with all the trimmings of a night club but without the booze.

6. **The Commodore Ballroom, Vancouver**: It was magic to play in. The view from the stage was dreamlike and took you back to the 1930s and 1940s, and the sound was impressive for a large hall. Also remembered by many performers because it had a room where two older women served coffee and tea to members of the crowd who wanted to steer clear of liquor.

7. **El Mocambo, Toronto**: More than once it played host to a variety of international pop stars and legendary icon bands. It was by no means fancy, but the "in your face" intimacy the room brought to both performers and the audience made it special.

8. **Capitol Theatres, Coast-to-Coast**: In the 1920s, a variety of movie palaces were built and although they had various monikers over the years, mostly because of their connection to film production houses in the United States, many wound up with the name Capitol Theatre posted on the sign over the sidewalk. They offered many young musicians and entertainers their first opportunity to play before seated patrons who were there to listen and watch your performance in a "concert" format.

9. **The Tabu Room, Ottawa**: In the basement of Ottawa's Beacon Arms Hotel, the Tabu Room was home base for my 1970s rock group Canada Goose. Every Thursday, Friday, and Saturday the band held court for about 250 mostly middle-aged swingers, many attired in leisure suits and bell bottoms, who would gather, have a good time, sometimes fight, and usually listen to the music.

10. **The Retinal Circus, Vancouver**: Toward the end of the 1960s, Canada caught up to the United States in the age of love, peace, and psychedelia and as a result a number of large entertainment spaces sprung up in Canada's major cities. Among the best was The Retinal Circus, which catered to a variety of musical formats, from hard rock to folk rock. It was outfitted with an in-house sound and lighting system, plus a psychedelic light show that was a show in itself.

List prepared by Richard Patterson, drummer in the 1960s and 1970s with The Esquires, 3's a Crowd, and Canada Goose.

RICHARD PATTERSON'S FAVOURITE FOLK HANGOUTS

1. Café Le Hibou, Ottawa

2. The Riverboat, Yorkville, Toronto

3. Smales Pace, London, Ontario

4. The New Penelope, Montreal

5. The Penny Farthing, Yorkville, Toronto

6. The Depression, Calgary

7. Yardbird Suite, Edmonton

8. Louis Riel Coffee House, Saskatoon

9. The Inquisition, Vancouver

10. The Bunkhouse, Vancouver

List prepared by Richard Patterson, drummer with 1960s folk rock group 3's A Crowd.

MAX FERGUSON'S FAVOURITE CANADIAN FOLK MUSICIANS
(with the exception of number one, in no particular order)

1. Ed McCurdy, Halifax, Nova Scotia.
2. Fiona Blackburn, Maple Ridge, British Columbia.
3. Bill Gallaher and Jake Galbraith, Victoria, British Columbia.
4. Barbara Ann Quigley, Moncton, New Brunswick.
5. Phyllis Morrissey, St. John's, Newfoundland.
6. The Barra MacNeils, Cape Breton, Nova Scotia.
7. Donald McGeoch, Brantford, Ontario.
8. Bob MacDonald, St. John's, Newfoundland.
9. Eileen McGann, Clagary, Alberta.
10. Tranby Croft, London, Ontario.
11. Pastime With Good Company, Vancouver, British Columbia.
12. Roger Helfrick, Calgary, Alberta.
13. Finest Kind, Ottawa, Ontario.
14. Tamarack, Guelph, Ontario.
15. Stan Rogers, originally from Hamilton, Ontario, died in a plane crash in 1983.

List prepared by Max Ferguson, host, humorist, and announcer on CBC Radio for more than fifty years. He was the longtime host of a folk music program broadcast on Saturday mornings.

Tranby Croft, shown here with current members and previous ones, is one of Max Ferguson's favourite folk bands.

FROM SEA TO SEA ...
SONGS ABOUT CANADA'S REGIONS AND HISTORY

1. **"Barrett's Privateers"**: The late Stan Rogers' stirring ballad is fictional but based on accounts of Canadian privateers who raided American ships in the eighteenth century.

2. **"Bud the Spud"**: Probably the most famous song about Prince Edward Island, courtesy of Stompin' Tom Connors.

3. **"Ca-na-da"**: Kids across Canada were singing Bobby Gimby's famous Centennial song in 1967 and gave him the nickname the Pied Piper of Canada.

4. **"Canadian Railroad Trilogy"**: Gordon Lightfoot's ode to the building of this country's railroads recalls an important part of our history.

5. **"Down by the Henry Moore"**: Few songs capture the feeling of downtown Toronto as well as this Murray McLaughlan song from 1975.

6. **"Gens du Pays"**: Gilles Vigneault's tune has been called Quebec's "national anthem" by many. An earlier and equally famous tune of his, "Mon pays," also speaks deeply to many Québécois.

7. **"The Hockey Song"**: Stompin' Tom Connors' tune about our national sport is heard at arenas across the country.

8. **"My Nova Scotian Home"**: Wilf Carter made a hit out of this song about his native province.

9. **"Something to Sing About"**: Oscar Brand's 1963 tune lyrically covers all regions of Canada and has been recorded many times.

10. **"The Wreck of the Edmund Fitzgerald"**: Gordon Lightfoot had an unlikely hit about the 1975 sinking of this Great Lakes ship.

11. **"Un jour, un jour (Hey Friend, Say Friend)"**: The official theme song of Expo '67 in Montreal was first written in French and then translated into English.

TEN CANADIAN JAZZ MUSIC CONTRIBUTORS
(alphabetical order)

1. **Jane Burnett:** flute/soprano sax/composer.

2. **Gil Evans:** piano/composer/arranger/leader.

3. **Maynard Ferguson:** trumpet/leader/composer.

4. **Diane Krall:** vocalist/piano.

5. **Rob McConnell:** valve trombone/composer/arranger/leader of Boss Brass.

6. **Phil Nimmons:** clarinet/composer/arranger/leader.

7. **Bert Niosi:** multi-instrumentalist/big band leader.

8. **Oscar Peterson:** piano/composer/leader.

9. **Don Thompson:** bass/piano/vibraphone/composer.

10. **Kenny Wheeler:** trumpet/flugal horn/composer.

List prepared by John Corcelli, jazz music consultant.

TOP TEN CANADIAN MUSIC VIDEOS OF ALL TIME
(In alphabetical order by artist's first name. All are "stellar examples of Canadian music and the videomaker's art.")*

1. Alanis Morissette, "Ironic," 1996.

2. Bryan Adams, "A Day Like Today," 1998.

3. Gowan, "Criminal Mind," 1986.

4. Maestro Fresh Wes, "Let Your Backbone Slide," 1989.

5. Mitsou, "Dis Moi Dis Mois," 1991.

6. Moist, "Tangerine," 1998.

7. Neil Young, "Rockin' in the Free World," 1990.

8. Rush, "Distant Early Warning," 1985.

9. Tea Party, "Sister Awake," 1997.

10. The Tragically Hip, "Ahead by a Century," 1996.

* *List prepared by Denise Donlon, Vice-President and General Manager of MuchMusic and MuchMore Music.*

FOURTEEN SIGNIFICANT POP SONGS BY CANADIANS SINCE 1950

1. **"Sh-Boom"**: Though purists might disagree, this song by the Crew-Cuts, four young crooners from Toronto, bridged the gap between rhythm and blues and the new style of music called rock 'n' roll, making it palatable for white audiences of the time.

2. **"Diana"**: The 1957 tune by Paul Anka hit number one and launched the Ottawa-born singer/songwriter and teen sensation into a long career in music.

3. **"Four Strong Winds"**: Canada has long had strengths in the folk music field, but this Ian and Sylvia classic would touch people in Canada and around the world.

4. **"Canadian Railroad Trilogy"**: Gordon Lightfoot had bigger hits and perhaps more well-loved songs during his long career, but this six-and-a-half-minute opus sums up the history of this country like no other. If it isn't already, it should be Canada's unofficial national anthem.

5. **"These Eyes"**: Yes, "American Woman" was a bigger hit, but this tune put The Guess Who front and centre in the international music scene of the 1960s and is as good an example of the strengths of the Bachman/Cummings songwriting team as any before or since.

6. **"The Weight"**: Fans of The Band may point to other songs as being better, but this was a major hit and a good example of how some Canadian boys could change the course of rock 'n' roll with their simple, straightforward approach to music.

7. **"Snowbird"**: This was the hit that launched Anne Murray's long career. A Grammy Award winner and the singer with the most Juno Awards in history, Murray was a familiar name on pop charts throughout the seventies, eighties, and nineties.

8. **"Born to be Wild"**: Steppenwolf gave us what was probably *the* anthem of the 1960s. Its introductory chords make you want to get in your car and head out on the highway long after your rebel days are over.

9. **"Helpless"**: Neil Young is arguably the most influential songwriter of his generation and has produced quality tunes for more than thirty years. This is just one of the many great songs from his collection.

10. **"The Circle Game"**: Songwriter Joni Mitchell has influenced hundreds of singer-songwriters and choosing just one of her songs is tough. But few could argue that this isn't one of her best.

11. **"Tears are Not Enough"**: The best of Canada's pop and rock musicians came together in 1985 under the name Northern Lights to record this song as a way to raise money for Ethiopians dying of starvation.

12. **"Everything I Do (I Do it for You)"**: This may not be Bryan Adams' best song, but it's certainly his most popular. Adams has stood tall among international performers and has built a solid career with hard-driving rock and catchy ballads.

13. **"You Oughta Know"**: This 1995 tune was just one of several that put Alanis Morissette on the international map and made her one of the most popular performers in the world.

14. **"My Heart Will Go On"**: Love it or hate it, this was the monster hit of the late 1990s and made Céline Dion an even bigger international superstar than she already was.

Fabulous Fact

The Crew-Cuts were just one of the successful groups that launched their careers at St. Michael's Choir in Toronto. Members of The Diamonds, known for many hits including "Little Darlin'," and The Four Lads, who had many charted songs, including "Moments to Remember," also got their start singing at St. Mike's.

BABY BOOMER MUSIC

ROCKIN' RANDY'S TOP FIFTEEN CANADIAN SINGLES: 1950s to the 1970s
(in alphabetical order by song)

1. **"Apricot Brandy"**: A punchy instrumental by Rhinoceros, a great band whose members hailed from a handful of great groups including Iron Butterfly and The Mothers of Invention.

2. **"As the Years Go By"**: One of my favourite Canadian million-sellers, this song by Mashmakhan demands lots of volume on the stereo.

3. **"Big Town Boy"**: A catchy tune that, for a while at least, made Shirley Matthews a big town girl.

4. **"Born to be Wild"**: The ultimate driving song by Steppenwolf, for the free spirit in all of us. Roll down the windows and turn it up loud.

5. **"Goodbye Baby"**: This move-your-feet Jack Scott tune from 1959 has to be played over and over and over — just ask my brother-in-law.

6. **"If I Call You by Some Name"**: The Paupers weren't terribly proud of this song, but it was the ultimate close-dancing number when the band played high school dances in Toronto in the late 1960s.

7. **"Just in Case You Wonder"**: The blistering lead guitar solo in this Ugly Ducklings single is etched in my brain forever.

8. **"Seasons in the Sun"**: Yes, it's on many a "worst Canadian singles" list but when you learn that Terry Jacks reworked the original Jacques Brel song after a close friend died of leukemia, you have to appreciate the song.

9. **"Shakin' All Over"**: This Chad Allan and The Expressions song is a Canadian classic. Enough said!

10. **"Signs"**: Canada's very own anti-establishment anthem by the Five Man Electrical Band.

11. **"The French Song"**: This Lucille Starr tune melts my heart every time I hear it.

12. **"The Weight"**: A classic from The Band that hits the turntable whenever I haul out the golden oldies collection.

13. **"Unless You Care"**: This early 1960s hit by Canadian teen idol Terry Black rates right up there with hits by American heartthrobs Bobby Vinton, Bobby Vee, and Bobby Rydell.

14. **"What the Hell I Got"**: With songs like this, it's no wonder Michel Pagliaro was once called Quebec's "undisputed king of rock and roll."

15. **"Wildflower"**: Skylark didn't do much after this song hit the top of the charts. But then, they didn't need to — "Wildflower" carved them a permanent place in Canadian rock music history.

List prepared by Randy Ray, co-author of Canadian Music Fast Facts.

MELODIC MARK'S TOP FIFTEEN CANADIAN SINGLES: 1950s to the 1970s
(in alphabetical order)

1. **"Can You Give it All to Me"**: A great Myles and Lenny single, especially when the violin solos come in where you might have expected electric guitar.

2. **"Cousin Mary"**: This marvellous laid-back tune is my favourite from Fludd, an underrated band that recorded several catchy 45s.

3. **"Every Bit of Love"**: Ken Tobias wrote wonderful melodic songs in the 1970s. This is Tobias at his best.

4. **"Free Man in Paris"**: Joni Mitchell is one those musicians who often had better album cuts than singles, but her ode to feeling "unfettered and alive" struck a chord with me.

5. **"Hurricane of Change"**: Murray McLaughlin also had better album cuts, but of his hits this tune still blows me away.

6. **"Lovin' Sound"**: Ian and Sylvia are better remembered for "Four Strong Winds," but I always liked the sound of this one better.

7. **"One Fine Morning"**: From the opening riffs and right on through on this high-energy classic, Lighthouse brought a rock tinged big-band sound to Canadian airwaves that still endures.

8. **"Opportunity"**: The Mandala were ahead of their time in the late sixties, which is why this song still sounds fresh and exciting today.

9. **"Pussywillows, Cat-tails"**: Gordon Lightfoot was Canada's foremost balladeer for good reason. This one's evocative and haunting.

10. **"Renaissance"**: Folksinger Valdy had successes with his own tunes, but his recording of this David Bradstreet song about a couple that "dance that old dance once more" is a standout.

11. **"Share the Land"**: With so many hits to The Guess Who's credit, how do you pick out their best? But this music-with-a-message song is my favourite. Check out Burton Cummings' vocals, particularly near the end.

12. **"Sour Suite"**: An underrated classic from The Guess Who. Burton Cummings' best ballad.

13. **"Sun Goes By"**: I've never been able to make out all the words to this, but I still love it. The musicians who made up Dr. Music peaked for this 1972 hit.

14. **"Three Rows Over"**: Yes, this Bobby Curtola song is pure bubble gum, but I've liked it ever since I was eight. And for the rest of my school years, I always checked out who was sitting three rows over and two seats down.

15. **"You Can't Dance"**: Great harmonies were a trademark of Jackson Hawke, and they soared on this song about being a band "playing in a bar uptown."

List prepared by Mark Kearney, co-author of Canadian Music Fast Facts.

GEN X MUSIC ...

RICHARD CROUSE'S FAVOURITE POP AND ROCK SINGLES: 1980s to the 1990s
(in alphabetical order)

1. **"Constant Craving," k.d. Lang:** A moving ballad from the woman who is, arguably, Canada's best song stylist.

2. **"Echo Beach," Martha and the Muffins:** Crisp, clean pop that rode the new wave boom to the top of the charts in Canada and abroad.

3. **"Funkmobile," Bass is Base:** A delicious soul-stew flavoured with generous portions of funk and R&B.

4. **"I'm an Adult Now," The Pursuit of Happiness:** A great three-minute rock song that shelves conventional rock songwriting cliches, and actually attacks its subject with a great deal of humanity. Oh, and it's funny too.

5. **"Let Your Backbone Slide," Maestro Fresh Wes:** This record represented something unheard of at the time — Canadian hip-hop on our homegrown charts. Ahead of its time, this one still sounds fresh today.

6. **"Listen To the Radio," Pukka Orchestra:** A remake of the Peter Gabriel/Tom Robinson song originally titled "Atmospherics."

7. **"Little Bones," The Tragically Hip:** Given the position the Hip occupy in Canada's pop pantheon, it would be considered a crime against the state not to include them on this list.

8. **"Little Kingdoms," Change of Heart:** A hard-rocking single from one of Canada's best, yet most underrated bands.

9. **"The Maker," Daniel Lanois:** Sublime. Ephemeral. In Lanois' hands this simple folk song becomes a supple soundscape, rich in texture and mood.

10. **"Mimi on the Beach," Jane Sibbery:** Whimsical and loopy, but at the same time graceful and literate, "Mimi on the Beach" is an impressively quirky song from one of Canada's great cult heroes.

11. **"Rockin' in the Free World," Neil Young:** Young in all his ragged glory — a string-busting wake-up call to those who thought Neil had become just another acoustic-guitar plucking folkie.

12. **"Sweet Jane," The Cowboy Junkies:** Part Velvet Underground, part Patsy Cline, this song earned the highest praise possible — songwriter Lou Reed said it is the best version yet of his 1960s classic.

13. **"'Til the Fever Breaks," The Jitters:** Like all Jitters' singles, this nugget is uncluttered effervescent popcraft that still sounds great on the radio or jukebox.

14. **"Too Bad," Doug and the Slugs:** Canada's sole purveyors of proto-punk barbershop quartet singing had many successes in the early eighties, but none match the unbridled fun of this record.

15. **"Underwhelmed," Sloan:** The debut single from Halifax wunderkids Sloan, and also the subject of the most bloated, wordiest sentence in all of Canadian rock music criticism (check out page 165 of *Mondo Canuck*).

List prepared by Richard Crouse, the author of several books, including Who Wrote the Book of Love.

SIX CANADIAN NOVELTY SONGS

1. **"Honky the Christmas Goose"**: Johnny Bower not only stopped pucks during his years with the Maple Leafs, but he probably stopped a few people in their tracks with this 1965 Christmas tune. Accompanying him on the song were Little John and the Rinky-Dinks.

2. **"Clear the Track (Here Comes Shack)"**: The Maple Leafs managed to notch another hockey song during their glory years in the sixties. This tune, performed by Doug Rankine and the Secrets and written by broadcaster Brian MacFarlane, was a number 1 tribute to "The Great Entertainer" Eddie Shack in 1966.

3. **"The Americans (A Canadian's Opinion)"**: At the height of the Vietnam War, outspoken broadcaster Gordon Sinclair talked from the heart about his feelings for our neighbours to the south in this unlikely hit. Recorded at CFRB studios in Toronto in 1973, it stayed on U.S. charts for four weeks in 1974.

4. **"Gordie Howe"**: The hockey legend had made his mark as the most prolific scorer in NHL history when Big Bob and the Dollars released this ode to the Detroit Red Wings star in 1963.

5. **"Take Off"**: Canadian hosers Bob and Doug McKenzie (SCTV stars Rick Moranis and Dave Thomas) teamed up with vocalist Geddy Lee of Rush to hit number 1 in Canada and crack the top twenty in the United States in 1982. Beauty, eh?

6. **"Don't Play Bingo Tonight, Mother"**: One of The Happy Gang's most successful songs, written in 1944, it tells the story of family urging a mother not to spend all her time at the bingo parlour.

People

THE TWELVE SEXIEST CANADIAN WOMEN

1. **Shania Twain:** Award-winning country music singer.
2. **Cynthia Dale:** Actress (Stratford Festival and TV series "Street Legal").
3. **Sarah McLachlan:** Award-winning singer-songwriter.
4. **Wendy Mesley:** CBC-TV broadcaster.
5. **Mary Pickford:** Silent film actress and producer.
6. **Gloria Reubens:** Television actress ("ER").
7. **Catherine O'Hara:** Comedian with "SCTV" and movie actress (*Home Alone, Waiting for Guffman*).
8. **Liona Boyd:** Classical guitarist and composer.
9. **Catriona LeMay Doan:** Olympic champion speed skater.
10. **Linda Evangelista:** Supermodel.
11. **Margo Timmins:** Lead singer and songwriter of the Cowboy Junkies.
12. **Neve Campbell:** Actress in television ("Party of Five") and movies (*Scream*).

Liona Boyd, Canada's First Lady of Guitar.
Photo by Keith Williamson.

THE TWELVE SEXIEST CANADIAN MEN

1. **Pierre Trudeau:** Former prime minister of Canada.
2. **Leonard Cohen:** Singer-songwriter and award-winning poet.
3. **Michael J. Fox:** Actor in movies (*Back to the Future*) and television ("Family Ties," "Spin City").
4. **Christopher Plummer:** Actor in theatre (*Barrymore*) and movies (*The Sound of Music, The Silent Partner*).
5. **Donald Sutherland:** Movie actor (*M*A*S*H, Ordinary People, JFK*).
6. **Kurt Browning:** Former world figure skating champion.
7. **Phil Fontaine:** Chief, Assembly of First Nations.
8. **R.H. Thomson:** Actor in theatre, television (*Glory Enough for All*), and movies (*Ticket to Heaven*).
9. **Lorne Greene:** Broadcaster (CBC Radio) and television actor ("Bonanza").
10. **Paul Gross:** Actor in theatre and television ("Due South").
11. **Robbie Robertson:** Singer-songwriter, most notably with The Band.
12. **John (J.D.) Roberts:** TV news anchor at CBS News, formerly at CITY-TV in Toronto.

Lists based on an informal (and highly unscientific) survey of friends, colleagues, and acquaintances from across Canada.

Paul Gross, star of "Due South," is one of Canada's sexiest men.
Photo by Tim Leyes

TEN GREAT CANADIAN QUOTATIONS FROM THE TWENTIETH CENTURY

1. "We must deliver power to such an extent that the poorest working man will have electric light in his house." — Sir Adam Beck, 1908, two years after assuming chairmanship of the Ontario Hydro-Electric Power Commission (now Ontario Hydro).

2. "Truly magnificent ... the sight was awful and wonderful." — General Sir Arthur Currie, April 9, 1917, in an entry in his war diary after commanding the Canadian Division during the Battle of Vimy Ridge, France.

3. "When I hear men talk about women being the angel of the home I always, mentally at least, shrug my shoulders in doubt. I do not want to be the angel of any home; I want for myself what I want for other women, absolute equality. After that is secured, then men and women can take turns at being angels." — MP Agnes Macphail, February 26, 1925, in the House of Commons.

4. "If you can't beat 'em in the alley, you can't beat 'em on ice." — Conn Smythe, 1952, owner of the Toronto Maple Leafs.

5. "I did it for Canada." — Swimmer Marilyn Bell, 1954, after becoming the first person to swim across Lake Ontario.

6. "There is more to marriage than four bare legs under a blanket." — Robertson Davies, 1957, *Love and Libel*, Davies' stage adaptation of his 1954 novel *Leaven of Malice*.

7. "I'm going to flood the rink." — Lucien Rivard, 1965. The convicted drug peddler told guards he was going to flood the prison ice rink just before he leapt over the wall at Bordeaux Jail, Montreal. His escape added to the controversy the Liberal government of the day was facing regarding possible bribe money for Rivard.

8. "In Pierre Elliott Trudeau, Canada has at last produced a political leader worthy of assassination." — Irving Layton, 1969, in his book *The Whole Bloody Bird*.

9. "A Canadian is someone who knows how to make love in a canoe." — Pierre Berton, 1973, in a magazine interview.

10. "I want to ask you gentlemen, if I cannot give consent to my own death, then whose body is this? Who owns my life?" — Lou Gehrig's disease victim Sue Rodriguez, November 1992, in a videotaped presentation to a House of Commons subcommittee, in which she sought amendments to the part of the Criminal Code that makes it a crime for one person to assist another's suicide.

TRUE ROMANCE ... TEN GREAT CANADIAN LOVE STORIES
IN THE TWENTIETH CENTURY

1. In 1923, architect Francis Rattenbury, designer of British Columbia's Parliament Buildings and Victoria's Empress Hotel, met Alma Pakenham, a beautiful musician who was half his age. A torrid love affair, his messy divorce, and their hasty marriage ensued, leading Victoria's society to censure the man once held in great esteem. The couple fled to England and twelve years later their love story gained international attention when Alma's teenaged lover killed Rattenbury and Alma killed herself.

2. World War I hero and former governor general Georges Vanier has been called the most important Canadian in history. He and his wife, Pauline, complemented one another in a way that improved Canadian society. The strength of the Vaniers' love for one another enhanced two already dynamic personalities with an elegance Canadians may never see again.

Georges and Pauline Vanier: A memorable romance. *Photo courtesy of National Archives of Canada: PA122356.*

3. In the 1930s, an Ojibway named Grey Owl burst onto the international lecture circuit. He credited his adored Mohawk wife, Anahareo, as his inspiration. Grey Owl toured the world clad in native attire addressing audiences that included royalty. Only at his death in 1938 did anyone, including his beloved, discover that Grey Owl was really Englishman Archibald Belaney, who had been married many times.

4. Canadian audiences cherished Hume Cronyn's and Jessica Tandy's careers and their relationship (even though Tandy wasn't Canadian). Both were established and accomplished actors when they married in 1942, but it was their performances together that were most remarkable. The couple remained deeply and happily committed to one another until her death in September 1994. Their last movie, *Camilla*, released in 1995, was lovingly dedicated to Tandy's memory.

5. In 1949, Eddie and Doreen Boyd were among war veterans and war brides establishing homes in Canada. Eddie, confident and handsome, would go places, Doreen was sure. She was right: He became the leader of the Boyd Gang, whose daring and profitable bank robberies held southern Ontario in awe during the early 1950s. Despite being surrounded by glamorous molls, Eddie remained in love with Doreen, who unquestioningly accepted her husband's illegal occupation.

6. Traditionally, Canadians don't do scandals. The tryst between Pierre Sévigny and Gerda Munsinger was an unlikely exception. Associate Minister of National Defence Sévigny was a decorated war hero and a proud patriot; Munsinger supplemented her income through prostitution and had once been arrested in her native Germany on spying charges. The love affair, which may have created a breach of national security, lasted from 1958 to 1961.

7. On March 5, 1971, Canadians awoke to learn that their fifty-two-year-old bachelor prime minister Pierre Trudeau had married twenty-two-year-old Margaret Sinclair, the daughter of a former Liberal cabinet minister. From then, through the birth of their three sons, to the couple's divorce in 1984, the world watched as the antics of Pierre and Margaret charmed, and occasionally embarrassed, Canadians.

8. In 1985, wheelchair athlete Rick Hansen left Vancouver to begin his Man in Motion tour of the world. His efforts raised $20 million for spinal cord research and raised worldwide awareness about the capabilities of people with disabilities. The tour also provided Hansen's physiotherapist Amanda Reid, with the opportunity to fall in love with Rick, as he had done with her the moment they met. Now married and with three daughters, they continue Hansen's mission.

9. Canadian hockey icon Wayne Gretzky married American dancer, model, and actress Janet Jones on July 23, 1988, an event of royal magnitude. The two attractive and accomplished young people were obviously very much in love and the country's collective hearts were stolen. Less than three weeks later those hearts were broken when Gretzky was traded from the Edmonton Oilers to the Los Angeles Kings.

10. In 1980, René Angélil wept as he listened to twelve-year-old Céline Dion's singing voice. Angélil, twenty-six years her senior, was married with children, including a son older than Céline. Under his auspices her singing career skyrocketed. In November 1994, Dion publicly declared her love for Angélil on her album *The Colour of Love*. They were married the following month.

List prepared by Barbara Smith, author of Passion and Scandal: Great Canadian Love Stories.

Snapshot

DIVORCE RATES PER 100,000 POPULATION

1921	1941	1961	1981	1995
6.4	21.4	36.0	278.0	262.2

Statistics Canada

LADIES FIRST ...
FIRSTS FOR CANADIAN WOMEN: 1900 to 1950
(Canadian women in the twentieth century broke new ground in many aspects of society. Here are some of their achievements.)

1. **Clara Brett Martin:** First woman barristor in Canada, 1901.

2. **Carrie Derick:** First woman to become a full professor in Canada, 1912, McGill University, Montreal.

3. **Alys McKey Bryant:** First woman to pilot an airplane in Canada, 1913, Vancouver.

4. **Annie Langstaff:** First woman to graduate with a law degree in Quebec, 1914. Forced to work as a legal clerk because the Quebec Bar refused to admit her.

5. **Elizabeth Smellie:** First woman appointed a colonel in the Canadian Army, 1915, as head of the Canadian Army nursing corps.

6. **Emily Murphy, Alice Jamieson:** Murphy of Edmonton and Jamieson of Calgary were the first women in the British Empire to be appointed police magistrates, 1916.

7. **E.M. Hill:** First woman architect in Canada, graduated from University of Toronto, 1920.

8. **Lydia Emelie Gruchy:** First woman ordained in the United Church, 1923.

9. **Eileen Volick:** First Canadian woman to earn a pilot's licence, 1928.

10. **Ethel Catherwood:** Canada's first woman gold medalist. She won the high jump at the Amsterdam Olympics with a jump of five feet three inches, 1928.

11. **Canada's Olympic Team:** The first time the team included women, Amsterdam Olympics, track and field, 1928.

12. **Mona Campbell:** First woman veterinarian in private practice, 1948.

FIRSTS FOR CANADIAN WOMEN: 1950 to 1999

1. **Winnie Roach Leuszler**: First Canadian to swim the English Channel, 1951.

2. **Jean Sutherland Boggs**: First woman in the world to head a national art gallery, National Gallery of Canada, Ottawa, 1966.

3. **Lorraine Carrie**: First woman elected president of a wing of the Royal Canadian Air Force, Wing No. 1, composed of women enlisted in the RCAF, 1969.

4. **Ada Mackenzie, Marlene Stewart Streit**: First women elected to the Canadian Golf Hall of Fame, 1970.

5. **Rosella Bjornson**: First North American woman jet pilot, Transair, Winnipeg, 1973.

6. **Grace Hartman**: First woman president of a national trade union, Canadian Union of Public Employees, 1975.

7. **Dr. Lois Wilson**: First woman to be elected as moderator of the United Church of Canada, 1980.

8. **Bertha Wilson**: First female Supreme Court Judge, Ottawa, 1982.

9. **Sharon Wood**: First woman from North America to scale Mount Everest, 1986.

10. **Sheila Hellstrom**: First woman Brigadier General in Canadian Armed Forces, 1988.

11. **Carol Anne Letheren**: First woman president of the Canadian Olympic Association, 1990.

12. **Manon Rheaume**: First woman to play in the National Hockey League. Played goal for the Tampa Bay Lightning in a pre-season game, 1992.

AUDREY McLAUGHLIN'S TEN COURAGEOUS WOMEN WHO HELPED CHANGE THE FACE OF CANADA

1. **Emily Murphy**: Talented and independent, Murphy built a career as a prominent journalist and author before becoming the first woman in the British Empire to be appointed a police magistrate in 1916 in Edmonton. A self-taught legal expert, she initiated the "persons" case, which saw the Judicial Committee of the Privy Council of Britain rule in 1929 that women were persons under the British North America Act and could be appointed to political positions.

Emily Murphy helped Canadian women gain recognition as persons.
Photo courtesy of National Archives of Canada: C5255.

2. **Pauline Jewett**: A veteran member of Parliament with the New Democratic and Liberal parties, Jewett was known for representing all of Canada in Parliament, not just her party. She was also a feminist, nationalist, and the first woman appointed president of Simon Fraser University in British Columbia and chancellor of Carleton University in Ottawa.

3. **Irene Spry**: Born in South Africa, Spry was a respected economist, historian, and social activist who was a professor and lecturer at a variety of universities, including the University of Toronto, University of Ottawa, and University of Saskatchewan during a seventy-year span. She was also an author, editor, and an Officer of the Order of Canada.

4. **k.d. Lang**: The provocative Consort, Alberta singer/composer, first broke into the music business with her band The Reclines in the early 1980s. She has

Pauline Jewett: At convocation ceremonies at Carleton University in Ottawa in 1991. *Photo by Mike Pinder.*

made her mark in the Canadian music industry by winning a number of awards, including Canadian Country Music Awards entertainer of the year in 1989, a Grammy Award in 1990, and Canadian Country Music Awards Album of the year in 1992. She is an Officer of the Order of Canada.

5. **Rosalie Abella**: A native of Stuttgart, Germany, Abella distinguished herself, from the 1970s onward, in many roles, including as a lawyer, Justice of the Ontario Court of Appeal, and as sole commissioner for the Royal Commission on Equality in Employment, which created the term and concept of employment equity in 1983–84. She's also a much-published author who wrote about access to legal services by the disabled and equality in employment.

6. **Martha Munger Black**: At age 70, this naturalist and adventurer from the Yukon Territory became only the second woman elected to serve in the House of Commons. She served as a Conservative from 1935 to 1940. Outside politics she was an authority on the flora of the Yukon and originated the craft of pressing, preserving, and mounting wild flowers.

7. **Agnes Macphail**: A country school teacher who was active in the farm movement, Macphail entered politics to represent the farmers of Grey County and was elected to the House of Commons in December 1921 as the country's first female member of Parliament. While in office in Ottawa and in Toronto as an MPP in the Ontario Legislature, she also devoted much of her time to such women's issues as prison reform and equal pay legislation, which was implemented in 1951 as a result of her efforts.

8. **Nellie McClung:** Known as Canada's first feminist and one of the most influential social activists in Canadian history, McClung built a modest career as a writer before embarking on a public career in 1911. She became a leading representative of the Woman's Christian Temperance Union and is widely credited with helping women win the right to vote in 1916. In 1921, she was elected to the Alberta legislature and over the years was known as a strong believer in the importance of home and family who frequently made clear demands for the equality of the sexes.

9. **Mary Two-Axe Early:** An aboriginal activist and founder of Equal Rights for Indian Women, she helped lead the fight to repeal sections of Canada's Indian Act that stripped aboriginal women of their status when they married non-natives. The act was amended in 1985, and she became the first woman to have her status officially restored.

10. **Margaret Atwood:** The Toronto writer has been described as "the leading feminist novelist of her generation" and "the outstanding novelist of our age." She was a leading poet before she was 30 and cemented her reputation in 1972 with the publication of two books — the nationalist novel *Surfacing* and *Survival*, a book of criticism. Other books, including *Alias Grace*, have attracted worldwide praise. She helped found the Writers' Union of Canada and joined other artists opposed to free trade with the United States in the late 1980s. Atwood has won dozens of awards, including the Giller Prize and the Governor General's Literary Award.

List prepared by The Honourable Audrey McLaughlin, Circumpolar Envoy for the Yukon Government and former leader of the federal New Democratic Party.

Nellie McClung helped women win the vote. *Photo courtesy of National Archives of Canada: C27674.*

PROMINENT CANADIANS ...
TWELVE CANUCKS WITH POSITIONS OF INTERNATIONAL IMPORTANCE IN THE
TWENTIETH CENTURY

1. **Vincent Massey:** The first Canadian government representative to the United States in the first diplomatic appointment made by Canada, 1926. It was significant because it demonstrated Canada's independence within the Commonwealth.

2. **Lester B. Pearson:** The former prime minister was elected president of the United Nations General Assembly, 1952.

3. **Paule-Emile Léger:** The archbishop of Montreal was appointed a cardinal by the Vatican, 1953.

4. **Blanche Margaret Meagher:** The career diplomat was the first woman in Canada to hold an ambassadorship when she was appointed Canada's envoy to Austria in 1962. And while in Vienna, she became Canada's representative at the International Atomic Energy Agency.

5. **Donald MacDonald:** The Canadian Labour Congress president was elected first non-European president of the ninety-one-nation International Confederation of Trade Unions, 1972.

6. **Sylvia Ostry:** An economist and public servant, Ostry was appointed head of the Department of Economics and Statistics, Organization for Economic Cooperation and Development in Paris, France, 1980.

7. **Stephen Lewis:** In a surprise move, the one-time leader of the Ontario New Democratic Party was named by the federal Conservative government as Canada's ambassador to the United Nations, 1984. Canada's first UN Ambassador was Leolyn Dana Wilgress, appointed in 1948.

8. **Lynn Williams:** The minister's son from Springfield, Ontario was the first Canadian elected to head the giant Pittsburgh-based United Steelworkers of America trade union, making him one of the few non-U.S. citizens to lead a major American labour body, 1984.

9. **Richard Pound:** A former medal-winning swimmer, he became a vice-president of the International Olympic Committee, 1987.

10. Norman Inkster: The one-time commissioner of the Royal Canadian Mounted Police served as president of France-based Interpol, the international association of police forces, 1992 to 1994.

11. Louise Arbour: The Ontario Court of Appeal judge became Chief Prosecutor for the International Criminal Tribunals for the former Yugoslavia and Rwanda, in The Hague, 1996. In 1999 she left the post after being appointed to the Supreme Court of Canada.

12. Adrienne Clarkson: One of Canada's leading television personalities, Clarkson was elected president of the prestigious IMZ-International Music Centre for leading audio/visual producers of cultural and arts programs, headquartered in Vienna, Austria, 1998.

Snapshot

Average Family Size

	1901	1951	1971	1991	1997
No. of Families	1,058,386	3,409,284	6,041,302	7,497,400	8,018,400
Average size	5.0 persons	4.0	3.5	3.1	3.0

Statistics Canada

FIFTEEN OF THE GREATEST CANADIAN HEROES

1. **Terry Fox:** Minus a leg lost to cancer, Fox attempted to run across Canada in 1980 in his Marathon of Hope to raise money for cancer research. But in September, near Thunder Bay, Ontario, cancer struck again and the run was called off. He died on June 28, 1981, at age 22, but not before $24 million was raised for his cancer research fund. Annual runs held in his name in Canada and around the world every September keep Fox's memory alive.

Terry Fox on the run. *Photo by Gail Harvey courtesy of the Terry Fox Foundation.*

2. **Lotta Hitschmanova:** A native of Prague, Czechoslovakia, she was founding director of Canada's Unitarian Service Committee and is remembered as the thickly accented voice on television commercials pleading with viewers to give generously to starving children. For thirty-seven years with USC Canada she was recognized as a leader in international development who initiated community development projects wherever war and poverty caused suffering.

3. **All men and women who served their country in times of war and peace,** including more than 100,000 who died from wounds or disease in the Boer War, World War I, World War II, the Korean War, and while keeping the peace in a variety of far-off lands.

4. **Cliff Chadderton**: Long-time chief executive officer of the War Amputations of Canada, a support organization for amputees which helped him after he lost part of his right leg in World War II. Under Chadderton's tireless leadership, War Amps branched out and helped Canada's thalidomide victims obtain government compensation. He also founded the War Amps' CHAMP program to help child amputees cope with their amputations, and he has long been active in the struggle for veterans' rights.

5. **Naomi Segal-Bronstein**: A Canadian activist who has dedicated her life to saving the sick and orphaned children of the third world by opening homes and clinics and bringing them to North American hospitals. During a 1997 television special, "Canadian Heroes: A Celebration of Excellence," it was reported that her work has saved sixty thousand children in Central America, Korea, Cambodia, and Vietnam.

6. **Hal Rogers**: Founder of Canada's Kinsmen Club and the man behind the Kinsmen "Milk-for-Britain" campaign, which, between 1941 and 1947, raised about $3 million and sent more than 50 million quarts of milk, in powdered form, to help millions of British school children combat malnutrition during and after World War II.

7. **Ken Taylor**: The former Canadian ambassador to Iran, who hid six American diplomats, then spirited them out of Tehran in January 1980 after Iranian militants stormed the U.S. embassy and took sixty-six hostages. Although some of the shine came off his accomplishment when an ex-Central Intelligence Agency agent claimed the CIA engineered the escape, Taylor is still remembered for his heroics.

8. **Nellie McClung**: Canada's first feminist and one of the most influential social activists in Canadian history. She was a leading representative of the Woman's Christian Temperance Union and is widely credited with helping women win the right to vote in 1916. As a member of the Alberta legislature, she frequently made clear demands for the equality of the sexes.

9. **Paul Henderson**: Few Canadians have been credited with deeds as momentous as the goal Henderson scored for Team Canada on September 28, 1972. The converted rebound, with thirty-four seconds remaining in the final game of the first ever Canada-Russia series, turned back a relentless Soviet Union advance in the climactic eighth match and gave Canada a win that may never be forgotten.

10. **René Marc Jalbert**: On May 8, 1984, Jalbert, Sergeant-at-arms at the Quebec National Assembly, subdued assassin Denis Lortie, who had killed

three people and wounded thirteen others in the assembly chamber. As bullets peppered the area, he convinced the heavily armed Lortie to allow several employees to leave, then spent four hours persuading the killer to surrender. In July 1984, Jalbert received the Cross of Valour for his courage, which almost certainly prevented a higher death toll.

11. **Rick Hansen**: Between 1985 and 1987, the Port Alberni, British Columbia wheelchair athlete raised $20 million for spinal cord research, rehabilitation, and wheelchair sports during a 792-day wheelchair odyssey known as the "Man in Motion" tour, which covered the equivalent of the distance around the world. In 1983, he shared Canadian athlete of the year honours with Wayne Gretzky.

12. **Norman Bethune**: A surgeon, inventor, political activist, and avowed Communist, Bethune's fame in Canada resulted mostly from his status as a hero in China, where in the 1930s, he was a tireless and inventive surgeon and propagandist who assisted China in its anti-Japanese war. He trained physicians for the Communist Party Army and braved death to save soldiers on the battlefield.

13. **Cardinal Paul-Émile Leger**: Appointed a cardinal of the Roman Catholic Church in 1953, Leger later served as a missionary among lepers and handicapped children in Cameroon, Africa. He was also involved in many humanitarian activities and was a recipient of the Pearson Peace Medal.

14. **Ben Wicks**: This internationally renowned author and cartoonist has written a series of children's literacy books and embarked on national speaking tours to help millions of young Canadians develop and strengthen their reading and writing skills.

15. **Vic Horner and Wop May**: Bush pilots who battled snowstorms and -40° weather in 1929 to fly anti-toxins to Fort Vermillion to stop a diptheria epidemic that threatened to wipe out Métis and Natives there. The pilots were apparently so frozen upon their return they had to be lifted from the cockpit.

List prepared with the assistance of listeners on radio stations CFRA in Ottawa and CFRB in Toronto.

TWELVE CANADIAN HEROES ...
THROUGH THE EYES OF ELEMENTARY SCHOOL STUDENTS

1. **Dr. Frederick Banting and Dr. Charles Best:** By discovering insulin as a treatment for diabetes they have saved many lives.

2. **Alexander Graham Bell:** A good role model because he believed in trying to do the impossible. Not only did he invent the telephone, but his airplane, the Silver Dart, made the first manned flight in the British Empire and his hydrofoil, the HD-4, held the record for more than a decade as the world's fastest watercraft.

3. **Billy Bishop:** A World War I flying ace who fought for our country.

4. **Dr. Roberta Bondar:** The first Canadian woman to go into space showed what can happen if you stay in school.

5. **The Canadian Military:** Members of Canada's Armed Forces have an international reputation for peacekeeping. All the Canadian military people that have fought were heroes. Many of them died trying to save our country.

6. **The Dionne Quintuplets:** These women brought hope to people during the Depression and endured a hard life. They showed us that it is wrong to use other human beings for entertainment.

7. **Terry Fox:** He is a hero because he ran across Canada to raise money for cancer research even after he had lost most of his leg to cancer. He never gave up. Since his death, people have kept organizing runs to raise money for cancer research.

8. **Wayne Gretzky:** The greatest hockey player who ever lived, a great role model, and one of the best Canadians ever. He had a dream to become a great hockey player, and he worked to fulfill it.

9. **Rick Hansen:** Going around the world in a wheelchair to help spinal research must have been very hard.

10. **Nellie McClung:** A teacher, novelist, and political activist, who went to the highest court of appeal as part of the "Famous Five" to have women recognized as persons. It would not be fair for women today if she had not done this.

People

11. **W.O. Mitchell:** He wrote great books and cared about our city. His writings show a comic view of life in Western Canada. He was so wonderful, he was able to have a school named after him.

12. **David Suzuki:** A hero because he cares so much about our ecological system and he does everything he can to save it. If we did not have his radio and TV shows we might not know about the ecological damage that is happening to our world.

List prepared by teacher Gary Edwards and his 1998–99 Grade 6 class at W.O. Mitchell Elementary School in Calgary, Alberta.

Snapshot

Elementary/Secondary School Enrollment

1920   1,928,000

1970   5,832,000

1980   5,100,000

1996   5,400,000

1998   5,600,000

Statistics Canada

NINE INFAMOUS CANADIANS IN THE TWENTIETH CENTURY

1. **Brian Mulroney:** No prime minister has altered the political landscape as much as Mulroney, whose government negotiated a free trade agreement with the United States, implemented the Goods and Services Tax, and, according to some, revived support for the Parti Québécois. For his efforts, not to mention years of scandals and party patronage, the boy from Baie-Comeau has been called the most loathed Canadian politician in the twentieth century.

2. **Arthur Meighen:** The controversial lawyer and former prime minister earned the hatred of many Canadians for championing conscription in World War I and World War II. And as acting minister of justice, he incurred the wrath of trade unionists by using troops and vicious emergency power to crush the Winnipeg General Strike of 1919.

3. **Alan Eagleson:** In 1998, the former hockey lawyer and player agent pleaded guilty to fraud and theft charges, was fined $1 million, and was thrown in jail for swindling players and stealing disability insurance money and Canada Cup money that was intended for the players' pension fund. He was later stripped of his Order of Canada medal, disbarred by the Law Society of Upper Canada and booted out of Canada's Sports Hall of Fame. He also resigned from the Hockey Hall of Fame.

4. **Ernst Zundel:** The Holocaust denier and advocate of Jewish conspiracies has been repeatedly accused over the past twenty years of violating Canada's hate laws and, in the process, has incurred the wrath of many Canadians.

5. **Harold Ballard:** People, especially long-suffering Toronto Maple Leafs fans, were never happy with the direction Ballard took the team in the 1970s and 1980s. "Pal Hal," as he was known, added insult to injury in 1972 when he was convicted on forty-seven charges of fraud and theft involving $205,000 in Maple Leaf Gardens' funds.

6. **Clifford Olson:** Canadians were outraged by his sex slayings of at least eleven Vancouver area children, for which he was charged in 1981, and many felt his life sentence on several counts of first degree murder wasn't sufficient punishment. His conviction once again raised the issue among Canadians of reinstituting the death penalty.

7 and 8. **Paul Bernardo and Karla Homolka:** The duo responsible for the murders of Leslie Mahaffy and Kristen French between 1990 and 1992 were tried in one of the most notorious murder cases in Canadian history. Even the

books written about the case have come under attack for being sensationalistic and not sensitive enough to the victims' plight. Bernardo was sentenced to life imprisonment while Homolka received two twelve-year sentences to run concurrently. She is eligible for parole in 2001.

9. **Ben Johnson:** Canadians were elated after Johnson won the 100 metres in the 1988 Olympics. But the cheers faded quickly after drug screening showed the Toronto athlete had tested positive for steroids. He was stripped of the gold medal and his actions led to an inquiry into drugs and sport in Canada that has had world-wide ramifications.

THE NAME GAME ...
TEN MEMORABLE NICKNAMES

1. **America's Sweetheart**: Toronto-born actress Mary Pickford, who was the leading actress of the silent film era.

2. **Wild Goose Jack**: Legendary conservationist Jack Miner, who started a 370-acre waterfowl sanctuary in 1904 near Windsor, Ontario, as a refuge for thousands of migrating birds.

3. **The Pied Piper of Canada**: Musician Bobby Gimby earned the nickname for his Centennial song "Ca-na-da," which featured the voices of young Canadians. Gimby was often pictured leading children in a march while they sang the song.

4. **The Gentleman Bandit**: U.S.-born thief Bill Miner, who pulled off Canada's first train robbery in 1904 when he held up a Canadian Pacific Railway train at Mission Junction, British Columbia. During heists he often apologized to his victims.

5. **The First Lady of the Guitar**: Classical guitarist Liona Boyd was tagged with this nickname in a 1970s magazine article. Born in London, England, but a resident of Canada since age 6, she is one of the world's leading classical guitar players and has more than lived up to her First Lady status.

Sam Sniderman founded one of the largest chains of record stores in the country, and came to be known as "Sam the Record Man."
Photo courtesy of Sam Sniderman

6. The Hawk: Although he was born in the United States, singer Ronnie Hawkins was a fixture at Toronto's Hawk's Nest Tavern on Yonge Street in Toronto in the 1960s and gave many Canadian musicians their start, including members of The Band.

7. A Man Called Intrepid: Winnipeg-born William Stephenson, who gained fame as a master spy during World War II.

8. Lucius "Christmas Time" Parmalee: Once referred to as the greatest forger Canada has ever produced, he often plied his trade in large cities. He picked up the name because in the festive season he often used clergymen's garb to persuade bank tellers to approve rubber cheques to help the poor at Christmas.

9. Vern "Dry Hole" Hunter: This roughneck experienced a long record of worthless holes until February 13, 1947, when he struck oil near Leduc, Alberta. His strike started the Alberta oil boom.

10. Sam the Record Man: Sam Sniderman began selling records in Toronto in 1937 and founded a record store chain that grew into 123 outlets across Canada. He received the Order of Canada in 1976 and the Walt Grealis Juno Award in 1989 for supporting Canadian artists and their music.

Fabulous Fact

"Wild Goose Jack" Miner's Windsor-area bird sanctuary is more than just a stopover for tired birds. Since the early 1900s, aluminum bands have been attached to more than 200,000 birds to help decipher their migratory travels and flight patterns and assess age classes and the survival of different sexes.

NOTORIOUS CANADIAN MURDERERS

1. **Omar Roberts:** In August 1922, Roberts poured gasoline on Elora Gray and set fire to her and his house in Kemptville, Nova Scotia, because she had turned down his marriage proposal and was in love with another man. Police found Gray before she died, however, and she was able to tell them what Roberts had done. Roberts was found guilty of murder and hanged in November 1922.

2. **Evelyn Dick:** She was charged with murder after the March 1946 killing of her husband John Dick and their baby. Later that year she was found not guilty in one of the most sensational murder trials in the country's history, but then found guilty at a new trial in 1947. Dick was sentenced to life. She was paroled in 1958 after serving eleven years in prison, and then disappeared.

3. **Steven Truscott:** He was found guilty of the June 9, 1959 murder of Lynn Harper in Clinton, Ontario, and sentenced to life. Truscott has claimed innocence from the start, and after serving a total of ten years in prison he was paroled. He now lives under an assumed name and is happily married with children and grandchildren. DNA testing was to be done to see if any more about the case could be found out.

4. **Dale Merle Nelson:** In 1970, he killed and mutilated members of two families in West Creston, B.C. He gave himself up several hours later and said that alcohol and drugs made him commit murder. But at his trial in March 1971 he was found guilty and sentenced to life in prison.

5. **The FLQ Murderers:** On October 17, 1970, during the FLQ crisis, the strangled body of Pierre Laporte, a Quebec cabinet minister, was found in the trunk of a car in St. Hubert, Quebec. Paul and Jacques Rose, Francis Simard, and Bernard Lortie were charged in 1971 with kidnapping and non-capital murder, and later all were convicted and sentenced to prison terms ranging from eight years to double life.

6. **Dwayne Archie Johnston:** In 1971 a Cree woman, Helen Betty Osborne, was murdered in The Pas, Manitoba. No one was initially found guilty, although many townspeople had an idea who might have done it. The case was re-opened in 1986 and though four men were charged with the crime, only Johnston was convicted and sentenced to life. A book was written on the case and in 1991 made into the movie *Conspiracy of Silence*.

7. **Peter Demeter:** Christine Demeter, Peter's wife, was found dead in their Mississauga, Ontario, home in July 1973. The wealthy property dealer wasn't originally a suspect because he had been out shopping with friends. However, police concluded that he had hired someone to do the murder for him, and Demeter was eventually arrested and charged with the crime. On December 4, 1974, Demeter was sent to prison for procuring the murder of his wife.

8. **Saul Betesh:** He was found guilty of first degree murder of Toronto shoeshine boy Emanuel Jaques. Betesh had raped, strangled, and eventually drowned the twelve-year-old boy. He was sentenced to life in prison with no chance of parole for twenty-five years for the July 1977 murder. Three others were also arrested for the killing: two were found guilty, and one not guilty.

9. **Fernand Robinson:** Torontonians were shocked by the murder of lawyer Barbra Schlifer in her apartment building in April 1980. Schlifer had been sexually abused and stabbed several times. Robinson confessed to the killing two years later, was found guilty of first degree murder in May 1984, and sentenced to life in prison with no chance of parole for twenty-five years. The Barbra Schlifer Commemorative Clinic was set up in 1985 to help female victims of violence.

10. **Clifford Olson:** Canada's most notorious serial killer was charged in August 1981 with eleven counts of first degree murder in connection with the slayings of Vancouver area children. He was sentenced to life in prison with no chance for parole for twenty-five years. Olson has also boasted of killing and burying several more victims.

11. **Colin Thatcher:** The Saskatchewan politician was charged with murdering his ex-wife Jo Ann in 1983. His trial in 1984 gained national attention. Thatcher was sentenced to life, and his appeal in 1985 was turned down. The case was later turned into the movie *Love and Hate.*

12. **Allan Legere:** He was convicted in June 1986 for murdering a shopkeeper, but later escaped and committed other murders. Legere was then convicted in November 1991 for several murders that took place in the Miramichi area of New Brunswick and sentenced to life in prison.

13. **Marc Lepine:** On December 6, 1989, Lepine killed fourteen female engineering students at École Polytechnique at the University of Montreal. He then killed himself. The "Montreal Massacre" has since become a symbol of violence against women and is commemorated each December across the country.

14 and 15. **Paul Bernardo and Karla Homolka:** This married couple gained notoreity for the 1991 murder of Leslie Mahaffy and the 1992 murder of Kristen French, both high school students. In one of the most sensational and widely covered cases in Canadian history, Bernardo was sentenced to the maximum term of life imprisonment with no possibility of parole for twenty-five years. He was later declared a dangerous offender, and will spend the rest of his life in prison, with no possibility for parole. Homolka received two twelve-year sentences to run concurrently. Homolka was eligible for parole in 1997, but didn't apply. She will be eligible again in 2001.

16. **Francis Carl Roy:** In July 1986, eleven-year-old Alison Parrott disappeared from her Toronto home and her body was found two days later. But it wasn't until ten years later that Roy was arrested. He was found guilty of first degree murder in April 1999 and was sentenced to life with no chance of parole for twenty-five years. An appeal was pending.

INNOCENT ...
FIVE WRONGLY ACCUSED CANADIANS

1. **Donald Marshall Jr.**: Charged with a murder in Nova Scotia in 1971 and sentenced to prison, Marshall was found innocent more than ten years later. A report from January 1990 said the justice system failed him and a month later the Nova Scotia government apologized. Marshall received $270,000 plus a monthly payout.

2. **David Milgaard**: Charged with the 1969 rape and murder of Gail Miller, a Saskatchewan nursing assistant, Milgaard was found guilty and spent twenty-three years in prison before being exonerated for the crime in 1992. As compensation, he and his family received a record $10-million settlement from the Saskatchewan and Federal governments in 1999 .

3. **Guy Paul Morin**: Morin was arrested in 1985 for the murder of Christine Jessop, who had disappeared the previous October and whose body was found two months later. Morin was originally acquitted, but was re-tried and convicted in 1992. He was released on bail several months later and finally exonerated and acquitted in 1995 based on DNA evidence. Morin got $1.2 million from the Ontario and federal governments for the wrongful conviction.

4. **Susan Nelles**: The Toronto nurse was prosecuted in 1981 for murdering four babies at the Hospital for Sick Children who had died suspiciously. Nelles found herself under the glare of national media coverage, but eight months later the charges were thrown out because of lack of evidence against her. A $3.5-million inquiry into the matter did little to clarify the matter, and in January 1985 Justice Samuel Grange said Nelles had been wrongly accused.

5. **Gregory Parsons**: Convicted in 1994 of murdering his mother Catherine Carroll three years earlier, Parson was later cleared of the crime based on DNA evidence. He received an apology from Newfoundland's Justice Department in November 1998.

Politics

PRIME MINISTER-SPEAK ...
TEN MEMORABLE QUOTATIONS BY CANADIAN PMs IN
THE TWENTIETH CENTURY

1. "The British Empire first, and, within the British Empire, Canada first." — Sir Robert Borden.

2. "The story of a nation's heroes is the fountain from which it draws the wine of its later life." — Arthur Meighen.

3. "Not necessarily conscription, but conscription if necessary." — William Lyon Mackenzie King.

4. "The West is not thinking, the West is drinking." — R.B. Bennett.

5. "I've lived history, I've made history, and I know I'll have my place in history." — John Diefenbaker.

6. "I didn't say what I said when I said it. What I meant to say when I didn't say it was that I wouldn't have said what I said when I did say it." — Lester Pearson.

7. "It is more important to maintain law and order than to worry about those whose knees tremble at the sight of the army." — Pierre Trudeau.

8. "If I am beaten, it will be because of image." — Joe Clark.

9. "As for us, we have only been in power for two months, but I can tell you this: Give us twenty years, and it is coming, and you will not recognize this country. Moreover, the whole area of federal-provincial relations will also be completely changed." — Brian Mulroney.

10. "No prime minister can hit a home run every time he stands up at the plate — prime ministers can sometimes miss the ball completely.... When it happens ... I don't lose my step, I don't even take steroids, I just work harder and run the stairs faster." — Jean Chrétien.

TEN MEMORABLE POLITICAL NICKNAMES

1. **Bible Bill**: William Aberhart, leader of the Social Credit Party in Alberta from 1935 to 1943.

2. **Wacky**: William Andrew Cecil Bennett, British Columbia's Social Credit premier from 1950 to 1972.

3. **The Chief**: John Diefenbaker, Canada's prime minister from 1957 to 1963.

4. **The Three Wise Men**: Jean Marchand, Gérard Pelletier, and Pierre Trudeau, who in the 1960s embarked on the task of saving federalism in Quebec.

5. **Hell on Wheels**: Charlotte Whitton, who as mayor of Ottawa in the 1950s and 1960s was the first woman to head a Canadian city.

6. **The Tiny Perfect Mayor**: David Crombie, while mayor of Toronto from 1973 to 1978.

John Diefenbaker: The Chief. *Photo courtesy of National Archives of Canada: PA57930.*

7. Ti-Poil (meaning Old Baldy or small hair, in English): René Lévesque, leader-founder of the Parti Québécois and premier of Quebec from 1976 to 1985.

8. Joe Who: Joe Clark after being elected leader of the federal Progressive Conservative Party in 1976.

9. The Rat Pack: Liberal backbench MPs, Sheila Copps, John Nunziata, and Sergio Marchi in the 1980s.

10. The Logger Lawyer from Lorne: Elmer MacKay, Conservative Member of Parliament in Nova Scotia and holder of several federal cabinet posts between 1971 and 1993.

Snapshot

Federal Government Employees

1911:   20,016

1941:   66,937

1971:   250,672

1991:   415,977

1997:   338,594

Statistics Canada

TEN GREAT CANADIAN POLITICAL SCANDALS, CRISES, AND AFFAIRS

1. **King-Byng Affair**: Prime Minister Mackenzie King was defeated in the House of Commons and advised Governor General Lord Byng to dissolve Parliament and call an election in 1926. Byng refused, insisted on King's resignation and called on Opposition leader, Arthur Meighen, to form a government. King accused Byng of acting unconstitutionally — which was not the case — but the mood of the electorate was on King's side and in the next election, King defeated Meighen.

2. **The Beauharnois Scandal**: Became public in 1931–32 when committees of the House of Commons and Senate investigated allegations that Beauharnois Light, Heat, and Power Co. had made $700,000 in contributions to the federal and Quebec Liberal parties in return for permission to divert the St. Lawrence River thirty kilometres west of Montreal to generate hydroelectricity. No connection was ever established between the donations and the power policy of the Mackenzie King government, but a senator and Liberal Party campaign treasurer lost their jobs. The scandal caused no long-term damage to the Liberal Party.

3. **"Wild Bill" Hawrelak**: First elected as mayor of Edmonton in 1951, Hawrelak in the late 1950s was found to have used his office for personal gain on a number of occasions, including purchasing land for his brother-in-law, then intervening as mayor to have it rezoned for development, a move that substantially increased its worth. A judicial inquiry forced his resignation in the early 1960s but in 1963 he was re-elected, before being dismissed again in 1964 by an Alberta court after becoming involved in shady land dealings. Amazingly, he was re-elected in 1974.

4. **The Munsinger Affair**: While associate minister of national defence in the Diefenbaker government between 1958 and 1961, Pierre Sévigny had an affair with Gerda Munsinger, a Montreal divorcée who had emigrated from East Germany. Munsinger was known to police as a prostitute who had had contact with Communist intelligence services. A Royal Commission criticized Diefenbaker for allowing Sévigny to remain in cabinet but found no security breach.

5. **The Rivard Scandal, 1964–65**: A Montreal lawyer was offered a $20,000 bribe by an assistant to the Liberal minister of immigration to get bail for Lucien Rivard, a narcotics smuggler. There was also a promise of money for Liberal Party coffers and the fact that Rivard escaped from a Montreal prison with remarkable ease. Prime Minister Lester Pearson claimed his justice

minister, Guy Favreau, had told him nothing of the affair and refused to accept the minister's offer to resign. In the end, most of those tainted by the affair were French-Canadians and those who publicized the scandal were accused of being anti-French.

6. Tunagate and Other Dirt: Federal Fisheries Minister John Fraser resigned his cabinet post in September 1985 after a public disagreement with Prime Minister Brian Mulroney. Fraser had approved the release of one million cans of tuna tested as unfit for human consumption. A string of other scandals or events that displayed questionable ethical behaviour involving nine other ministers would follow, involving Mulroney's environment minister, defence minister, and industry minister, to name a few. Within the Conservative Party, this spate of scandals would come to be known as the "Mulroney sleaze factor."

7. The Fantasy Gardens Affair: In 1984, two years before he became British Columbia's premier, Bill Vander Zalm and his wife Lillian bought a property in a suburb of Vancouver, which was eventually developed into the Fantasy Gardens World theme park. When it began losing money, they sold it to a Taiwanese entrepreneur who had been feted by the premier's office and was considering making other investments in B.C. An investigation later showed Vander Zalm had violated several of his own conflict of interest guidelines by mixing business with his personal affairs and taking a mysterious $20,000 cash payment. The premier resigned as leader of the Social Credit Party, which later suffered a resounding defeat in the 1991 election. By the end of the century the party was nearly irrelevant in B.C.

8. Fraud in the Saskatchewan Conservative Government: Known as the biggest political scandal ever in the Prairies, it involved numbered companies, false expense accounts, honest mistakes and incompetence between 1986 and 1999. Twenty-one Saskatchewan Conservatives, including several cabinet ministers in Premier Grant Devine's government, were charged with an assortment of frauds totalling $1 million. As of early 1999, fifteen people had been convicted, including five who went to jail.

9. Tainted Blood: At least 1,200 Canadians of all ages were infected with the deadly AIDS virus and thousands more contracted hepatitis C after receiving blood transfusions between 1980 and 1990. Blame for the suffering has been lain with the Red Cross, public health officials, bureaucrats, and politicians in what has been called "the greatest preventable medical scandal" in Canada's history.

10. Canadian Airborne Regiment: In 1993, four members of the elite Canadian Airborne Regiment, who were in Somalia for a peacekeeping mission, were charged with the torture and beating death of a Somali civilian. In 1994, Private Elvin Kyle Brown was convicted of manslaughter and torture and sentenced to five years in prison. In 1995, a leaked videotape of an Airborne hazing ritual depicted drunken troops forced by their comrades to simulate sex acts and eat feces, vomit, and urine-soaked bread. The video also showed a black soldier on a leash with the words "I love the KKK" scrawled on his back. The government disbanded the regiment later in 1995.

NINE OF THE BIGGEST FEDERAL ELECTION VICTORIES IN THE TWENTIETH CENTURY

(Based on popular vote):

Party/Leader	Number of Votes	Percentage of Votes	Margin of Victory
March 26, 1940			
Liberal W.L. Mackenzie King	2,536,214	54.9	24.3
Conservative Robert Manion	1,416,257	30.6	
September 4, 1984			
Conservative Brian Mulroney	6,278,697	50.03	22.01
Liberal John Turner	3,516,486	28.02	
June 27, 1949			
Liberal Louis St.-Laurent	2,929,391	50.1	20.4
Conservative George Drew	1,742,276	29.7	
March 31, 1958			
Conservative John Diefenbaker	3,910,852	53.7	19.9
Liberal Lester Pearson	2,459,700	33.8	
June 2, 1997			
Liberal Jean Chrétien	4,994,377	38.5	19.1
Reform Preston Manning	2,513,070	19.4	

August 10, 1953

Liberal Louis St.-Laurent	2,819,813	50.0	17.0
Conservative George Drew	1,751,215	33.0	

October 14, 1935

Liberal W.L. Mackenzie King	1,955,727	44.4	14.6
Conservative Richard Bennett	1,311,459	29.8	

June 25, 1968

Liberal Pierre Trudeau	3,696,945	45.5	14.1
Conservative Robert Stanfield	2,554,880	31.4	

June 11, 1945

Liberal W.L. Mackenzie King	2,170,625	41.4	13.7
Conservative John Bracken	1,455,453	27.7	

Snapshot

The Federal Debt and Canadians' Share:

	Net Debt	Net Debt Per Person
1940:	$ 3.2 billion	$ 288
1960:	$ 12.0 billion	$ 677
1980:	$ 72.1 billion	$ 2,853
1990:	$357.8 billion	$13,484
1997:	$583.1 billion	$19,247

Finance Canada

**FLEETING FAME ... FOUR TWENTIETH CENTURY PRIME MINISTERS
WHO WERE TURFED FROM OFFICE — QUICKLY!**

1. John Turner, Liberal. 80 days: June 30–September 17, 1984.

2. Arthur Meighen, Conservative. 89 days: June 29–September 25, 1926.

3. Kim Campbell, Conservative. 135 days: June 13–October 25, 1993.

4. Joe Clark, Conservative. 273 days: June 4, 1979–March 3, 1980.

**Prime Minister Arthur Meighen:
Not long on the job.** *Photo
courtesy of National Archives
of Canada: PA28132.*

WARREN ALLMAND'S TWELVE MOST SIGNIFICANT POLITICAL EVENTS

1. October Crisis, murder of Pierre Laporte, kidnapping of James Cross: 1970.

2. Newfoundland enters Confederation: 1949.

3. Vincent Massey appointed Canada's first Canadian-born governor general: 1952.

4. Supreme Court of Canada replaces the Judicial Committee of the Privy Council of the United Kingdom as the last court of appeal: 1949.

5. Winnipeg General Strike: 1919.

6. Abolition of the death penalty: 1976.

7. Battle of the North Atlantic during World War II, Canadian frigate and destroyers run supply convoys to England.

8. James Bay and Northern Quebec Agreement, the first major native land claims settlement in the modern era, with James Bay Cree and Inuit: 1975.

9. Prime Minister John Diefenbaker cancels Avro Arrow: 1959.

10. Adoption of Canada–U.S. Free Trade Agreement: 1988.

11. Election of first separatist government in Quebec, 1976, and defeat of separation referendum in 1980.

12. Nunavut Territory established: 1999.

List prepared by Warren Allmand, president of the International Centre for Human Rights and Democratic Development and a former Member of Parliament for thirty-one years.

TEN OF THE MOST SIGNIFICANT POLITICAL EVENTS OF THE TWENTIETH CENTURY

1. The Wilfrid Laurier Government's campaign to open the west to European immigrants in the early 1900s. Hundreds of thousands of immigrants settled the Prairie provinces and created Canada's breadbasket to the world.

2. King-Byng Wing-Ding. In 1926, Liberal Prime Minister Mackenzie King was defeated in the House of Commons and advised Governor General Lord Byng to dissolve Parliament and call an election. Byng refused, insisted on King's resignation and called on the Opposition leader, Arthur Meighen, to form a government. King accused Byng of acting unconstitutionally, which was not the case, but the mood of the electorate was on King's side and in the next election, he defeated Meighen. King's election win showed the public clearly favoured the prime minister as controller of Parliament, rather than a "foreign" head of state who had tried to overrule the political leader who headed the Canadian government.

3. Person's case. In 1928, in Edwards v. the Attorney General of Canada, the Privy Council concluded that women were "persons," and as a result, could be appointed to the Senate.

4. Prairie radicalism gave birth to the Co-operative Commonwealth Federation in 1933, forever offering the electorate a leftist alternative to the more moderate Liberals and creating a body within which innovative liberal ideas could be debated and developed.

5. Igor Gouzenko, a cipher clerk, gave himself up and revealed a Russian spy ring operating out of Ottawa in the mid-1940s. The scandal marked the outbreak of the Cold War, which dominated East-West relations for the next four decades and inspired countless spy novels.

6. The election of Jean Lesage in 1960: Father of the Quiet Revolution, Lesage, as leader of the Quebec Liberals, put an end to the Catholic Church's absolute control of Quebec society and launched the province into a period of self-evaluation and growth.

7. Introduction of medical care insurance in 1962 by the Co-operative Commonwealth Federation government of Tommy Douglas in Saskatchewan introduced this predecessor to a national health insurance plan which, after considerable debate, was in place in all provinces and territories by 1972.

8. The flag debate, 1964. Lester Pearson severed another significant tie with Britain.

9. Declaration of the War Measures Act during the FLQ crisis of 1970. In using this act, Pierre Trudeau ended the separatist movement's fling with terrorism and turned it into a political movement.

10. Patriation of the constitution in 1982. The final symbolic milestone in Canada's development as an independent nation.

List prepared by Gary May, an editor at The Ottawa Citizen, *who from 1981 to 1986 was Parliament Hill correspondent for* The London Free Press.

Snapshot

Labour Unrest in Canada

	Strikes/Lockouts	Employers	Workers	Person Days Lost
1901	99	285	24,089	737,808
1931	88	266	10,738	204,238
1951	259	646	102,870	901,740
1971	569	n/a	239,631	2,866,570
1991	463	n/a	253,000	2,516,000
1997	279	n/a	254,000	3,570,000

Statistics Canada

TWELVE WOMEN WHO BROKE POLITICAL GROUND DURING THE TWENTIETH CENTURY

1. **Nellie McClung:** Widely acclaimed as Canada's first feminist, she was a leading representative of the Woman's Christian Temperance Union and led the fight to give women the right to vote in western Canada in 1916.

2. **Louise McKinney:** In 1917 she was the first woman in Canada to be elected to a provincial legislature when she won a seat in Alberta.

3. **Agnes Campbell Macphail:** She was the first woman to be elected to the House of Commons when she won the Ontario riding of Grey South East in 1921 — the first election in which women had the right to vote.

Agnes Macphail, the first woman elected to the House of Commons. *Photo courtesy of National Archives of Canada: PA127295.*

4. **Cairine Reay Wilson:** In 1930, she was the first woman appointed to the Senate.

5. **Mary Teresa Sullivan:** Became Canada's first female municipal councillor when she was sworn in as a member of Halifax city council in 1936.

6. **Charlotte Whitton:** First woman mayor of a major Canadian city, Ottawa, 1951.

7. **Ellen Loucks Fairclough:** The Ontario MP became the first federal female cabinet minister in 1957 with her appointment as secretary of state in the government of John Diefenbaker.

8. **Rosemary Brown:** In 1972, she was the first black woman elected to the provincial legislature in British Columbia.

9. **Ione Christiansen:** First woman commissioner of the Yukon, 1978.

10. **Jeanne Sauve:** Named Canada's first female governor general in 1983. She was also the first woman Speaker of the House of Commons and the first female MP from Quebec to be a cabinet minister.

11. **Audrey McLaughlin:** First woman to lead a national political party in Canada and North America when she was elected leader of the federal New Democratic Party in 1989.

12. **Kim Campbell:** In 1993 she became the country's first female prime minister. She was also the first woman to lead the federal Progressive Conservative Party.

Snapshot

Ups and Downs:
A Sampling of Unemployment Rates in Canada Between 1923 and 1998

1923	1933	1943	1953	1963	1973	1983	1993	1998
3.8%	19.3%	2.1%	3.0%	5.5%	5.5%	11.5%	11.2%	8.3%

Statistics Canada

Science

TEN SIGNIFICANT SCIENTIFIC DISCOVERIES INVOLVING CANADIANS

1. Discovery of insulin for the treatment of diabetes, Toronto, in 1922 by Frederick Banting and Charles Best: Banting shared his Nobel Prize, Medicine, winnings with Best in 1923. Banting was born in Alliston, Ontario, while Best was the son of a Canadian-born physician but was born in Maine.

2. Mapping the visual cortex of the brain, enabling medical practitioners to determine where different vision processing tasks take place, such as lines, brightness, and colour: Work done at Harvard University by David Hubel of Montreal in the 1960s and 1970s. Hubel shared the Nobel Prize, Medicine, in 1981 with Torsten Wiesel, who was Swedish.

3. Development of site-based mutagenesis, a new way of creating mutations in living organisms to produce improved plants and animals: The discovery was made in the early 1980s in Vancouver by Michael Smith, who moved to Vancouver from England in 1956. Smith won the Nobel Prize, Chemistry, in 1993.

4. Characterization of free radicals, which are crucial to understanding the mechanism in countless chemical reactions: The discovery was made in Ottawa in 1959 by Gerhard Herzberg, who came to Canada in 1935 from Hamburg, Germany. He won the Nobel Prize, Chemistry, in 1971.

5. Invention of the CCD chip for camcorders and telescopes, which takes light and converts it into digital data that can be manipulated by computers and electronics to form images in camcorders and TV cameras: Willard Boyle of Amherst, Nova Scotia, was co-inventor of the chip in 1969 at Bell Laboratories in New Jersey.

6. Development of computerized weather forecasting systems now used worldwide: The theories were developed in Montreal and Boulder Colorado between the 1970s and 1990s by Roger Daley, who was born in London, England, but grew up in West Vancouver.

7. Development of the Ricker curve used worldwide to determine sustainable fisheries catches: The theories were developed at the Fisheries Research Board of Canada in Ottawa and Nanaimo in the 1950s and 1960s by William Ricker, a native of Waterdown, Ontario.

8. Theory of plate tectonics, the notion that the earth's crust is made up of a series of floating plates: Developed during the 1970s in Toronto by Ottawa native John Tuzo Wilson.

9. Discovery of the t-cell receptor, a key to the understanding of the human immune system: Discovered in 1983 in Toronto by Tak Wah Mak, who came to Canada from China in the early 1970s.

10. Ellucidation of the geometry of higher dimensions, such as the fourth dimension, which can be very useful to comprehend cosmological concepts such as space-time and computer networks: Developed by H.S.M. Coxeter, who came to Toronto in 1937 from London, England.

List prepared by Barry Shell, Research Communications Manager, Simon Fraser University, and author of Great Canadian Scientists.

Snapshot

What it costs to learn your ABCs:
Annual University Tuition Fees to Obtain a Bachelor of Arts Degree (full-time student):

	1909	1939	1949	1999
University of Saskatchewan	$ 30	$ 90	$175	$3,000
University of Toronto	$ 50	$145	$180	$3,835
University of Western Ontario	$123	$125	$230	$4,252
McGill University	$ 61	$215	$250	$1,668.30 *
				$3,168.30 **

* (Canadian citizens who are residents of Quebec)
** (Canadian citizens from outside of Quebec)

BLAST OFF ...
TEN SIGNIFICANT EVENTS IN OUTER SPACE

1. September 29, 1962: Canada launches the Alouette I satellite to study the ionosphere, becoming the third country in space after Russia and the United States.

2. July 20, 1969: U.S. spacecraft Apollo 11 lands on the moon with Canadian-built landing gear.

3. November 9, 1972: Launch of Anik A-1, the first of a series of Canadian satellites. Canada becomes the first country with a domestic communications satellite system in geostationary orbit (moving so as to remain above the same point on the earth's surface).

4. November 13, 1981: Launch of Canadarm aboard Space Shuttle *Columbia*. This remote manipulator system was mounted on the shuttle and successfully moved payloads in and out of the shuttle bay.

5. October 5, 1984: Marc Garneau becomes the first Canadian in space aboard Space Shuttle *Challenger*.

Marc Garneau, Canada's first man in space. *Photo courtesy of Canadian Space Agency.*

6. September 29, 1988: Canada signs an intergovernmental agreement /memorandum of understanding to participate in the international space station project.

7. March 1, 1989: Creation of the Canadian Space Agency to promote the peaceful use and development of space and ensure space science and technology provide social and economic benefits to Canadians.

8. September 12, 1991: Canada's Wind Imaging Interferometer (WINDII) is launched aboard NASA's Upper Atmospheric Research Satellite (UARS) to provide new measurements of the physical and chemical processes taking place at altitudes ten to three hundred kilometres above the earth's surface.

9. January 22, 1992: Roberta Bondar becomes the second Canadian and first Canadian woman in space aboard Space Shuttle *Discovery*.

10. November 4, 1995: RADARSAT is launched. It is Canada's first earth observation satellite and first non-communications satellite since 1971. It can provide images of the earth's surface day and night, in any climate condition, to clients around the world.

List prepared by Mac Evans, president, Canadian Space Agency.

WHAT'S UP DOC? ...
TWELVE NOTABLE DOCTORS IN THE CANADIAN MEDICAL HALL OF FAME

1. **Dr. Maude Abbott:** A pioneering female doctor, Abbott was a world famous pathologist and renowned authority on heart defects. She wrote on congenital heart disease in *Modern Medicine*, a classic medical text.

2 and 3. **Dr. Frederick Banting and Dr. Charles Best:** Their discovery of insulin changed the lives of millions around the world who suffer from diabetes.

4. **Dr. Murray Barr:** His identification of a sex chromatin body ushered in a new era in research and diagnosis of genetic disorders and led to a better understanding of disorders associated with mental retardation.

5. **Dr. Henry Barnett:** Did vital work in the area of stroke prevention and the preventive aspects of aspirin.

6. **Dr. James Collip:** Provided vital contributions to Banting and Best in their insulin work and later enhanced his reputation with the study of hormones.

7. **Dr. Douglas Copp:** Did important research on the effects of radiation on bone marrow and discovered calictonin, which regulates the level of calcium in the blood.

8. **Dr. Charles Drake:** Gained worldwide fame by perfecting surgical techniques for repairing brain aneurysms.

9. **Dr. Jacques Genest:** Was the pre-eminent investigator in ways to treat high blood pressure.

10. **Dr. Wilder Penfield:** A neurosurgeon who helped further the understanding of brain-related disorders, epilepsy, and brain scars resulting from trauma.

11. **Dr. Louis Siminovitch:** In addition to his key roles in establishing important medical research institutions in Canada, he was also instrumental in discovering the genetic causes of muscular dystrophy and cystic fibrosis.

12. **Dr. Michael Smith:** A Nobel Prize winner for chemistry in 1993, Smith has been a pioneer in the field of genetics and the manipulation of DNA.

SIGNIFICANT BREAKTHROUGHS BY CANADIAN PHYSICIANS

1. **Dr. Roberta Bondar**: Conducted back pain experiments aboard the 1992 Space Shuttle *Discovery* to determine how the body changes in space.

2. **Dr. Bruce Chown and Dr. Jack Bowman**: Developed methods for diagnosis, treatment and prevention of RH disease in pregnant women.

3. **Dr. Jean Dussault**: Discovered a blood test to identify newborns with thyroid deficiency and subsequently prevent severe mental retardation in these infants.

4. **Dr. Oleh Homykiewicz and Dr. Andre Barbeau**: Discovered the use of levodopa, a synthetic compound, for the treatment of Parkinson's disease.

5. **Dr. Robert Korneluk**: In collaboration with an international team of scientists, located the defective gene responsible for myotonic dystrophy, a rare, slowly progressive hereditary disease involving the muscles.

6. **Dr. Lap-Chee Tsui**: Identified the defective gene responsible for cystic fibrosis.

7. **Dr. Claude De Montigny**: Initiated the use of lithium in the treatment of depression.

8. **Dr. William Mustard**: Devised an operation to correct the "blue baby" heart defect.

9. **Dr. Robert Noble**: Discovered an effective anti-cancer drug, vinblastine sulfate, which helps control the growth of cancers.

10. **Dr. Hans Selye**: A world-famous pioneer and popularizer of research on biological stress in humans, he theorized that stress plays some role in the development of every disease. He founded the International Institute of Stress in 1977, through which he increased the understanding of stress.

11. **Dr. Arthur Vineberg**: A cardiovascular surgeon who developed a surgical procedure for the relief of angina.

12. **Dr. Ronald Worton**: Identified the defective gene responsible for Duchenne muscular dystrophy.

List prepared with the assistance of the Canadian Medical Association.

GOOD MEDICINE ...
TEN OF THE MOST SIGNIFICANT DEVELOPMENTS IN CANADIAN HEALTH CARE

1. The Canadian Hospital Association, the first association dedicated to hospital advocacy at the federal level, was founded in 1931. In 1995, the association changed its name to the Canadian Healthcare Association to reflect the broadening scope of its membership to health services across the continuum of care. CHA is the first national association to represent the concerns of the health-care sector across the broad spectrum of care at the national level.

2. Saskatchewan became the first province to insure hospital services in 1947. This is important because previously access to hospital and medical services was based on the ability to pay.

3. In 1957 the federal government enacted the Hospital Insurance and Diagnostic Services Act. This established for the first time a cost-shared approach to financing hospital and diagnostic services on a roughly 50–50 basis for all provinces and territories.

4. In addition to hospital and diagnostic services, coverage was extended in 1966 for the first time to include medical services through the Medical Care Insurance Act. This provided coverage for visits to and services provided by physicians outside hospitals.

5. The Canada Assistance Plan (CAP) was enacted in 1966 to provide cost-sharing to the provinces and territories for social services and income assistance programs. For the first time, through CAP, federal funding was provided for health-care-related services such as homemakers, rehabilitation, assistive devices, homes for special care, and counselling. As well, some provinces provided subsidiary health services through CAP.

6. All provinces had signed on to the Medical Care Insurance Act by 1971. For the first time in Canada, Canadians could have access to hospital and physician services wherever they lived based on need and not on the ability to pay.

7. Quebec was the first province to establish a network of local community health organizations (known as Local Community Services Centres, or CLSCs) in 1972. These organizations are managed by boards whose mission is to offer preventive services, curative services, rehabilitation, and reintegration into society for the people in their jurisdiction. This is important because it extended access to needed community health services.

8. Manitoba was the first province to formally establish a provincial home care program in 1974. The mission of this program is to ensure the provision of home health care services to Manitobans to support independent living in the community.

9. The Canada Health Act replaced the Hospital Insurance and Diagnostic Act and the Medical Care Insurance Act in 1984. This was the first time the five principles of universality, comprehensiveness, portability, accessibility, and public administration were introduced to Canadian health care for hospital and physician services.

10. In 1989, the federal Department of Health and Welfare published the first comprehensive review of existing institution-based, community-based, and home-based adult long-term care services in Canada. The review was important because there was a patchwork of long-term care services in Canada, and a comprehensive review gave a clear picture of what was available in each province and territory.

List prepared by the Canadian Healthcare Association.

Snapshot

Percentage of Births that Took Place in Hospitals

1926	1946	1966	1974	1996
17.8%	67.6%	99.2%	99.7%	99.2%

Statistics Canada

LOG ON ...
CANADA'S TEN MOST IMPORTANT INFORMATION TECHNOLOGY INNOVATIONS

1. **The Global Village**: In 1964, Marshall McLuhan published a book entitled *Understanding Media* which helped Canada and the world understand the changes technology and communications were bringing about in society.

2. **Packet-switching**: Northern Electric, now Nortel Networks, in 1972 developed the X-25 protocol, which allows information to be sent over telephone lines in digital packets. The technology allows voice conversations, financial data, and video signals to be jumbled together to fill all of the carrying capacity of the transmission facility whether it be copper wire, fibre-optic, or wireless, and still be patched back together at the receiving end so quickly that the transmissions seemed to be happening in real time. This is the technology of the Internet.

3. **Java**: In 1995, Canadian James Gosling of American company Sun Microsystems developed Java, an object-oriented programming language. The technology-based software let many different kinds of computers, consumer gadgets, and other devices communicate with one another more easily.

4. **Radio**: In 1900, Reginald Fessenden transmitted the world's first wireless spoken message and six years later, the first two-way voice transmission. Fessenden is credited with the discovery of the super-heterodyne principle, the basis of all modern broadcasting.

5. **Communications Theory**: Harold Adams Innes in 1950 published *Empire and Communications*, a book that deals with the role of communications in various societies throughout history. Innes showed the connection between communications technology and the ability of different empires to survive and prosper.

6. **High-Speed Debugging Compilers**: Between 1965 and the 1980s, researchers at the University of Waterloo in Waterloo, Ontario, developed the first widely used high-speed compilers with good compile-time and run-time error diagnostics. This allowed programmers to write in easy languages, then compress code into a form computers liked; it also showed programmers what was wrong when their computer programs didn't work. These developments revolutionized the teaching of programming and software development in general.

7. **Fibre Gratings:** In 1978 at the Communications Research Centre in Ottawa, Dr. Kenneth Hill discovered photosensitivity in optical fibres. This discovery allowed scientists to make wavelength selective optical devices at low cost. The different frequencies of light could each carry different conversations or data streams at the same time through the same strand of fibre. The technology has made long distance communications much less expensive.

8. **Local Area Networks for Microcomputers:** The University of Waterloo in 1981 developed the first local area networks, or LANs, for microcomputers. The networks were created as soon as the first Macintosh computers and IBM personal computers were available. LANs let all computers in an office communicate with one another.

9. **IMAX Film System:** Graeme Ferguson, Robert Kerr, Roman Kroitor, Bill Shaw, and Bill Breukelman developed this giant-screen, large-format film medium, which uses the largest film frame in movie history and multi-track sound systems. The first Imax images premiered in 1970; the first permanent Imax theatre followed at Toronto's Ontario Place in 1971.

10. **Anik 1 Geo-stationary Commercial Satellite:** Developed in 1972 by Telesat Canada, it enabled Canada to become the first country to employ satellites for domestic communications.

List prepared by Michael Robinson, senior research associate, the Information Technology Association of Canada.

Fabulous Fact

The Ottawa area is known as "Silicon Valley North" thanks to the burgeoning high-technology industry, which produces everything from high-speed telephone switches to innovative computer software. In 1999, more than nine hundred technology companies provided jobs for approximately fifty thousand people.

Sports

GREATEST HOCKEY PLAYERS OF ALL TIME
(in order by position)

GOALIE:

1. **Terry Sawchuck:** Many consider him the greatest ever. His crouching style was innovative and helped him get his name on the Vezina Trophy four times. He recorded 103 shutouts during his twenty-one-year career.

2. **Jacques Plante:** A creative and talented goalie who won seven Vezina trophies, six with the great Canadiens' teams of the 1950s, and one jointly with Glenn Hall of the St. Louis Blues. He was at the top of his game in the 1950s and early 1960s, but was superb enough to later help less-talented teams such as the St. Louis Blues and the Toronto Maple Leafs.

3. **Glenn Hall:** He was called "Mr. Goalie" and his Calder Trophy, seven first-team all-star berths, eighty-four shutouts, and three Vezina trophies solidify him as one of the best.

4. **Ken Dryden:** A cool performer who played his best when the pressure was on, Dryden was a five-time first team all-star and winner of the Vezina Trophy five times in a relatively short, eight-year career.

5. **Dominik Hasek and Bill Durnan** (tie): Hasek's style is unorthodox but in his goaltending career the Dominator's record has been stellar. In his first eight seasons he has won five Vezina Trophies and back-to-back Hart Trophies. Durnan was one of the best goalies in hockey's "old days," thanks to lightning-quick hands and the ability to stymie shooters by changing hands with his goal stick. He won six Vezina Trophies and had six first-team all-star berths in just seven NHL seasons.

DEFENCE:

1. **Bobby Orr:** Some consider him the perfect hockey player, and though he won the Norris Trophy as the best defenceman eight times, he also changed the game with his offensive skills. Bad knees kept him from having a longer and probably greater career.

2. **Doug Harvey:** A seven-time winner of the Norris Trophy, even though such an award didn't exist for the first six years of his career. Many consider him the best defensive defenceman ever.

3. **Eddie Shore**: A fearless and talented player with great skating skills that made him an offensive threat as well. And he did it long before Orr.

4. **Denis Potvin**: Some considered him the equal to Orr during the years they were in the league together. Potvin had similar offensive skills, but was a better bodychecker.

5. **Ray Bourque**: A superb all-round defenceman with many Norris Trophy wins. He has been favourably compared to Orr.

6. **Larry Robinson**: Creative with the puck, a decent goal scorer and able to deliver devastating bodychecks, Robinson was a six-time all-star and double Norris Trophy winner. His twenty-year career saw him win six Stanley Cup rings.

7. **Red Kelly**: Though he also excelled as a forward, he was a great defensive defenceman early in his career and played on many Stanley Cup winners.

8. **Paul Coffey**: A great all-around defenceman who was a superb skater, playmaker, and goal-scorer.

9. **Brad Park**: Overshadowed during his career by Orr, Park was a five-time first-team all-star who had exceptional defensive skills.

10. **Dit Clapper**: The NHL's first twenty-year player, this six-time all-star made the smooth transition from right wing to defence eleven years into his career. Power, precision, and a knack for avoiding mistakes were Clapper's hallmarks.

CENTRE:

1. **Wayne Gretzky**: He's called "The Great One" for good reason. Gretzky holds so many records and has won so many awards it's hard to keep track, and even in the twilight of his career he was still outshining most everyone in the game.

2. **Mario Lemieux**: The only player who has come close to matching Gretzky's offensive skills, he was also a great playmaker, skater, and leader.

3. **Jean Beliveau**: A smooth and majestic player who was not only a perennial all-star, but a great leader who won ten Stanley Cups during his career.

4. **Howie Morenz**: A speedy skater who had a flair for scoring dramatic goals. One of the best players in the first half of the century.

5. Mark Messier: The man they call "Moose" is known as much for his leadership and dressing room presence as his ability to score big goals that turn around games. He is a six-time Stanley Cup winner and has five all-star selections and two Hart Trophies to his credit.

LEFT WING:

1. Bobby Hull: "The Golden Jet" was the dominant player of his time, a great skater, legendary goal-scorer, and underrated checker and penalty killer.

2. Ted Lindsay: One of the toughest players in the game, a great goal-scorer, and first team all-star eight times.

3. Frank Mahovlich: A gifted skater and stickhandler with a huge slapshot, "the Big M" could turn a team into a champion, as he did on several occasions. He won the Calder Trophy in his first season with the Toronto Maple Leafs and played on six Stanley Cup winners.

Frank Mahovlich, one of the all-time great left wingers.
Photo courtesy of Graphic Artists/Hockey Hall of Fame.

4. Dickie Moore: Although his career was plagued by injuries, Moore persevered to win two Art Ross Trophies, including in 1957–58 when he played with a broken wrist for the final three months of the season. Maurice Richard once called him the best left-winger he ever played with.

5. **Johnny Bucyk**: Often lost in the shadow of Bobby Orr and Phil Esposito, hard-hitting Bucyk was one of the league's premier wingers but not until later in his career. After turning 32, he had seven thirty-goal seasons, including his first fifty-goal year. He won the Lady Byng Trophy twice and retired in 1978 as the fourth-leading NHL goal and point producer of all time.

RIGHT WING:

1. **Gordie Howe**: Until Gretzky came along, most considered him the greatest player ever. And with the kind of record he piled up over thirty-four incredible years he's certainly the greatest right winger in the history of the game.

2. **Maurice Richard**: "The Rocket" was the dominating player of his day, an exciting and excellent goal-scorer who played with intensity and skill rarely matched.

3. **Guy Lafleur**: One of the dominant players of the 1970s, he was fast, scored a bucket of goals, and was a winner.

4. **Mike Bossy**: The New York Islander winger was one of the most prolific scorers in NHL history, notching fifty or more goals in nine consecutive seasons and helping his team to four consecutive Stanley Cups.

5. **Charlie Conacher**: Six feet one inches of determination and possessing the hardest shot in the league in the 1930s, Conacher was a hockey legend. He was a five-time all-star, won two Art Ross Trophies, scored more than thirty goals in four of his twelve seasons, and held or shared the league goal-scoring lead five times.

TEN GREATEST CANADIAN FOOTBALL LEAGUE PLAYERS: PRE-1950

(in no particular order)

1. **Lionel Conacher:** Outstanding all-everything. Canada's athlete of the first fifty years of the twentieth century. Ted Reeve once stated that meeting Conacher head-on was always a shattering event. He scored fifteen points for the Argonauts in the 1921 Grey Cup game before he had to leave to play hockey that night.

2. **Norm Perry:** Running back with Sarnia Imperials, referred to by some as the greatest running back in Canada. Playing in Sarnia meant less publicity.

3. **Brian Timmis:** Hamilton power runner and sometimes middle wing (tackle), dubbed the "Old Man of the Mountain." Consistently tore off gains before being gang tackled.

4. **Greg Kabat:** Outstanding back and linebacker with powerhouse Winnipeg teams of the thirties. He was tough and hardnosed offensively and defensively.

5. **Fritz Hanson:** Fast and powerful back with Winnipeg, star of the 1935 Grey Cup game when the west won for the first time.

6. **Harry Batstone:** Versatile runner and all-around athlete for the Argonauts and Queen's who had an uncanny knack of timing on running and extension plays.

7. **Ted Reeve:** A Balmy Beach player with tremendous grit. He played every game with 100 percent determination and had the ability to inspire teammates with his play.

8. **Joe Krol:** The original triple threat. He passed, ran, and kicked for the Toronto Argonauts. Dubbed the "King," he sometimes seemed to be the whole team.

9. **Tony Golab:** Ottawa's "Golden Boy," a powerful runner who could carry a team with his play or on his back.

10. **Herb Trawick:** His career spilled over into the fifties but he made a huge impact in Montreal as a guard, tackle, and linebacker.

TEN GREATEST CANADIAN FOOTBALL LEAGUE PLAYERS: POST-1950
(in no particular order)

1. **Doug Flutie:** The outstanding player of the nineties, his play with three CFL teams led to the phrase "Flutieball" to describe his remarkable athletic ability during a contest.

2. **Jackie Parker:** Mr. Everything — quarterback, halfback, defensive back. He always found a way to win.

3. **Ron Lancaster:** The Saskatchewan quarterback was probably the best in the game at "reading" defences and reacting to them.

4. **George Reed:** A powerful and dependable fullback with Saskatchewan who performed consistently in every game he played. Teams virtually conceded him one hudred yards and tried to minimize the number after that.

5. **Wayne Harris:** Perhaps the best linebacker in terms of range of movement and diagnostic reads and reactions.

6. **Johnny Bright:** A powerful fullback who was able to dominate a game with his ability. He was a cornerstone of the twin-fullback system he operated in with Normie Kwong.

7. **Hal Patterson:** During his years with Montreal and Hamilton, Patterson was an intense competitor with speed and catching ability who ran with fire in his eyes whether on a kickoff or after catching a pass.

8. **Roger Nelson:** An offensive lineman and tackle for Edmonton who consistently made the block he was assigned and looked around for more. Consistent quality was his trademark.

9. **Russ Jackson:** An outstanding quarterback with great athletic ability who developed into a quality passer, better each year. He retired too early, at the peak of his career.

10. **Herb Grey:** Nicknamed "Oink" by his teammates because he was never afraid to stick his nose into any situation. He played guard and defensive end and sometimes nose guard.

Lists prepared by Frank Cosentino, a former CFL quarterback and author of Canadian Football: The Grey Cup Years *(1969) and* A Passing Game *(1995).*

THE FALL CLASSICS ...
TEN GREATEST GREY CUP GAMES
(in order)

1. **Saskatchewan 43, Hamilton 40 in 1989**: The greatest Grey Cup game ever, it featured many lead changes and outstanding plays, including Tony Champion's touchdown catch in the dying minutes. But Dave Ridgway's field goal with less than ten seconds to go gave Saskatchewan the victory.

2. **Edmonton 38, Toronto 36 in 1987**: Two evenly matched teams in a game that featured great passing, exciting touchdowns (particularly Henry "Gizmo" Williams touchdown return of a missed field goal), several lead changes, and a winning field goal in tl e last minute. This game was one of the most thrilling ever.

3. **B.C. Lions 26, Baltimore 23 in 1994**: It was Canada versus the U.S. in the first Grey Cup where a Canadian-based team faced an American one. A fake field goal attempt involving Darren Flutie was key, as was a controversial fumble call against Baltimore that many thought should have been a touchdown for them. But it was Lui Passaglia's final field goal on the last play of the game that sealed it for B.C.

4. **Edmonton 26, Montreal 25 in 1954**: This game had it all. Montreal was heavily favoured, thanks to the passing arm of Sam Etcheverry, but they faced a tough Edmonton team and lost the game on one of the most memorable turnovers in Grey Cup history. Chuck Hunsinger of Montreal was given the ball and flipped what he claimed was a forward pass. The officials ruled it as a fumble, which Jackie Parker of Edmonton picked up and ran ninety-five yards for a touchdown in the dying minutes.

5. **Edmonton 26, Ottawa 23 in 1981**: Ottawa was a twenty-two-point underdog in this classic, but led 20–0 by the second quarter. Edmonton battled back, and Dave Cutler kicked a winning field goal in the dying seconds to win it.

6. **Ottawa 23, Saskatchewan 20 in 1976**: A memorable Grey Cup classic that had the east Rough Riders battling the west Roughriders. On a cold day at CNE Stadium, Tony Gabriel broke the hearts of Saskatchewan fans with his last-minute touchdown catch.

7. **Winnipeg 35, Hamilton 28 in 1958**: A see-saw battle that was the first Grey Cup of the newly formed CFL (amateur teams up till then were also eligible for the cup). An action-packed game that featured a star performance by

Winnipeg's Jim Van Pelt. He passed, ran, caught passes, and kicked to score a then-record twenty-two points.

8. **Sarnia 26, Ottawa 20 in 1936:** Sarnia led 12–0, but Ottawa came back to tie. Sarnia got the lead again, but Ottawa pulled within six points. In the last three minutes of the game, Ottawa got to Sarnia's eleven-yard line but failed to score on a third-down gamble.

9. **Toronto 43, Edmonton 37 in 1996:** One of the highest-scoring Grey Cup games ever despite being played in blowing snow. Many players starred, but the Argos got a brilliant performance from quarterback Doug Flutie, who proved he could play in any kind of weather.

10. **Winnipeg 28, Hamilton 27 in 1962:** Known as "The Fog Bowl," it was the great Grey Cup that few people saw. The two teams staged an exciting game that saw the lead change hands a few times, but fog rolling in from Lake Ontario reduced visibility. With just over five minutes left in the game and Hamilton trailing by a point, the game was stopped and the remaining time was played the next day. The game ended with Hamilton trying to score a single point, but the punt fell short of Winnipeg's end zone.

Fabulous Fact

The original Grey Cup cost forty-eight dollars to make and was supposed to be awarded to amateur football clubs only.

THE CHANGING FACE OF SPORT ...
TWELVE CANADIAN INNOVATIONS

1. **Slingshot Goal Post:** Developed by Canadian Football League scout Jim Trimball and his neighbour Joel Rottman in the 1960s as a way of making it safer to score touchdowns because there is one goal post six feet inside the end zone, rather than two posts on the goal line. First introduced in 1967 at the Montreal Autostade and now universally used.

2. **Eye Protection:** In 1979 the Canadian Hockey Association ruled that all minor hockey players must wear Canadian Standards Association-approved face protectors attached to CSA-approved helmets. Much of the credit goes to Toronto eye physician and surgeon Dr. Tom Pashby, who spearheaded a CSA committee that was responsible for writing standards for eye protection. The protectors replaced models that allowed sticks to come in contact with the eyes.

3. **The Brill Bend:** This reverse jumping style originated with Canadian high jumper Debbie Brill in the 1960s, around the same time American Dick Fosbury was developing the "Fosbury Flop." Brill's bend helped her win gold medals at the 1970 Canada Games and the 1971 Pan-American Games. She was the first woman in North America to clear the six-foot barrier.

4. **The Death Spiral:** Developed and first performed in international figure skating competition in 1948 by Canadians Suzanne Morrow and Wally Distelmeyer, it is a circular move in which the man lowers his partner to the ice and swings her in a circle while she is arched backward gliding on one foot with her head almost touching the ice.

5. **The Fox 40 Whistle:** Introduced in 1987 by part-time basketball referee Ron Foxcroft of Hamilton, Ontario, this "pealess" whistle has no internal movable parts to obstruct its sound or to stick, freeze, or jam up from overblowing, and its high-pitched trill cuts through crowd noise. Users in more than one hundred countries include the Canadian Football League, the National Basketball Association, the U.S. Coast Guard, and Boy Scouts of America.

The Fox 40 Classic Whistle: All-Canadian and used around the world. *Photo courtesy of Fox 40 International Inc.*

6. **Slide Delivery in Curling:** Most experts agree that the modern slide delivery, which gives greater control and more accuracy because curlers can hold on to the rocks longer, was introduced in 1930 at the St. John's Curling Club in Winnipeg by the Ken Watson team. However, other Canadian curlers such as Bob Dunbar, Frank Cassidy, and Gordon Hudson, experimented with a shorter slide delivery earlier in the century.

7. **Horse Race Starting Gate:** Invented in the early 1900s by Philip McGinnis, a racetrack reporter from Huntingdon, Quebec. Previously, horse races started with the throwing of a flag, often causing arguments because jockeys and horses left early. The gates were used at most race tracks in North America until electric gates took their place.

8. **Numbers on baseball uniforms:** St. Thomas, Ontario-born baseball player Jack Graney was a pioneer in many ways. In 1916, as a member of the Cleveland Indians, he was the first major league batter to wear a number on his uniform. The concept didn't improve the game but it certainly helped fans more easily identify players.

9. **Curved hockey stick:** There are several schools of thought on who invented the curved blade. One has it that while playing with the Toronto Maple Leafs in the early 1960s, forward Andy Bathgate used to soak his blades in hot water and bend them under dressing room doors to create a bow that produced shots that gave goaltenders nightmares. Others say Stan Mikita and Bobby Hull of the Chicago Blackhawks were the innovators with Mikita accidentally breaking a stick under a door, then showing Bobby Hull how it altered the flight of the puck. Hull, later, is said to have curved a stick on a stove.

10. **The Bubble Machine:** Invented in Pointe Claire, Quebec, in 1971 by Olympic diving coach and former diver Herb Flewwelling. The device uses high pressure jets to mix air with water, forming a mound of bubbles that softens the impact and reduces injuries when new and difficult dives are tried. The device is used by divers from around the world.

11. **Laser Sailboat:** Since being designed by Ottawa native Bruce Kirby in 1969 and going into production in 1971 in Pointe Claire, Quebec, more than 167,000 of this small "cartop" sailboat have been sold around the world. The Laser is considered the biggest sailboat racing class on the globe and in 1996 was given Olympic status. There are licensed builders in the U.S., U.K., Japan, Australia, Chile, and South Africa.

12. **Short Track Speed Skates:** Developed by former Canadian speed skater Raymond Laberge and introduced at the world championships in 1982, they feature a blade that can be adjusted for ice conditions and to make turning easier. They also have high boots which permit skaters to go down very low on turns and corners. The skates have helped increase skating speed to sixty kilometres per hour from twenty-nine kilometres per hour and were instrumental in gaining short track recognition as a new Olympic sport.

A friend tries out Bruce Kirby's first Laser in Connecticut, 1971. *Photo by Bruce Kirby.*

Snapshot

Sales from Vending Machines

1958: $ 26,331,000

1975: $249,960,000

1985: $367,317,000

1995: $391,434,000

Statistics Canada

CANADIANS WHO HAVE WON THE BOSTON MARATHON

(Note: Ronald J. MacDonald of Antigonish, Nova Scotia, won the second Boston Marathon ever in 1898. Canadians have also won in various Masters' age categories).

1. **Jack Caffery** of Hamilton won the 1900 marathon in 2:39:44. Two other Canadians, Bill Sherring and Fred Hughson, finished second and third. Caffery won again in 1901.

2. **Tom Longboat** of the Six Nations Reserve near Brantford, Ontario, won the 1907 race easily and became the most famous runner of his day.

3. **Fred Cameron** of Amherst, Nova Scotia, was victorious in the 1910 marathon.

4. **Jimmy Duffy**, who was born in Ireland but emigrated to Toronto, ran in a white shirt with a maple leaf and the word "Canada" when he won in 1914. He was killed in a World War I battle a year later.

5. **Eduourd Fabre** from Montreal was a champion snowshoe racer who battled a chest cold and hot weather to win the 1915 marathon.

6. **Johnny Miles** of Sydney Mines, Nova Scotia, was a cocky kid who upset a strong field to win the 1926 event and returned to Canada a hero. He was living in Hamilton, Ontario, in 1929 when he won the Boston Marathon again.

7. **Dave Komonen**, a Finnish-born runner who moved to Toronto and later Sudbury, Ontario, won in 1934 after placing second the year before.

8. **Walter Young** was an unemployed carpenter from Verdun, Quebec, who was promised a job on the town's police force if he won the marathon. He did so in 1937.

9. **Gerard Côté** of St. Hyacinthe, Quebec, who worked with the same trainer as Young, won easily in 1940. While serving with the Canadian army and battling a sore heel, he won again in 1943 in a then-record time. On leave the following year he won at Boston a third time, and then a fourth and final time in 1948.

10. **Jerome Drayton** of Toronto was already a world-class racer when he won the 1977 event.

11. **Jacqueline Gareau** of Montreal won the women's division in 1980, an event best remembered because Rosie Ruiz had been mistakenly declared the winner at first but was later disqualified for not running the full race.

12. **Andre Viger** of Sherbrooke, Quebec won in 1984 in the wheelchair division, the first year wheelchair entrants became official. He won in this category again in 1986 and 1987.

Fabulous Fact

Bill Sherring of Hamilton, Ontario, was the only Canadian to win an Olympic gold medal in the marathon. He finished first in the 1906 Games in Athens.

ON THE PODIUM ...
GREATEST CANADIAN OLYMPIANS — SUMMER GAMES

Ever since the 1904 Olympics, when Étienne Desmarteau became the first to win gold (in the fifty-six-pound throw) while competing as a Canadian, Canada has had many Games heroes and multiple medal winners who performed at the top level when it counted or at a consistently high level in more than one Olympics. In order, they are:

1. **Percy Williams:** His double gold victories in the 100-metre and 200-metre sprints in Amsterdam in 1928 have never been matched by Canadian sprinters.

Percy Williams, a great Canadian Olympian. *Photo courtesy of National Archives of Canada: PA150993.*

2. **Marnie McBean and Kathleen Heddle:** Canada's first triple gold medallists. They won their first two golds in pairs rowing and as part of the eights crew in Barcelona in 1992, then captured first place in a different event, double sculls, in Atlanta in 1996.

3. **George Hodgson:** He won his two gold medals in 1912 in the 1500-metre freestyle swim and the 400-metre freestyle, breaking world records along the way.

4. **Donovan Bailey:** He claimed the title "the world's fastest man" by winning gold in Atlanta in the 100-metre sprint. Then he anchored the Canadian team to another gold in the 4 x 100-metre relay.

5. **Carolyn Waldo**: In a sport that's harder than it looks, Waldo won a silver in synchronized swimming in 1984, then came away from the Games in Seoul in 1988 with two gold medals.

6. **Alex Bauman**: In the 1984 Olympics in Los Angeles (which was boycotted by some Eastern European nations), he captured gold in the 400-metre individual medley swim while smashing the world record. A few days later he won gold in the 200-metre version of the same event, also in world record time.

7. **Victor Davis**: He captured gold in the 200-metre breaststroke in 1984 in world record time and a silver in 100-metre breaststroke the same year, again beating the previous world record. He won a silver in the 4 x 100-metre medley relay in 1984 and another silver in the same event in 1988.

8. **Fanny Rosenfeld**: As part of the strong Canadian women's team in the 1928 Olympics (which also included high jump gold-medallist Ethel Catherwood), Rosenfeld stood out winning silver in the 100-metre sprint and leading her team to gold in a world-record performance in the 4 x 100-metre relay. She was named Canada's outstanding female athlete of the first fifty years of the century.

9. **Anne Ottenbrite and Mark Tewksbury** (tie): Swimmers who won a medal of each colour. Ottenbrite did it in 1984 — a gold in the 200-metre breast stroke (the first Canadian woman swimmer to ever win Olympic gold), silver in the 100-metre breast stroke, and bronze in the 4 x 100-metre medley relay, while Tewksbury captured gold in Olympic-record time in the 100-metre backstroke in 1992, silver in the 4 x 100-metre medley relay in 1988, and bronze in the same event in 1992.

10. **Phil Edwards**: He's the best example of an athlete who gave consistently strong performances over several years. He won five bronze medals at middle distance races in the Olympics from 1928 to 1936.

Fabulous Fact

An honourable mention goes to Larry Lemieux, who left his second place position in the Finn sailing race in 1988 to rescue injured Singaporean sailors whose boat had capsized. Though he came in twenty-first, he was awarded a second place special award for his selfless act, an example of true Olympic spirit.

GREATEST CANADIAN OLYMPIANS — WINTER GAMES
(in order)

1. **Gaetan Boucher:** Won silver in 1980 in the 1000-metre speed skate in Lake Placid, New York, then two golds in the 1000- and 1500-metres and a bronze in the 500-metres in 1984 in Sarajevo, Yugoslavia.

2. **Myriam Bedard:** She won bronze in the 15-kilometre biathlon in Albertville, France, in 1992, and then double gold in Lillehammer, Norway, in 1994 in the 7.5-kilometre and 15-kilometre events.

3. **Nancy Greene:** The heroine of the 1968 Olympics in Grenoble, France, Greene won gold by an almost three-second margin in the giant slalom and silver in the slalom.

4. **Barbara Ann Scott:** She became Canada's sweetheart after following up her world championship win in 1947 by winning the gold medal in figure skating in 1948 in St. Moritz, Switzerland. Her athletic style that featured several jumps changed women's figure skating forever.

5. **Catriona LeMay Doan:** She had all of Canada applauding her gold medal in the 500-metre speed skate and bronze in the 1000-metres in Nagano, Japan, in 1998.

6. **Anne Heggtveit:** Won gold in 1960 in the slalom by a margin of more than three seconds over her nearest rival. Her victory helped inspire Nancy Greene.

7. **The Toronto Granite Hockey Team:** In the 1924 Olympics in Chamonix, France they dominated the sport like no other team has since. They captured gold by winning by such scores as 33–0 and 22–0 and the final over the U.S. 6–1. And an honourable mention to all the Canadian hockey teams between 1920 and 1952 who had a 37–1–3 record and scored 403 goals with only 34 against.

8. **Susan Auch:** A strong performer who captured silver in the 5000-metre speed skate in Lillehammer, Norway and silver in the 500-metre in Nagano, Japan.

9. **Brian Orser and Elvis Stojko** (tie): Orser was a world figure skating champion who won two silver medals in two separate Olympics and just missed gold on both occasions. In 1984, he won the long and short free-skate programs but still couldn't catch Scott Hamilton. In 1988 in Calgary, he was narrowly defeated for gold by Brian Boitano by the slimmest of margins.

Stojko, who's also been world champion, skated brilliantly in 1994 in Lillehammer, Norway, and won silver. Battling an injury in 1998, he still managed another silver.

10. **Barbara Wagner and Robert Paul**: They captured Canada's first and only gold medal in pairs figure skating in 1960. Their brilliant and poised performance so impressed the judges that all of them awarded the pair first place.

Fabulous Fact

The only Winter Olympic Games ever held in Canada took place in Calgary in 1988. Canada won no official gold medals that year.

Sports

BRIAN WILLIAMS' MEMORABLE CANADIAN OLYMPIC MOMENTS
(from Games he has covered)

1. Ben Johnson wins and is disqualified in Seoul, South Korea, 1988.

2. Donovan Bailey wins the 100 metres in Atlanta, 1996 (the first Canadian to win and keep the gold since Percy Williams in 1928).

3. Canada wins the men's 4 x 100-metre relay in Atlanta, 1996.

4. Rowers Marnie McBean and Kathleen Heddle win gold in Atlanta, 1996. The third Olympic gold for each!

5. Karen Lee-Gartner wins gold in the women's downhill at Albertville, France, 1992 (first ever downhill gold for a Canadian).

6. Alex Baumann wins two swimming gold medals in Los Angeles, 1984.

7. Gaetan Boucher wins two speedskating gold in Sarajevo, Yugoslavia, 1984.

8. Greg Joy wins silver in the high jump in Montreal, 1976.

9. Lennox Lewis wins boxing gold in Seoul, South Korea, 1988 (the first Canadian gold in boxing since Horace "Lefty" Gwynn in Los Angeles, 1932).

10. NHL players arrive in Nagano, Japan, for the 1998 Winter Games.

11. Sylvie Bernier wins diving gold in Los Angeles, 1984.

12. Brian Stemmle's gutsy performance in the men's downhill at Nagano, Japan, in 1998. He was leading when he went off the course near the finish.

Brian Williams is a sports broadcaster for CBC-TV who has covered several Olympic Games.

WHO'S ON FIRST? ...
TWELVE BEST CANADIAN-BORN BASEBALL PLAYERS
(in order)

1. **Ferguson Jenkins:** The greatest player to come from Canada and the only Canadian in the Baseball of Hall of Fame in Cooperstown, New York. Jenkins, from Chatham, Ontario, won twenty games a year six seasons in a row, the Cy Young Award in 1971, and finished with 284 wins and 226 losses. He threw more than three thousand strikeouts in his career.

2. **Larry Walker:** A perennial league all-star, batting champion in 1998, and National League Most Valuable Player in 1997, the only Canadian to achieve this honour. So far in his ten-year career, the Maple Ridge, British Columbia native has already hit more than two hundred home runs.

3. **Jeff Heath:** A two-time all-star who had seven seasons batting .300 or better, Heath, from Fort William, Ontario, had a career average of .298, had 1447 hits, and 194 home runs .

4. **Terry Puhl:** The Melville, Saskatchewan, native had three seasons batting .300 or better, a career .993 fielding average, played more than 1500 games in fifteen seasons with the Houston Astros, and had the most career stolen bases by a Canadian with 217.

5. **John Hiller:** In his fifteen years with the Detroit Tigers, Hiller, from Toronto, compiled 125 saves, including a then-record thirty-eight saves in 1973. He threw more than one thousand strikeouts and finished with an 87–79 record.

6. **George Selkirk:** In nine seasons he batted .290, including five seasons of .300 or better. Born in Huntsville, Ontario, Selkirk played in two all-star games and hit 108 home runs during his career.

7. **George Gibson:** The London, Ontario-born catcher played 1,213 games. Although he only batted .236 during his career, he was a superb defensive player who later managed in the big leagues.

8. **Russ Ford:** A three-time twenty-game winner, including winning twenty-six for the New York Yankees in 1910, Ford, of Brandon, Manitoba, finished with a 99–71 record over seven seasons.

9. **Pete Ward:** The Montreal-born player won the Sporting News American League Rookie of the Year Award in 1963 and over 973 games in his career hit .254 and slugged ninety-eight homers.

10. **Reggie Cleveland**: The first Canadian to pitch in the World Series, Cleveland, from Swift Current, Saskatchewan, amassed a 105–106 record over several seasons.

11. **Frank O'Rourke**: He had more than one hundred hits in six different seasons, led American League second basemen in fielding percentage one year, and had a career .254 batting average over fourteen seasons. O'Rourke, from Hamilton, Ontario, was later a baseball scout for many years.

12. **Jack Graney**: During his fourteen seasons he batted .250 and twice led the league in bases on balls. The St. Thomas, Ontario native was also the first person to pitch to Babe Ruth in the major leagues.

Catcher George "Mooney" Gibson, shown here with batter Arthur Raymond, was one of the best baseball players to ever come out of Canada.
Photo courtesy of the London Free Press Collection of Photographic Negatives, D.B. Weldon Library, University of Western Ontario. Copy taken from a photo from Sporting News, 1910.

Fabulous Fact

Jack Graney was the first ex-ballplayer to broadcast a game on radio.

FIVE GREAT CANADIAN-BORN FEMALE BASEBALL PLAYERS
(All played in the All-American Girls Professional Baseball League in the 1940s and 50s.)

1. **Mary "Bonnie" Baker** from Regina, Saskatchewan: A star catcher in the league, Baker batted .235 over her long career of 921 games.

2. **Helen Callaghan** (St. Aubin) from Vancouver British Columbia: Her hitting power earned her the nickname the "female Ted Williams." Callaghan was a batting champion in 1945, stole 354 bases, and had a .257 career batting average.

3. **Olive Little** from Poplar Point, Manitoba: One of the fastest pitchers in the game, she threw the league's first no-hitter and finished her career with 57 wins and 43 losses.

4. **Helen Nicol** (Fox) from Ardley, Alberta: Nicol was a two-time league pitching champ who won 31 games in 1943. She had a career ERA of 1.89 and finished with 163 wins and 118 losses.

5. **Evelyn Wawryshyn** (Moroz) from Tyndall, Manitoba: A first team all-star in 1950, she had a career batting average of .266.

OOPS!...
TEN SPORTS GAFFES

1. Donald Linden of Canada won a silver medal in the 1500-metre walk at the 1906 Olympics in Athens. However, officials agreed that the American who won gold had used improper footwork. They offered to re-stage the event and while Linden showed up, the American didn't. Still, the judges let the original medal results stand.

2. In the 1920 Olympics in Antwerp, the Canadians had no flag for the march into the stadium for the Opening Ceremonies. Flag bearer Archie McDiarmid marched in the procession carrying a bare flag pole.

3. James Ball of Winnipeg made some mistakes in the 400-metre final that cost him gold at the 1928 Olympics. He didn't break out of his lane in the home stretch to move toward the curb as was allowed and thus ran a greater distance than the others. And just before the finish he looked around for his competitors, which cost him time. He lost by two-tenths of a second to American Ray Barbutti.

4. During the 1957 Grey Cup, Ray "Bibbles" Bawel was running toward the Winnipeg goal line with no one in front of him. A spectator near the sidelines tripped Bawel and prevented him from getting the touchdown. Winnipeg was penalized half the distance to the goalline, and Hamilton later scored and eventually won 32–7. The spectator eventually apologized to Bawel and sent him a gold watch.

5. In the dying seconds of the 1971 Grey Cup, the Toronto Argonauts had the ball deep in Calgary Stampeders territory. Argos' running back Leon McQuay fumbled the ball on the slippery turf and Calgary recovered, preserving the win. Toronto hadn't won the Grey Cup since 1952 and wouldn't win again until 1983.

6. At the world curling championship in Germany in 1972, the U.S. team, led by Bob Labonte, appeared to defeat the Canadian team in the tenth end. As the team began to cheer, Labonte lost his balance and kicked a Canadian stone, moving it as he fell. A subsequent measurement allowed Canada to tie the game and then go on to win it in an extra end. Labonte swore Canada would never win a world championship again and his "curse" held true until 1980.

7. In 1973, Montreal mayor Jean Drapeau claimed that the upcoming 1976 Olympic Games "can no more have a deficit than a man can have a baby." But incredible bungling, greed, and corruption led to the Games costing $1.5 billion. Taxpayers were still paying more than two decades later.

8. Steve Smith scores on his own net. The Edmonton Oilers were chasing their third consecutive Stanley Cup in the 1985-86 playoffs when Edmonton defenceman Steve Smith inadvertently banked the puck into his own net off goalie Grant Fuhr's leg. The third period miscue — which gave the Calgary Flames the win in game seven — was a heartbreaker because it ended the Oilers' bid to win their third straight cup. The Oilers won again in 1987 and 1988. Had they won in 1986, the Oilers would have won five straight cups, a feat only accomplished by the Montreal Canadiens.

9. Canadians cheered as Ben Johnson won gold in the 100-metres in Seoul at the 1988 Olympic Games. But a drug test indicated Johnson used an anabolic steroid, and he was stripped of the gold. The event led to a full-scale inquiry into drug use among Canadian athletes.

10. Instead of the gold medal, Sylvie Frechette of Canada got a silver medal after a Brazilian judge inadvertently misrecorded her score in synchronized swimming at the 1992 Barcelona Games. Although officials admitted the mistake, the results stood. Frechette accepted her fate graciously, but was rewarded retroactively with the gold medal sixteen months later.

FOURTEEN MEMORABLE SPORTS QUOTATIONS

1. "The Olympic Games are attended by the world's best athletes and judged by the world's worst officials." — J.A. Jackson, Canadian Olympic official at the 1924 Olympics in Paris after a wrestling decision went against Canada despite the rules not supporting it.

2. "So I'm supposed to be world champ. Crushed apples! No more fun now." — Sprinter Percy Williams, writing in his diary after winning the gold medal at the 1928 Olympics.

3. "He shoots, he scores." — The most famous sports quotation in the history of sports in Canada, Foster Hewitt, who covered Maple Leaf and National Hockey League games from 1923 to 1985. First said in 1933, during a game between the Toronto Maple Leafs and the Boston Bruins.

4. "All I could think, as I ran, was I hope I don't get a cramp." — Running back Vic Washington of the Ottawa Rough Riders, discussing his eighty-yard run that was a crucial turning point in the 1968 Grey Cup.

5. "It will take an act of God to beat us Saturday." — Leo Cahill, coach of the Toronto Argonauts on November 19, 1969, after his team beat Ottawa in the first game of a two-game total-point series 22–14. In the following game, Ottawa, led by quarterback Russ Jackson, trounced the Argos 32–3 to win the series 46–25 and go on to the Grey Cup.

6. "When I scored that final goal, I finally realized what democracy was all about." — Paul Henderson, 1972, after scoring the goal that would propel Canada to a narrow series victory in the first ever Canada-Soviet Union hockey series.

7. "All pro hockey athletes are bilingual. They speak English and profanity." — Gordie Howe, 1975, as quoted in *The Toronto Star*.

8. "I'm proud of the fact that I only hit one ball out of bounds in my first year on the tour. On that one I was right in the middle of my backswing when my bra strap broke." — Golfer Cathy Sherk, 1979.

9. "I try consciously not to let anybody down. I think that's important. Players trust me. The minute the trust ends then there's nothing; that goes for everybody." — Alan Eagleson, sports lawyer, executive director of the National Hockey League Players Association, as quoted in the book *The Eagle: The Life and Times of Alan Eagleson* (1982).

10. "I skate to where the puck is going to be, not where it's been." — Wayne Gretzky, 1985, describing his intriguing insight into how one can be trained to anticipate future conditions and change in a hockey game.

11. "I have never, ever knowingly taken illegal drugs, and I would never embarrass my family, my friends, my country and the kids who love me." — sprinter Ben Johnson, after being stripped of his gold medal at the 1988 Summer Olympics for using banned anabolic steroids.

12. "Everybody is in goo-goo land." — Al Morrow, Canadian rowing coach after his team's medal successes at the 1992 Olympic Summer Games.

13. "I had this feeling like I was on my way to hell and now I'm on my way to heaven, riding on a cloud." — Kicker Lui Passaglia of the B.C. Lions on how he felt about missing a field goal late in the game and then making one in the last seconds to beat the Baltimore team 26–23 in the 1994 Grey Cup.

14. "It's a gut feeling, something that I really believe is right.... I have peace of mind. It's the right decision." — Wayne Gretzky, April 16, 1999, while announcing his retirement from the National Hockey League after twenty seasons.

TWELVE DISTINCT SPORTS NICKNAMES

1. **Big-Chief-Shoot-the-Puck**: George Armstrong was known as the "Chief" when he played for the Toronto Maple Leafs, partly because of his mother's Iroquois heritage. He was given the longer nickname by Alberta's Stoney Indian tribe in the mid-50s when his Allan Cup winning senior hockey team toured western Canada.

2. **The Rifle**: Montreal Alouettes quarterback and coach Sam Etcheverry earned this nickname in the 1950s during a Canadian Football League career that saw him throw 1,630 completions and 174 touchdowns.

3. **Le Grande Orange**: When popular slugger Rusty Staub was hitting homers and playing the outfield for the Montreal Expos from 1969–71 and playing first base in 1979, his shock of red hair got him this nickname. He hit eighty-one homers with the Expos and his batting average was over .300 twice.

4. **The Chicoutimi Cucumber**: Netminder Georges Vezina picked up this moniker based on his place of birth and because opponents said he was as cool as a cuke when he tended the nets for the Montreal Canadiens from 1917 to 1926. The Vezina Trophy, the NHL's highest honour for netminders, is named after him.

Georges Vezina, "The Chicoutimi Cucumber." *Photo courtesy of National Archives of Canada: C29549.*

5. **Wildfire**: Known as Canada's first sports hero of the twentieth century, marathon runner Tom Longboat picked up this nickname for a winning streak on the track that included winning the Boston Marathon in April 1907 and outrunning international champion Alfie Shrubb in 1909 in a run for the professional championship of the world.

6. **The Mistake by the Lake**: Referred to CNE Stadium in Toronto in the 1970s and 1980s after the football stadium was remodelled to house the Toronto Blue Jays, who began playing there in 1977.

7. **The Shawville Express**: Frank Finnigan, so named because he usually rode a train into Ottawa from the Ottawa Valley community of Shawville when he played for the Ottawa Senators in the 1920s and 1930s.

8. **The Old Man of the Mountain**: Brian Timmis, a player with the Hamilton Tigers football team (before they became the Tiger-Cats). He picked up the nickname from sports columnist Ted Reeve in the 1920s and 30s because he was the team's mainstay for many years.

6. **Dipsy Doodling Dandy**: Max Bentley, who played in the NHL from 1940 until 1954 with the Chicago Black Hawks, Toronto Maple Leafs, and New York Rangers, was tagged with this name because of his finesse with the puck.

10. **The Production Line**: One of the greatest hockey lines ever assembled, made up of three hockey greats with memorable nicknames of their own, "Terrible" Ted Lindsay, Sid "Old Boot Nose" Abel, and "Mr. Hockey" Gordie Howe.

11. **William "Torchy" Peden**: So called because a sportswriter once described him in a race as a "flame-haired youth (who) led the pack like a torch." He has been described as Canada's greatest cyclist for his accomplishments in the 1920s, 30s, and 40s.

12. **The Pumper**: Alberta jockey Johnny Longden acquired this name because of the way he pumped his arms vigorously near the finish line to get more out of his horse.

IN THE HACK ...
TEN IMPORTANT MALE CURLERS

1. **Dr. Murray MacNeill:** The skip of the first Canadian championship team.

2. **Ken Watson:** A three-time Canadian champ, Watson revolutionized the slide delivery by sliding out farther from the hack before letting the stone go. This allowed for better control and accuracy.

3. **Matt Baldwin:** A three-time Brier winner and well-known for his "off ice" carousing.

4. **Ernie Richardson:** He's the only skip to win four Briers, a record that may never be broken.

5. **Ron Northcott:** A three-time champion and Alberta's best player.

6. **Don Duguid:** A two-time Brier champion who has become a leading curling commentator on television.

7. **Al Hackner:** Another two-time winner who threw the "most famous shot in curling" — a thin double takeout — in the 1985 Brier final. It's now referred to simply as the Hackner Shot.

9. **Ed Werenich:** He won the world championship twice and revolutionized curling with his aggressive style of play. He's considered to be the best "money" player of all time.

10. **Russ Howard:** A two-time Brier champion and sensational shotmaker who is given credit with devising the free-guard zone.

Fabulous Fact

An honourable mention goes to Paul Gowsell. The long-haired two-time world junior champion from Alberta is considered by some to have popularized push brooms in Canada in the 1970s. Today Canadian curlers favour push brooms over the traditional corn broom by about 9 to 1.

TEN IMPORTANT WOMEN CURLERS

1. **Joyce McKee:** The first Canadian women's champ and a five-time winner of it (though not always as skip) during her career.

2. **Vera Pezer:** She was a four-time winner of the Canadian championship, three times as skip from 1971–73.

3. **Lindsay Sparkes:** A two-time Canadian champ who has gone on to make her mark as a coach. She was also a member of the gold medal team that won at the Calgary Olympics in 1988.

4. **Linda Moore:** A Canadian champ who skipped the gold-medal team at the Calgary Olympics. Has also made a name in curling broadcasting.

5. **Marilyn Bodogh:** A two-time world champ who brought an aggressive style to the women's game.

6. **Heather Houston:** A great strategist among women curlers, she won two Canadian championships and a world championship.

7. **Sandra Schmirler:** She's won three Canadian titles, three world titles, and Olympic gold in Nagano in 1998. Many consider her the best ever.

8. **Connie Laliberte:** A two-time Canadian champion, world champion, and perennial contender for the title.

9. **Robin Wilson:** She was on two Canadian championship teams and has run the Scott Tournament of Hearts since 1982.

10. **Colleen Jones:** A two-time Canadian champ who's also made her mark as a broadcaster. She's appeared in more than twenty national championships, more than any other Canadian curler.

Colleen Jones is one of Canada's top curlers. *Photo courtesy of* **Sweep! Curling's Magazine.**

FORE! ...
TEN GREATEST MALE GOLFERS

1. **George S. Lyon:** An outstanding Canadian amateur who won the national amateur title eight times and the gold medal the only time golf was played in the Olympics in 1904.

2. **Sandy Somerville:** A six-time Canadian amateur champion and the first Canadian to win the U.S. Amateur. Also scored the first hole-in-one at the Masters.

3. **Stan Leonard:** He won numerous Canadian and three Professional Golf Association (PGA) Tour events despite not playing regularly there until his 40s.

4. **Al Balding:** He was the first Canadian to win in the U.S. on the PGA Tour and was a multiple winner at Canadian events.

5. **George Knudson:** He won more PGA Tour events than any other Canadian with one of the finest swings in the game. Also became a great teacher.

6. **Nick Weslock:** A great Canadian amateur player and winner of four national amateur crowns.

7. **Moe Norman:** An eccentric player recognized by many as the game's best ball striker, he also won many Canadian tournaments.

8. **Gary Cowan:** He won the U.S. Amateur twice as well as many events in Canada and had a solid international record.

9. **Dave Barr:** To date, he's earned more money than any other Canadian on the PGA Tour and has won regularly at Canadian events.

10. **Doug Roxburgh:** A multiple winner of the national amateur title with a strong international record.

TEN GREATEST WOMEN GOLFERS

1. **Ada Mackenzie:** This pioneering woman golfer won several national amateur titles and founded the first women-only golf club (the Ladies' Golf Club of Toronto) in Canada.

2. **Marlene Streit:** A winner of Canadian, U.S., British, and Australian amateur titles. Arguably Canada's greatest golfer ever, male or female.

3. **Sandra Post:** She's the only Canadian to win a major championship, the Ladies' Professional Golf Association (LPGA) title, and won eight other LPGA tournaments.

4. **Jocelyne Bourassa:** An LPGA rookie of the year who won the du Maurier Classic on home soil. She has run that tournament since 1983.

5. **Cathy Sherk:** In one year, she won the U.S., Canadian, and World amateur titles, and later played on the LPGA tour.

6. **Barb Bunkowsky:** During her distinguished career in professional golf, she won on the LPGA Tour.

7. **Dawn Coe-Jones:** She's earned more than $2 million on the LPGA Tour so far, and was also a Canadian amateur champion.

8. **Gail Graham:** A top amateur player who has won twice on the LPGA Tour.

9. **Lisa Walters:** She was a top B.C. amateur and set the record of lowest four-round score on the LPGA Tour (-23) in 1998.

10. **Lorie Kane:** She was Canada's female athlete of the year in 1997 and has so far won more than $1 million in just a few years on the LPGA Tour.

MILESTONES IN CANADIAN FIGURE SKATING

1. 1930: Cecil Eustace Smith becomes Canada's first skater to win a medal at the World Championships, winning a silver in New York City.

2. 1948: Barbara Ann Scott wins senior Canadian, European, World, and Olympic titles, becoming the first North American to win all four in the same year, the first Canadian figure skater to win an Olympic gold medal, and the first to win back-to-back world titles. Also in 1948, Suzanne Morrow and Wallace Distelmeyer are the first pair to perform the death spiral (in its present-day low position) at an international competition.

3. 1960: Barbara Wagner and Robert Paul become Canada's first pairs team to win a medal at an Olympic Winter Games, winning gold at Squaw Valley, USA.

4. 1962: Donald Jackson performs the first triple Lutz in competition at the World Championships in Prague, Czechoslovakia.

5. 1963: Donald McPherson becomes the first Canadian male to hold three titles simultaneously — Canadian, North American, and World — without having won any of them previously. He is also the youngest male to win the World title.

Elvis Stojko shows his stuff. *Photo by Brian Dole.*

6. 1965: Petra Burka performs the first triple Salchow in international competition at the World Championships in Colorado Springs, USA, and in the process wins the world title.

7. 1978: Vern Taylor performs the first triple axel in competition at the World Championships in Ottawa.

8. 1988: Kurt Browning performs the first quad toe-loop in competition at the World Championships in Budapest, Hungary. In the same year, Tracy Wilson and Rob McCall become Canada's first ice dancers to win an Olympic medal — a bronze at the Winter Olympics in Calgary, Alberta.

9. 1991: Elvis Stojko performs the first quadruple combination jump (quad-toe/double toe) in competition at the World Championships in Munich, Germany.

10. 1997: Elvis Stojko performs the first quadruple toe-loop/triple toe loop in skating history in the Champions Series Final at Hamilton, Ontario.

List prepared by the Canadian Figure Skating Association.

IT HAPPENED IN CANADA ...
TWENTY CANADIAN SPORTS FIRSTS IN THE TWENTIETH CENTURY

1. George Orton of Strathroy, Ontario, may have been competing for the Americans, but he was the first Canadian to win an Olympic gold medal when he captured first place in the 2500-metre steeplechase event in Paris, in July, 1900. Montreal policeman Étienne Desmarteau was the first to win Olympic gold while competing for Canada when he won the 56-pound hammer throw at the St. Louis Olympics, in September, 1904.

2. Babe Ruth hit his first professional home run as a member of the Providence Grays, during a game in Toronto on September 5, 1914.

3. The voice of hockey, play-by-play man Foster Hewitt, announced his first hockey broadcast over Toronto radio station CFCA on March 23, 1923.

4. Lela Brooks of Toronto won a world speed skating championship in Saint John, New Brunswick, becoming the first Canadian woman to be a sports world champion in 1926.

5. Clint Benedict of the Montreal Maroons was the first goalie to wear a mask in a hockey game in the 1929–30 season.

6. Detroit Red Wings great Gordie Howe scored his first NHL goal on October 16, 1946.

7. The Toronto Huskies of the Basketball Association of America became Canada's first major professional basketball team: 1946.

8. Marilyn Bell became the first person to swim Lake Ontario, a distance of fifty-one kilometres, on September 9, 1954.

9. The first Canadian Football League regular season game that was played in the United States. The Hamilton Tiger-Cats beat the Ottawa Rough Riders 24–18 in Philadelphia on September 14, 1958.

10. Northern Dancer became the first Canadian horse to win the Kentucky Derby: May 2, 1964.

11. Dave Bailey became the first Canadian to break the four-minute mile (3:59.1) on June 11, 1966.

12. Montreal was awarded Canada's first major league professional baseball franchise on May 27, 1968.

13. Sandra Post became the first foreign player to win the LPGA Championship on June 24, 1968.

14. In Rome, George Knudson and Al Balding were the first Canadians to win golf's World Cup on November 17, 1968.

15. Cindy Nicholas was the first woman to complete a return, non-stop swim of the English Channel on September 7, 1977.

16. Steve Podborski won the men's downhill skiing World Cup, the first non-European to do so on March 5, 1982.

17. Vickie Keith was the first marathon swimmer to swim the English Channel using the butterfly stroke on July 10, 1989.

18. Kurt Browning became the first Canadian male to win successive world figure skating championships in March, 1990.

19. Wayne Gretzky became the first National Hockey League player to score 2,000 points on October, 23, 1990.

20. Toronto Blue Jays were the first team based in Canada to win baseball's World Series on October 24, 1992.

Travel
& Leisure

ON THE ROAD AGAIN ...
THE TEN MOST SCENIC DRIVES

1. **British Columbia via the Sunshine Coast and Inside Passage to Prince Rupert**: From Horseshoe Bay, Vancouver, take the ferry to Langdale, then drive the spectacular "Sunshine Coast" to Powell River. Cross by ferry to Comox on Vancouver Island, then continue northward to Port Hardy. Ride the ferry from Port Hardy up the Inside Passage to Prince Rupert for more spectacular scenery.

2. **Newfoundland's Viking Trail and Labrador coast**: Make sure to take in Gros Morne National Park, as well as historic Viking and Basque settlements.

3. **The Icefield Parkway between Banff and Jasper**: Drive in either direction through Banff and Jasper National Parks for some truly majestic mountain scenery. Stop off at the Athabasca Glacier.

4. **Yukon Gold Seekers' Trail**: Starting in Skagway, Alaska, trace the prospectors' trail over the Chilkoot Pass, through Whitehorse and down the Yukon River to Dawson City. Then, for good measure, loop through a small slice of Alaska and skirt magnificent Kluane National Park before returning to Whitehorse.

5. **Cape Breton's Cabot Trail**: Enjoy some of Nova Scotia's finest scenery.

The beautiful Cabot Trail in Cape Breton, Nova Scotia, is one of Canada's most scenic drives. *Photo by Catherine Blake.*

6. **Shore of Lake Ontario:** The lakeshore route from the Quebec border to Toronto's eastern suburbs via the Thousand Islands and Kingston.

7. **Toronto to Ottawa via Algonquin Park:** Drive through Ontario's "Cottage Country" and Algonquin Park to the Ottawa River and on to Canada's capital city.

8. **The Fundy Coast:** From Amherst, Nova Scotia to New Brunswick's Fundy National Park and on to Saint John and St. Andrews.

9. **Nova Scotia's south shore and Annapolis Valley:** From Halifax around the Nova Scotia peninsula's south shore.

10. **PEI's Blue Heron Drive:** Take in the famed P.E.I. National Park as well as the south shore.

List prepared by Pam Hobbs and Michael Algar, authors of Visitors Guide — Canada *and other publications.*

Snapshot

Vehicle Registrations in Canada

1916:   128,328

1956:   4.2 million

1975: 11.2 million

1997: 17.4 million

Statistics Canada

EIGHT MEMORABLE VACATIONS IN CANADA

1. Sailing on a thirty-seven-passenger Russian icebreaker from Greenland to Churchill, Manitoba, travelling along the coast of Baffin Island, where you'll visit Inuit communities and see such animals as walruses and whales.

2. Taking the train across Canada. A classic journey that has been popular for decades.

3. Whale watching on the St. Lawrence River near the mouth of the Saguenay River, Quebec.

4. Visiting Bathurst Inlet Lodge, on the edge of the Arctic Ocean in Nunavut. Fly in by bush plane and stay in a historic Hudson's Bay Company fur trading post. It offers distinctive landscapes, lush vegetation, accessible wildlife, and intriguing history.

5. Hiking and horseback riding in and around Jasper Park Lodge (Jasper National Park). Ice Skating on Lake Louise and enjoying other winter sports in Banff National Park.

6. Rafting or canoeing to Bathurst Inlet by way of the Burnside River and Arctic Waterways.

7. Hiking the rainforests of Vancouver Island where wilderness beauty is incomparable. Ocean kayaking and sport fishing are also available here.

8. Seeing polar bears close up in Churchill, Manitoba. A popular trip for many non-Canadians as well.

List based on an informal survey of Canadian professional travel writers.

TEN POPULAR CANADIAN ATTRACTIONS IN 1997

	Attraction	Attendance
1.	Eaton Centre, Toronto, Ontario:	2,404,000
2.	Canada's Wonderland, Maple, Ontario:	1,794,000
3.	Harbourfront, Toronto, Ontario:	1,670,000
4.	Old Quebec City, Quebec:	1,625,000
5.	Old Port, Montreal, Quebec:	1,513,000
6.	Ontario Place, Toronto, Ontario:	1,510,000
7.	CN Tower, Toronto, Ontario:	1,338,000
8.	Stanley Park, Vancouver, British Columbia:	1,247,000
9.	Metro Zoo, Toronto, Ontario:	1,161,000
10.	West Edmonton Mall, Edmonton, Alberta:	1,074,000

Print Measurement Bureau.

Totem poles in Vancouver's Stanley Park. *Photo courtesy of Tourism Vancouver.*

TEN POPULAR FESTIVALS AND EVENTS IN CANADA IN 1997

	Event	Attendance
1.	International Jazz Festival, Montreal, Quebec:	1,148,000
2.	Canadian National Exhibition, Toronto, Ontario:	1,107,000
3.	Benson & Hedges Symphony of Fire, Toronto, Ontario:	745,000
4.	L'International Benson & Hedges, Montreal, Quebec:	641,000
5.	Winterlude Festival, Ottawa, Ontario:	566,000
6.	Calgary Stampede & Exhibition, Calgary, Alberta:	546,000
7.	Pacific National Exhibition, Vancouver, British Columbia:	539,000
8.	Festival D'Été de Québec: Quebec City, Quebec:	481,000
9.	Benson & Hedges Symphony of Fire, Vancouver, British Columbia	478,000
10.	Just For Laughs Festival, Montreal, Quebec:	457,000

Print Measurement Bureau.

Action at the Calgary Stampede. *Photo courtesy of Calgary Stampede.*

TEN BEST LIVING MUSEUMS
(in alphabetical order)

1. Acadian Historic Village, near Caraquet, New Brunswick.

2. Barkerville Historic Park, Barkerville, British Columbia.

3. Fort Edmonton Park, Edmonton, Alberta.

4. Fort Langley National Historic Park, Fort Langley, British Columbia.

5. Fortress of Louisbourg National Historic Park, Louisbourg, Nova Scotia.

6. Kings Landing Historical Settlement, near Fredericton, New Brunswick.

7. L'anse aux Meadows National Historic Park, Newfoundland.

8. Old Fort William, Thunder Bay, Ontario.

9. Ste-Marie Among The Hurons, Midland, Ontario.

10. Upper Canada Village, Morrisburg, Ontario.

List prepared by Pam Hobbs and Michael Algar, authors of Visitors Guide — Canada *and other publications.*

Snapshot

Top Five Countries Visited by Canadians:

1970	1997
United States	United States
United Kingdom	United Kingdom
France	Mexico
Germany	France
Switzerland	Germany

Statistics Canada

TEN MOST POPULAR DOMESTIC AIR ROUTES
(by number of passengers)

1. Montreal–Toronto

2. Toronto–Vancouver

3. Ottawa–Toronto

4. Calgary–Vancouver

5. Calgary–Toronto

6. Toronto–Winnipeg

7. Edmonton–Vancouver

8. Halifax–Toronto

9. Calgary–Edmonton

10. Edmonton–Toronto

Snapshot

Top Five Countries of Origin for Visitors to Canada:

1958	1970	1997
United States	United States	United States
United Kingdom	United Kingdom	United Kingdom
Germany	Germany	Japan
Netherlands	France	France
France	Netherlands	Germany

Statistics Canada

ARE WE THERE YET? ... TEN GREAT PLACES TO TAKE KIDS
(In alphabetical order)

1. Anne of Green Gables House (PEI National Park and *Anne of Green Gables Review* at the Confederation Centre Theatre).

2. Barkerville Historic Park, Barkerville, British Columbia.

3. Botanical Garden of Montreal (including Insectarium and Biodome).

4. Butchart Gardens, near Victoria, British Columbia.

5. Fortress of Louisbourg National Historic Park, Louisbourg, Nova Scotia.

6. Kings Landing Historical Settlement, near Fredericton, New Brunswick.

7. Ontario Science Centre, Toronto, Ontario.

8. Old Fort William, Thunder Bay, Ontario.

9. Royal Tyrrell Museum, Drumheller, Alberta. (Also the museum's field station in Dinosaur Provincial Park.)

10. Upper Canada Village, Morrisburg, Ontario.

List prepared by Pam Hobbs and Michael Algar, members of the Society of American Travel Writers and frequent contributors to Canadian and U.S. magazines and newspapers.

The Ontario Science Centre in Toronto is one of the best places to take your children. *Photo courtesy of the Ontario Science Centre.*

CANADA'S TOP TEN BEERS

(The following are the ten fine Canadian examples of the brewer's craft, some of which, alas, are no longer available.)
(in alphabetical order)

1. *Creemore Springs Premium Lager* — Creemore Springs Brewery, Creemore, Ontario. A refreshing example of a pure and simple lager, made with local spring water.

2. *Hermannator Ice Bock* — Vancouver Island Brewery, Victoria, British Columbia. Probably the best of few dopplebocks brewed in Canada. Rich, slightly sweet with a warm and lasting finish.

3. *Iron Duke Strong Ale* — Wellington County Brewery, Guelph, Ontario. A big, solid ale that lives up to its name, with a rich, complex, but well-balanced malty flavour.

4. *La Seigneuriale Triple* — La Brasserie Seigneuriale, Boucherville, Quebec. This bottle-conditioned brew, in the Belgian style, has a feisty, memorable taste not usually associated with "Canadian" beer.

5. *Maudite* — Unibroue, Chambly, Quebec. The power of this bottle-conditioned beer is legendary, as is the lasting spicy flavour and its bitter-sweet earthiness.

6. *Russian Imperial Stout* — Tall Ship Ale Co., Squamish, British Columbia. An old style of beer given new life, with all the traditional, solid, "dark" flavours intact and bottle-conditioned for long life.

7. *Salzburger Lager* — Creek Brewery and Restaurant, Vancouver, British Columbia. A great Canadian version of a Vienna-style draught lager with impressive toasty malt flavours and perfectly balanced hopping.

8. *Spinnakers Cask IPA* — Spinnakers Brewpub, Victoria, British Columbia. Probably the best IPA I've ever tasted in North America, with a big, bright, Pacific Northwest hop character, gravity-fed from the cask.

9. *St. Ambroise Oatmeal Stout* — Brasserie McAuslan, Montreal, Quebec. This bottled "biere noire a l'voine" has all the robust, lasting character a good oatmeal stout should have.

10. *Thor's Hammer Barley Wine* — Hagar's Brewing Company, North Vancouver, British Columbia. A yearly, limited bottle edition old ale that improves with age — a promising, delicious brew for toasting any millennium!

List prepared by Dave Preston, a certified beer judge, member of the North American Guild of Beer Writers, and director of the Great Canadian Beer Festival.

Snapshot

Canada's Best Tourist Sites in 1999

1. Outdoor Site: Calgary Zoo
2. Indoor Site: Maritime Museum of the Atlantic in Nova Scotia
3. Cultural Event: FrancoFolies de Montreal in Quebec
4. Sports Event: Alcan Canadian International Dragon Boat Festival in British Columbia
5. New Attraction: Hopewell Rocks, New Brunswick
6. National or International Attraction: Kings Landing Historical Settlement, New Brunswick

List based on selections made by a jury of media, tourism, and business representatives.

CANADA'S TEN BEST WINES

(In Canada's very young fine-wine growing history these vintages set the pace in various style categories)

(in no particular order)

1. Gehringer Brothers 1997 Riesling Ice Wine, British Columbia. Dessert Wine.

2. Mission Hill 1997 Grand Reserve Gewurztraminer Icewine, British Columbia. Dessert Wine.

3. Henry of Pelham 1995 Riesling Icewine, Ontario. Dessert Wine.

4. Inniskillin 1991 Vidal Icewine, Ontario. Dessert Wine.

5. Burrowing Owl 1998 Pinot Gris, British Columbia. White Wine.

6 Chateau des Charmes 1994 Chardonnay, St. David's Bench Vineyard, Ontario. White Wine.

7. Tinhorn Creek 1995 Merlot, British Columbia. Red Wine.

8. Sumac Ridge 1997 Sauvignon Blanc, British Columbia. White Wine.

9. Thirty Bench 1995 Cabernet Reserve Blend, Ontario. Red Wine

10. Hillebrand 1995 Cabernet Franc Showcase Unfiltered, Ontario. Red Wine

List prepared by the editors of Wine Access, Canada's Essential Wine Buyers Guide *(416-596-1480 or at www.warwickgp.com/wineaccess).*

Fabulous Fact

At the Challenge International du Vin 1999, considered to be the Olympics of wine, Canadian ice wines captured seven top prizes.

AT THE PLATE...
TEN POPULAR ALL-CANADIAN EATS IN THE TWENTIETH CENTURY

1. **Pablum**: The popular baby food was invented and named by doctors Drake, Brown, and Tisdall in 1929 at Toronto's Hospital for Sick Children. There's even a bit of humour in the name, since it derives from the Latin word *pabulum* which means "horse feed" or "animal fodder."

2. **Son-of-a-Bitch-in-a-Sack**: This boiled chuckwagon pudding from Alberta is aptly named, due to its horrible taste. Canada has a tradition of colourful names for puddings. Consider also bugger-in-a-bag, from Cascapedia Bay in northern New Brunswick, where fresh raspberries and pudding ingredients are boiled in a cotton bag that has been oiled and floured.

3. **Pets de Soeur**: Literally translated as "nun's farts," these are little dessert pastries that look like cinnamon rolls, and illustrate a hefty dollop of good-natured but anticlerical humour in many Quebec expressions.

4. **BeaverTails®**: The Hooker family perfected this hit food of Ottawa's annual Winterlude Festival, in which whole-wheat pastry dough is rolled into a shape vaguely reminiscent of a beaver's tail. It is fried in hot vegetable oil and then painted with butter and sprinkled with a variety of tasty toppings, such as garlic and cheese, and cinnamon and sugar.

BeaverTails® Pastry: A unique Canadian treat. *Photo courtesy of Harrison Baker Photography.*

5. **Labrador Tea:** This was and still is a staple drink of Canada's north. It is made by steeping the crushed, dried leaves of a common northern evergreen shrub, *Ledum groenladicum*, a member of the heath family of plants.

6. **Winnipeg jambuster:** A local name for a large and scrumptious jelly doughnut made near the intersection of Portage and Main.

7. **Scrunchins:** This Newfoundland favourite is made from fried cubes of fat-back pork, often served over what may be the provincial dish of The Rock — fish and brewis, itself a dish of cod and hard tack biscuit often accompanied by vegetables, all boiled together with the cod.

8. **Nanaimo Bar:** Named after the city on Vancouver Island, this dessert treat is now popular across Canada. It is little cut squares consisting of Graham wafer crumbs and a sweet, sugary cream filling and slathered with a layer of chocolate.

9. **Sockeye Salmon:** This frisky Pacific fish has a Canadian name from the Coast Salish language, where *suk-kegh* means, aptly enough, "red fish."

10. **Poutine:** Quebec's gift to lunch-counter food is a hearty serving of thick-cut French fries topped with fresh cheese curds and hot gravy. Surprisingly, the French word *poutine* originally derived from the English word "pudding."

List prepared by Bill Casselman, author of Canadian Food Words, *published by McArthur & Company, Toronto.*

SEVEN OUTSTANDING BOTANICAL GARDENS OPENED IN CANADA
IN THE TWENTIETH CENTURY

1. **University of British Columbia Botanical Garden, Vancouver, British Columbia:** One of the oldest existing Canadian gardens devoted to teaching, research, and introducing new plants, it was set up in 1916 and has several diverse displays including the Nitobe Memorial Garden.

2. **VanDusen Botanical Garden, Vancouver:** Operated by the Vancouver Board of Parks and Recreation and established in 1972, it is known for ornamental displays, including roses.

3. **Devonian Botanic Garden, Edmonton:** Formed in 1959 by the University of Alberta as Canada's most northerly botanical garden in Canada where work is carried out on the hardiness of ornamental plants.

4. **Royal Botanical Gardens, Burlington:** The only such garden in Canada to have a royal charter, it was established in 1941 and includes vast nature trails along with extensive collections of lilacs, irises, and roses.

5. **Montreal Botanical Gardens, Montreal:** Founded in 1931 by renowned Quebec botanist frére Marie-Victorin, a university professor who also established the Botanical Institute in Montreal. The conservatory and outdoor displays feature a collection of ten thousand rosebushes.

6. **New Brunswick Botanical Gardens, Saint-Jacques:** Located along the Saint John River Valley, a total of eight gardens and two arboreta are included in this attraction, which opened in 1993.

7. **Memorial University of Newfoundland Botanical Garden, St. John's:** This woodland setting opened in 1977 and specializes in natural displays designed to reclaim diminished butterfly and insect species.

List prepared by Marlene Orton, a freelance writer and passionate gardener who lives in the country near Ottawa.

TWELVE FAVOURITE BOARD GAMES PLAYED BY CANADIANS
(but not necessarily invented by Canadians)

	Game	Year Invented
1.	Monopoly	1935
2.	Trivial Pursuit	1982
3.	Yahtzee	1956
4.	Scrabble	1948
5.	Twister	1966
6.	Trouble	1986
7.	Battleship	1967
8.	Guess Who	1988
9.	The Memory Game	1966
10.	Clue	1949
11.	Sorry	1932
12.	The Game of Life	1960

TEN MOST POPULAR EXERCISES AMONG CANADIANS
(in order)

1. Walking

2. Home Exercises

3. Bicycling

4. Swimming

5. Jogging/Running

6. Weight Training

7. Fishing

8. Bowling

9. Baseball or softball

10. Golfing

TEN POPULAR ALL-CANADIAN WORDS

1. **Wonderbra®**: This famous brassiere was invented in 1964 by Canadian Louise Poirier for Canadelle, a Canuck lingerie company later bought by Playtex.

2. **Deke**: To deke somebody out is to trick them by a feint. The Canadian hockey slang verb is a direct contraction of the verb, to decoy. If you pretend to take a shot, if you feint a move and draw an enemy defenceman out of position, if you do anything to decoy the opposition, you have pulled a big deke.

3. **Calgary Redeye**: This a beer mixed with tomato juice. And there's red in your eye!

4. **Kerosene**: A Canadian discovered kerosene and invented the kerosene lamp. Dr. Abraham Gesner first demonstrated his product at a public lecture on Prince Edward Island in 1846. He named it by using the Greek work for wax, *keros*, and added -ene, a common ending of chemical terms applied to names of alcohols and certain distillates.

5. **Gopher**: The word entered English on our prairies as settlers heard traders from Quebec using their name for the burrowing rodent. They called it *gaufre gris*, "the grey honeycomb," because its interlocking tunnels resemble a honeycomb.

6. **Mush! Mush!**: This command to northern sled dogs to go forward looks on the surface as if it might have derived from an Inuit expression. But it was an English hearing of voyageurs' French, originally "*Marche! Marche!*," which in Quebec was first shouted to a team of horses. So Mush! is just Giddyup! in old Quebec French.

7. **Muskeg**: In the Cree languages of Canada, *muskak* means "swamp." In Chipewyan, a related language, *muskig* is a "grassy bog."

8. **Robin Storm**: This a term for a very late snowfall in southern Canada.

9. **Gone to the Sand Hills**: The expression is used as a synonym for "dead" by some Albertans. It originated with the Blood people in the sandy hill country south of Lethbridge who call their heaven the Sand Hills.

10. **Rock Doctor**: This nugget of Canadian mining slang is a playful synonym for geologist.

List prepared by Bill Casselman, author of Casselman's Canadian Words, *published by McArthur & Company, Toronto.*

THIRTEEN TERMS AND PHRASES COINED IN THE TWENTIETH CENTURY

1. **Hands Up!**: Although he wasn't a Canadian, American bandit Bill Miner is believed to have originated this hold-up command and was likely the first to use it in Canada. Miner ordered a train crew to put their hands up in 1904 when he pulled Canada's first train robbery in Mission Junction, British Columbia.

2. **Pogey**: Used to describe the financial relief given by the government to unemployed Canadians. The term probably came from the word "pokey," which in the 1920s referred to a place that catered to people who were down and out. Its modern meaning has been around since World War II.

3. **D-Day Dodgers**: Coined by Lady Nancy Astor, a sharp-tongued British member of Parliament, it refers to World War II war veterans, including thousands of Canadians, who were stationed in Italy at the time of the D-Day invasion at Normandy, France, on June 6, 1944. Although Lady Astor claimed it was an innocent remark, it was greeted angrily by troops in Italy. To this day Canadian "D-Day Dodgers" continue to meet on a regular basis.

4. *Kemo Sabe*: A phrase forever associated with Jay Silverheels, the Indian athlete and actor born Harry Smith on the Six Nations Indian reserve near Brantford, Ontario. Silverheels was the Lone Ranger's faithful companion Tonto in radio, television, and movie productions between 1949 and 1958. The phrase is said to have meant either "don't understand" or "trusty scout."

5. **The Medium is the Message**: In addresses in Vancouver, British Columbia and Omaha, Nebraska, in 1958 and 1959, Toronto communications theorist and University of Toronto professor Marshall McLuhan coined the phrase "the medium is the message." McLuhan's contention was that different media require different levels of sensory involvement on the part of the user when information is transferred. Since each medium affects the user's perception of it differently, each message is also perceived differently. To McLuhan, it is the shifts in perceptions that hold the key to the meaning of the message.

6. **Red Tory**: A term popularized in Canada in 1966 by political scientist Gad Horowitz. It defines "a conscious ideological Conservative with some 'odd' Socialist notions or a conscious ideological Socialist with some 'odd' Tory notions. Its opposite is a "blue Grit," a non-progressive Liberal.

7. **Fuddle Duddle**: After being accused of uttering the "f"-word in the House

of Commons in February 1971, Prime Minister Pierre Trudeau denied the charge as "an absolute untruth," telling a reporter what he really said was "fuddle duddle."

8. Corporate Welfare Bums: Coined in 1972 by New Democratic Party Leader David Lewis, this phrase referred to corporations large and small that avoided paying their fair share of business taxes, as well as those businesses which pressed all levels of government for additional grants, concessions, subsidies, depreciations, and incentives.

9. Let the Eastern Bastards Freeze in the Dark: Message on bumper stickers in Alberta during the oil crisis of 1973 to reflect Albertans' anger with Prime Minister Pierre Trudeau's National Energy Policy.

10. Cineplex: Coined in 1978 by Toronto film exhibitor Nat Taylor, former head of the Famous Players movie theatre chain and partner in the Cineplex Corporation. The term combines the words cinema and complex and refers to the installation of multiple movie screens in one movie theatre.

11. Take off, eh?: A quip made popular by Rick Moranis and Dave Thomas, better known as the McKenzie brothers, Bob and Doug, on the 1980s Canadian comedy television show SCTV.

12. A cannonading shot: During his lengthy career as play-by-play man for the Montreal Canadiens, Danny Gallivan used this term to describe many a player's booming shot. The term, and the broadcaster, retired in 1984.

13. Generation X: The generation of North Americans born in the mid-1960s who are in no hurry to find themselves because they give equal value to education and life experience. The term has been around since the 1970s, but came into popular use in 1991, after Canadian fiction writer Douglas Coupland used it as the title of his first novel.

The Future

WHAT TO EXPECT ...
TWELVE SURPRISES OF THE TWENTY-FIRST CENTURY

1. **A Century of Disruptions:** The magnitude and frequency of the disruptions that will occur throughout the century will surprise us and catch us unprepared.

   • The use of nuclear weapons in a regional war.
   • The further disintegration of the social fabric of every society.
   • The use of biological weapons by terrorists.
   • The havoc of a five-foot rise in sea levels, due to melting polar ice.
   • The worldwide shortage of capital caused by one disruption after another.
   • Items 2–9 below.

2. **Life Beyond Earth:** The confirmation of life beyond our Earth will excite and confound life on the Earth.

3. **The 150-Year Life:** Due to the ability to replace diseased cells and organs with ones we have grown in a lab, lifespans will gradually expand to 150 years by 2100. The questions of when to end one's life, how to make psychological and organizational room for younger generations, how to cope with double and triple "sandwich generations," and the obligations of one generation to another will become pressing and disturbing issues.

4. **Bio-computers:** They will perform many roles better and cheaper than "the real thing," from fixing plumbing, to cleaning out our arteries, to filing tax returns. The result will be a massive shift in what society thinks is a "good" job — away from doctor, lawyer, accountant, plumber to philosopher, entertainer, and who knows what else.

5. **The Dominion of Western Canada:** Quebec will stay. But, frustrated by the inability of the governments of Canada, Quebec, and Ontario to cope with the new global realities, the four Western provinces and the two Western territories will create a new country — the Dominion of Western Canada.

6. **A Post-Westphalian World:** At every level, from individuals to the globe, sovereignty — self-contained independence — is eroded. Sovereign levels of governments (local, provincial, federal, global) will be replaced by a global network of nested and interpenetrating governing systems. No person or government has the right to do just what they want, without considering the affects of such behaviour on the whole planet.

7. **Second Order Governments**: The long-held view that it is "the job of governments to govern, to decide for us" will fade away. Canada will be the first country to elect a party committed to the view that the role of governments is the second order work of designing and facilitating systems and processes which encourage and enable persons, families, communities, corporations, and whole societies to become self-governing.

8. **Post-Industrial Societies and Economies**: Public wakes will be held to mark the end of the Industrial Age and its emphasis on production and consumption being the highest meaning in life. The Post-Industrial Society will revolve around the growth and maturation of persons. The overriding commitment will be that each person becomes fit to live with and participates in co-creating a world fit to live in. Every business, school, church, and government will struggle to learn these new roles and be judged by their capacity to contribute to this higher purpose. The business of business will no longer be business.

9. **The Rediscovery of Home and Community**: We will no longer have to leave home and community to go to work to create wealth, go to school to learn, go to the mall to acquire goods, go to the hospital to heal, and go outside to play. For the first time in three hundred years all these central human functions will be done from home. This will greatly facilitate new commitments to families, communities, and re-knitting the social fabric.

10. **The End of Universities**: The demand for higher learning will force governments to end the monopoly held on higher learning by universities and colleges. Higher learning will be treated as any other commodity or service — as long as the standards are met, any group can offer any educational experiences. Costs will come down and choice will proliferate.

11. **Bio-Robots**: There will be intelligent personal robots — not mechanical devices with artificial intelligence, but bio-robots, bred and modified from existing beasts to serve as companions. There will be some form of bio-control to keep them loyal. This will raise the deep-seated fear of "bio-beasts," e.g. Frankenstein.

12. **A 24/7 World**: Virtually all activities will be continuous — twenty-four hours a day, seven days a week. It will be possible to make a contribution to work going on in any place in the globe, from any place on the globe, at any time.

Added Note: Given all that the twenty-first century will bring, we will be surprised by the capacity of human persons and human organizations to grow into new forms of truly adult maturity required to meet these conditions. All in all, the century will be one of deepening hope as it becomes clear that we can learn our way into fundamentally new ways of living together.

List prepared by Ruben Nelson, who is president of Square One Management Ltd. in Alberta, a pioneer of futures research in Canada, and past president of the Canadian Association of Futures Studies.

Acknowledgements

After writing this book of lists, it would be only logical to draw up yet another list — one that would offer thanks to all of the people that have helped us on this project. However, we'll spare you.

But this book could never have been launched without the help of the many people who prepared lists or contributed ideas, data, and pertinent information to lists we wrote ourselves. Someone once said, "if you want something done, ask a busy man." Well, we asked many busy men and women for help and despite jam-packed schedules, they came through with flying colours. Their names appear on their lists, and we thank each of them for their fine work.

The names of many others do not appear on lists. They are folks who helped with ideas, lent an ear as we tossed around the concept of the book, and offered valuable input. To list all of their names would be a book in itself but several deserve special thanks for their efforts. They are: Janis Ray, for spending long hours in archives and libraries in search of books and photographs, for inputting information, proofreading, and most importantly, for moral support; Catherine Blake, for her photography and sage advice; Dan and Rachel Bériault, Ollie and Sally Kuehn, Richard Patterson, Louise Rachlis, Bryan Ray, Harold Wright, Gary and Madeleine Jeffries, Ed Janiszewski, John Firth, Arlene Gehmacher, Arthur McCudden, Judy Noordermeer, Carolyn Dobel, and all the folks on Pwac-L.

Also, a special thanks to the Library of Parliament and staff at the Ottawa Public Library, in particular those at the Alta Vista Branch, who tracked down dozens of books needed to research this book. And a tip of the hat to staff at the London Public Library and University of Western Ontario Library for their help in finding vital information in their excellent collections.

We'd also like to acknowledge Barbara Crowder and the various Canadian Clubs in Ontario for taking an interest in our Canadian-oriented books, including this one, and inviting us to speak to their members. To all the bookstore managers and staff who have already shown an interest in this book, in lining up signings, and for past support, we say thank you. Many radio hosts also helped by getting us on the air to solicit their listeners' input as we gathered material for this book, and we'd be remiss in not thanking them, particularly Jim Richards at CFRB in Toronto, Gary Michaels at CFRA in Ottawa, and Arthur Black and Chris Straw at CBC in Vancouver.

Finally, we've also appreciated the special attention from the folks at The Dundurn Group for their enthusiasm, ideas, and professionalism from the minute we began work on this book. A big thanks to all of them.

Mark Kearney and Randy Ray

Printed in the USA
CPSIA information can be obtained
at www.ICGtesting.com
JSHW012019140824
68134JS00033B/2778